The Republic of
TRANSKEI

Chris van Rensburg Publications (Pty) Ltd
P.O. Box 25272 Ferreirasdorp 2048 Johannesburg
Republic of South Africa

Captions to colour plates on introduction pages in order of appearance.

Paramount Chief the Honourable K. D. Matanzima, Prime Minister of Transkei.

Indigenous forests in the hills of Pondoland.

The Honourable B. J. Vorster, Prime Minister of the Republic of South Africa.

Cattle on a beach on the Wild Coast of Transkei.

Thembu boy dressed for the dance.

The Magwa Falls near Lusikisiki.

Bhaca man dressed in his best finery.

Huts in the mountains near Engcobo.

Unrehearsed elegance in Pondoland.

Wild Coast, with 'hole in the wall' formation in background.

Thembu woman with unusual headdress.

The picture at the front of the book shows a Bomvana family walking near the 'hole in the wall' on the Wild Coast.

The picture at the back of the book shows four well-dressed Thembu men on their way to town.

First Edition 1976.
ISBN 908393 06 7   (De Luxe Edition)
ISBN 908393 07 5   (Standard Edition)

Additional information on Transkei is available from the Information Division of the Transkeian Department of Foreign Affairs, Private Bag, Umtata 5100.

The Republic of
TRANSKEI

Foreword

by the Prime Minister of Transkei
Paramount Chief the Honourable K. D. Matanzima

As a sovereign nation, Transkei now leaves the Republic of South Africa. However, Transkei is inseparably bound by geography, history and economics to the other parts and peoples of South Africa, for better or for worse. We are determined that it shall be for better: and this is a fit occasion to outline the philosophy that will guide our new nation.

We believe that the worth of all men, as human beings, must be recognised: but that all men are not equal and deserve different rewards, each according to his capacity, effort and contribution to society.

Already Transkei has given all Black people of South Africa a new dignity by blazing the trail, in the manner we have, to sovereign nationhood. Violence debases human dignity: and strife, brute force, intimidation and terrorism have too often been the means, on this and other continents, for the entry of states into the community of independent nations. Instead, by choosing together with the Republican Government the path of peaceful negotiation, Transkei has enhanced the status and reputation of our own people and of Black men everywhere. It will be our endeavour, by the example we set as a stable, responsible and just nation, to go on doing so.

Transkei will be a democratic State, the essential principles and practices of democracy being deep-rooted in our own traditional institutions. Before Marx, before Magna Carta, these principles were operating in African society. We totally oppose the Marxist doctrine in politics and economics, and align ourselves with the democratic countries of the world.

Transskei will be a non-racial state: but while we reject all discrimination based on race, colour or creed, we are equally opposed to enforced integration. Freedom of association means the right to associate with one's own as well as with others.

Since it became self-governing some 13 years ago, Transkei has achieved its administrative goal. With the celebrating now of its sovereignty, it has achieved its constitutional goal. Only one goal remains – economic development which is the *sine qua non* of true independence. In the first place it is agriculture in Transkei, with its immense potential, that must be revitalised: at the same time manufacturing industry must be expanded for the wealth it generates and for the employment it offers to the surplus population siphoned off the land by the process of agricultural revitalisation.

This will be done within the system of free enterprise and the profit motive. There will in Transkei be no distribution of wealth in equal shares, but according to deserts. We recognise that the progress of Transkei will depend upon the efforts of our own people, but also that we cannot succeed alone. Our progress and that of the other parts and peoples of Southern Africa demands co-operation among all. The natural and human resources and the particular capacities of this association complement one another: and we subscribe to the contention that there is in Southern Africa a *common wealth* to which all must be free to contribute and from which all must be free to draw.

The signing of a document of independence does not constitute the final phase in our political evolution: there is no such thing as finality or an ultimate solution in politics. Already, as leader of Transkei, I look forward to a wider dispensation in which each man's loyalty to his own community and nation will be woven with loyalty to Southern Africa which separately, but jointly also, we are destined to share.

Umtata
October 1976

Foreword

by the Prime Minister of the Republic of South Africa
the Honourable B. J. Vorster

It is right and proper that a publication such as this should appear on Transkei on the eve of that territory's independence.

The people of Transkei have always been distinct from all the other peoples of Southern Africa. Throughout all the years it has always been their aim to maintain and uphold their traditions. In this they have achieved a remarkable degree of success. With their leaders they have participated in establishing a Xhosa nation to which we may all look as an example.

A nation that preserves and upholds that which is its own will survive. A nation that upholds and defends all that is dear to it will find stability and security.

I wish to say to the people of Transkei that the government of the Republic of South Africa never doubted their good faith, integrity and resolve to develop their country. We are now on the eve of Transkei's independence which has been brought about by people and their leaders who never failed to show courage and enthusiasm for the task.

I believe that all will be well with Transkei and it is my prayer that Almighty God will extend his hand in protection over Transkei and its people. I also believe that the friendly relations which have always existed between Transkei and the Republic of South Africa will be maintained and even extended after Transkei has become an independent state.

Pretoria
October 1976

This book tells the story of Transkei, the world's newest nation-state which was granted independence on 26 October 1976. The guardian country responsible for guiding it to constitutional maturity is what is today the Republic of South Africa, of which Transkei was an integral part for more than 66 years.

Transkei is situated in the south-east of Southern Africa, south of the South African province of Natal and the independent Kingdom of Lesotho. It has a resident population of some two million (with a similar number of its people working and living, temporarily or continuously, across its borders in the Republic), a coastline of 250 kilometres and a total area of 41 100 square kilometres – twice the size of Israel and larger than the Netherlands. It is a well-watered country of majestic mountains, rolling hills, perennial rivers and temperate climate, with an agricultural potential as rich as any in Africa.

Transkeians are a proud people, nurtured on an elaborate set of traditions and customs which have not only stood the test of time, but have also provided a true and trusted framework for their national development to sovereign independence. But their pride is leavened by a gentle and spontaneous humour and joy of living. It is almost as if custom decrees that among Transkeians there is a time to be solemn and a time to laugh: and at every opportunity the young people will dance and sing.

Why has this territory now been excised from South Africa, and the Transkeians given their sovereignty?

To answer that question the pages of history must be turned back some two centuries. In the early 1770s – more than a hundred years after the Cape had been settled by the Dutch – pioneer White Afrikaner farmers, having moved eastward across a vast unpopulated expanse of land, came into contact with a Black people who had occupied for a century and more much of the eastern seaboard of what was later to become the (British) Cape Colony. These Black people were the vanguard of the southerly migration of large numbers of Bantu tribes, who originated in the distant past in the vicinity of the Great Lakes of Central Africa. The group of tribes that reached furthest south were the Xhosa-speaking people; and by the middle of the 16th century they were settled in the corridor between the southern reaches of the Drakensberg and the seaboard, roughly the area which is now Transkei.

Modern Transkei came into existence as a result of a series of British annexations of Xhosa territory to the Cape Colony. The process began with the incorporation of Fingoland and Griqualand East in 1879 and ended with the annexation of Mpondoland in 1894. Prior to that there had been several attempts to fix a boundary between the territory of the Xhosa and that of the White pioneers. For more than a century the frontier was moved backward and forward, from one river to another, until the Kei River finally became the boundary in 1847. Hence the name of the country – Trans-kei.

Meanwhile other Black ethnic groups had settled in other parts of what eventually

became British South Africa. Over a period of about 25 years in the 19th century they were repeatedly uprooted and decimated, and their remnants scattered in perhaps the most devastating chapter of internecine warfare in Africa's history. This time of terror is generally referred to as the Mfecane, and was initiated by the Zulu tyrant Shaka.

One result was that the White Afrikaner pioneers – who had become increasingly disenchanted with British colonial rule at the Cape and from 1836 had moved ever further north into the subcontinent – were able to establish themselves in unsettled or abandoned tracts of land. There they founded the two independent republics of the Transvaal and Orange Free State, but after a three-year war for their independence against the British Empire they were defeated in 1902 and incorporated in British South Africa, which then comprised four colonies (Transvaal, Orange Free State, Cape and Natal) and three Black homelands or protectorates (Bechuanaland, Basutoland and Swaziland).

The Union of South Africa, predecessor of the Republic of South Africa, came into being in 1910. Afrikaners, who had fought and lost the first wars of national independence on the African continent, and British South Africans were united now in Africa's pioneer venture in decolonisation. *Included* in the Union were the Transkei and seven other scattered Black homelands which had previously been associated administratively with one or other of the constituent colonies. *Excluded* were the three protectorates. However the inhabitants of neither the homelands nor the protectorates were consulted concerning their destiny, since in those days, almost 70 years ago, White rule and decision-making on behalf of people of colour was regarded (by a White-dominated world) as a desirable, proper and just arrangement.

The Second World War brought a profound change to this state of mind and affairs. The British Empire was the first to feel the full force of the new demand for self-determination and independence of all colonial peoples. In 1947 the Indian Empire gave way to the independent states of India and Pakistan (and much later, after a bloody civil war, was to produce a third sovereign state, Bangladesh).

On the African continent Ghana (in 1957) was the first of Britain's Black dependencies to be emancipated, to be followed in the 1960s by many others. Similarly, the French and Belgian African empires were precipitately liquidated; and much later, in the mid-1970s the Portuguese empire in Africa met the same fate.

With the birth of each new African nation, international pressure on the Republic of South Africa increased. It was demanded that she should abandon her "abhorrent" policy of separate development of the various Black peoples and introduce within a single state a one-man-one-vote dispensation to provide self-determination (and thus liberation) to all her peoples. She refused and stood condemned at the United Nations and capitals around the world – by some, for exploitation and oppression and by all, for moving stubbornly against the tide of history.

The truth is, however, that in her policies and the declarations of her leaders South Africa had anticipated by a generation and more the coming tide of history – and particularly the tide of decolonisation. In 1917 Prime Minister J. C. Smuts and in 1925 Prime Minister J. B. M. Hertzog both postulated the development of the Black peoples of South Africa to the stage where they would take charge in their own territories of their own destiny; and this is the policy which has been consistently followed and vigorously applied since the National Party came to power in 1948.

It was a policy devised by South Africa from her own experience of 300 years to meet her own special conditions. The means employed elsewhere for the self-determination and emancipation of dependent peoples could not, and cannot, be used in South Africa . . . for various cogent reasons.

First: In South Africa the metropolitan power cannot withdraw (leaving the emancipated people, for better or for worse, to their own devices), since here there *is* no metropolitan power. The Whites in South Africa are certainly not representatives of such a power. After three centuries and more there is no home across the seas they can return to. South Africa is their only home. Afrikaans, the mother tongue of the majority of the White nation, was developed in Africa – hence its name. Afrikaner nationalism, as has been shown, inspired the first wars of national independence against colonial power in Africa. In the course of those three centuries, and against all odds, the White people have fashioned their own distinctive nationhood, and here on the soil of Africa it lives on, or it perishes.

Second: Neither White nor Black can lay claim historically to all of South Africa. They are, alike, immigrant races; and by far the greater part of the country was never settled by Blacks at all. By every standard of international law – continuous occupation, undisputed control, effective administration – the White nation is entitled to those regions of South Africa which through the generations have been their homelands.

Third: The political systems of the White nation have throughout been Western. They are based on the Westminster model. Every five years the electorate has a choice of candidates representing a plurality of parties of different persuasions. The total attitude of Black people to government is different; and elsewhere on the continent the Western political forms inherited at the time of independence have been rejected by the Black states, one after the other. Instead, the single-party system or dictatorship of various kinds has been adopted, and is claimed by these states to be better suited to their temperament and circumstances. The evidence is overwhelmingly against the possibility of accommodating harmoniously in the same political system the Whites and Blacks of South Africa.

Fourth: A one-man-one-vote dispensation in a single state would be an absolute negation, in a population as mixed as South Africa's, of self-determination. It would inevitably mean the supremacy of the numerically strong – over the Whites, the Coloureds, the Indians and not least, the smaller Black national communities. It would represent a reckless disregard for ethnicity, which eminent authorities

maintain today "must be placed at the very centre of our concern for the human condition". That term is Professor Nathan Glazer's, of Harvard University.

Such are the reasons for the rejection by Pretoria of the prescription for emancipation adopted elsewhere. Pretoria's formula was different, and it was based four-square on the ideal postulated by the great champion of self-determination – President Woodrow Wilson of the United States – after the First World War, namely, that each ethnic group should, where possible, have a state of its own. In the case of the Black nations of South Africa this *was* possible since each had its traditional homelands.

Pretoria's policy of separatism which gave effect to Woodrow Wilson's ideal was clearly delineated only after the Second World War, but had been foreshadowed in the first years of Union. As early as 1913 – three years only after Union – legislation was passed by Parliament in Cape Town to protect for the Black people the territory of their homelands against acquisition by others. In 1936 the Bantu Trust and Land Act increased the area of the homelands by some 70 per cent to a total of 154 000 square kilometres – or some 13 per cent of the area of the Union. This allocation, following the setting aside of the protectorates in 1910 and of the homelands in 1913, meant that the original British South Africa was divided about equally between White and Black.

After the National Party came to power in 1948, the political development of the Black nations, based in the homelands, began. In 1951 the Bantu Authorities Act introduced a system of local government founded in traditional institutions and culminating in a territorial authority with a measure of jurisdiction over the homeland as a whole. This development was taken a decisive stage further with the Promotion of Bantu Self-Government Act of 1959, which provided the constitutional machinery for progress towards autonomy as a prelude to full independence. The White Paper which accompanied this Act envisaged the coming into being in due course of a Commonwealth in South Africa of politically independent but economically interdependent states.

Of the eight Black homelands, Transkei had always enjoyed the greatest degree of territorial and political cohesion. Its experience in local self-government in one form or another reached back more than a century; and these were the circumstances in which it progressed fastest under the 1959 legislation. In 1963 the South African Parliament passed the Transkei Constitution Act which bestowed on Transkei its own Legislative Assembly, Executive, national flag and anthem and the final phase had begun in its progress to a sovereign nation-state. The concept of the nation was as important as that of the state. As the Constitution Act was being prepared, the then Minister of Bantu Administration and Development (Mr De Wet Nel) declared: 'When we speak of freedom and self-determination for the Xhosa nation, we have in mind not only the geographical area of Transkei but its people everywhere in South Africa. Our concern is not only with political borders on a map but with the borders of national consciousness which hold all Xhosas together. Transkei will be the spring from which that national consciousness flows

but every Xhosa, wherever he may be in South Africa, will be given the fullest opportunity to share in it and to enrich it.'

The new Assembly, partly elected and partly composed of traditional rulers, was vested with powers of direct taxation on the citizens of Transkei, and authority to legislate on matters such as agriculture, education, roads and public works, the administration of justice, labour and social security. Through the 1960s and early 1970s other powers were progressively transferred from the South African Parliament to the Legislature in Umtata: and it was by now clear that the country was qualifying for sovereignty. During its 1974 session the Assembly appointed a recess committee from among its members to consider various implications of independence and to draft a constitution. Negotiations with Pretoria began at the end of that year. It was agreed then that Transkei would be granted independence within five years. In the event, it has come within less than two years.

A notable feature of the Transkei's constitution is that it was designed exclusively by Transkeians. Neither the South African Government nor any of its agencies had any share in the framing of it. This was a complete departure from the usual decolonisation process, where the metropolitan country had a decisive say in the constitution-making. Certainly, the Transkei constitution – which is largely based on that of 1963 when the territory was granted internal self-government – incorporates many aspects that are South African in nature, but this was the choice of the Transkeians themselves.

Preparation for independence was thorough. As has been pointed out, by the time Transkei was granted self-government in 1963, it had had more than a century of experience in local administration; and in this the traditional leaders at all times had a significant part. Political parties emerged only after 1963, when the first general election was held. In that and in both subsequent elections in 1968 and 1973 – in which Transkeians inside and across their borders participated – elected members numbered just under half the total complement of the Assembly; and throughout this transitional period the influence and authority of the traditional leaders contributed much to orderly and sustained progress. Now, after independence, they will continue to play the key and balancing role which is theirs in African society. The constitution lays down that the number of chiefs (75) will equal that of elected members.

The mass of the Transkeian people continue to regard their chiefs with deep respect. Prime Minister Matanzima himself preferred the designation Paramount Chief on the commemorative postage stamp which bears his image. The place given to the hereditary leaders in the new constitution could well provide Transkei with the political stability and continuity which has eluded the mass of black nations in the north, whose traditional forms of social organisation have been discredited and dismantled.

In other areas of Transkei's life, progress has been sound if not spectacular. The country has a long tradition of education stretching back over 150 years (the first schools established by missionaries are today household names among Trans-

keians). When the territory was granted self-government in 1963, 4 700 teachers were teaching 277 000 pupils in 1 600 schools. A year before independence more than 500 000 pupils were being taught in nearly 2 000 schools by about 10 000 teachers, all but 70 of whom were Black Transkeians.

Until recently most Transkeians seeking higher education attended the University of Fort Hare, which in 1970 became a full-fledged university with its own charter, serving primarily the people of Transkei and Ciskei (the other Xhosa homeland). A new national university for Transkei is planned, and as a first step a campus of Fort Hare was commissioned in February 1976 in Umtata, capital of Transkei. Halfway through the first year 131 students had enrolled in disciplines such as politics, public administration and economics.

A sound administrative structure has been built up over the years. In 1963, when Transkei was granted self-government, 455 of the 2 446 posts in the civil service were held by Whites seconded to Transkei by the South African Government. At independence, only 350 – or three per cent – of the 10 620 officials were White. The Government of South Africa has agreed to put White officials at the disposal of the Transkei Government for as long as they may be needed. The civil service of Transkei was reorganised to cope with additional functions that devolved at independence. No serious problems were encountered, thanks to the considerable body of experienced officials who by then had come up through the ranks.

The agricultural potential of Transkei is impressive. The average annual rainfall is much higher than for Southern Africa as a whole. Transkei is ideal stock-farming country and, as far as physical factors are concerned, much can be achieved in crop production, particularly under irrigation. Before this potential can be realised, however, several problems, some more serious than others, must be overcome. A major factor militating against the full utilisation of the country's agricultural resources of good soil and abundant water is the age-old system of land tenure which decrees that every family head has a right to graze and cultivate a piece of land. Every head of family in Transkei is therefore a 'farmer'. This means that the available farm land is divided into uneconomic units: farming is a way of life rather than an enterprise for economic gain. Where this type of subsistence farming is practised yields are low, but where land has been consolidated into larger units and modern methods are applied they are remarkably high. Both the Transkei Government and the Transkei Development Corporation have done much to promote project farming. Examples of such successful commercial enterprises are the Magwa tea estate and various Phormium tenax plantations which supply fibre for a large bag factory in Butterworth.

An area of some 300 000 hectares, or nearly seven per cent of the country, is suitable for afforestation. Some 70 000 hectares are under indigenous forest and 61 000 hectares have been put under plantations – mostly pine, eucalyptus and wattle. The plantations are managed by the Transkeian Department of Agriculture and Forestry, but the 28 sawmills are privately owned – including the newest which was commissioned in March 1976 at the cost of $3,6 million.

In recent years concerted efforts have been made to diversify the economy and so reduce Transkei's dependence on agriculture and create more job opportunities for Transkeians inside their own country. Up to now large numbers of them have had to sell their labour in neighbouring South Africa, but the Transkei Government is well aware of the need to develop the secondary and tertiary sectors of the economy so that the country's reliance on jobs beyond its borders may be reduced as far as possible.

The main agency for diversification and industrialisation is the Transkei Development Corporation which in 1976 had a share capital of $92 million. So far it has been instrumental in the establishment of 24 factories in Transkei – mostly in Umtata and in Butterworth which promise to become the nerve-centre of the country's industrial activity. Many of the factories were established on the 'agency' basis, in terms of which the South African Government offers entrepreneurs in the Republic's metropolitan areas generous incentives to move their plants to Transkei or to start new ones there. The main proviso is that such enterprises must be taken over by Blacks within a specified period, usually 25 years. The system will continue to operate following the coming of independence.

Africanisation of the tertiary sector, especially commerce, was virtually complete at independence. In this, too, the Transkei Development Corporation has played a significant role. Many Transkeian businessmen have been granted loans and given expert advice by the Corporation to launch their own ventures, mostly in the retail trade and transportation.

The national budget of Transkei exceeded $155,25 million in the financial year 1976-77. The largest votes were those concerned with human development and care, notably education and social security. Like most Third World countries, Transkei also has to cope with a population growth of awesome proportions. Every year there are many more pupils at school and more people requiring assistance in some form or other. This will be one of the country's main problems in future – to strike a balance between the demands on the exchequer of human development projects and those of physical development and job creation.

Meanwhile a sound foundation has been laid in all spheres in Transkei, and the progress and stability achieved to date suggest that the prospect for Transkei is measurably brighter than for many Black countries where comparable advantages (and particularly the close co-operation of highly-developed South Africa) in dealing with typical Third World problems are not available. Even now the *per capita* income in Transkei at more than $200 is higher than that of most other African countries; and the potential, both physical and human, for sustained improvement is there.

But the future of Transkei cannot be viewed separately from the rest of South Africa. As Prime Minister Matanzima observes in his foreword: 'Our progress and that of the other parts and peoples of Southern Africa demands co-operation among all. The natural and human resources and the particular capacities of this association complement one another'.

Contents

	Page
Chapter One	
The Country	7
Chapter Two	
The People – Historical Survey	25
Chapter Three	
The People – Way of Life and Culture	49
Chapter Four	
The Capital – Umtata	69
Chapter Five	
Education and Vocational Training	77
Chapter Six	
Health Services	97
Chapter Seven	
The System of Justice	111
Chapter Eight	
Agriculture	123
Chapter Nine	
Forestry	147
Chapter Ten	
Social Security	153
Chapter Eleven	
The National Economy and Demography	159
Chapter Twelve	
Political Evolution	193
Chapter Thirteen	
System of Government	225
Chapter Fourteen	
Transkei and the World	237
Chapter Fifteen	
Nature Conservation and Tourism	247

Acknowledgements

The publishers wish to place on record their sincere appreciation of the valuable assistance given by Transkeian Government Departments and South African Government Departments; in particular the Transkeian Department of the Chief Minister and Finance, Umtata; and the Publications Division of the South African Department of Information, Pretoria.

Contributors
Dr D. D. Arbuckle, the Transkeian Department of Health, Transkei.

Bureau of Economic Research for Bantu Development, Pretoria.

Mr P. J. A. Carstens, Transkeian Department of the Interior, Umtata.

Prof. W. C. Els, University of Fort Hare, Alice.

Mr G. Geldenhuys, Chief Information Officer, Department of the Chief Minister and Finance, Umtata.

Dr K. B. Hartshorne, Director of Education Planning, Pretoria.

The Honourable Mr Justice Munnik, Chief Justice of Transkei.

Mr H. Neville, Town Clerk (Retired), Umtata.

Mr P. M. Ntloko, Cultural Planner, Transkeian Department of Education, Umtata.

Mr D. M. Ntusi, Senior Education Planner (Retired) Umtata.

Prof. Gerrit Olivier, University of Pretoria, Pretoria.

Mr G. Seymour Wood, University of Fort Hare, Alice.

Prof. Dr P. Smit, University of Pretoria, Pretoria.

Mr G. Swanepoel, Transkeian Department of Agriculture and Forestry, Umtata.

Dr Denis Worrall, Cape Town.

Photographers
Argent, Godfrey, London; Elliott, Aubrey, Pretoria; McNally, Terence, Cape Town; Mertens, Alice, Stellenbosch; Prinsloo, Michael, Pretoria; Verwey, Walt Productions, Johannesburg; Ward, Peter, Umtata.

Summer has come and brought copious rains with it.
The grazing has been fully regenerated and all the
animals will do well this year, the first year of
Independence, and in the fertile valleys men and women
are tilling the soil and planting maize and vegetables.

Production manager
Barbara Norman-Smith

Design, layout and picture editor
Ernst de Jong Studios, Pretoria

Photo typesetting and litho reproduction
McManus Bros. (Pty) Limited, Cape Town

Printers
Hortors Printers, Johannesburg

Publishers
Chris van Rensburg Publications (Pty) Ltd., Johannesburg

*A Bhaca boy. The Bhaca are an important segment of
the population of Transkei and originally hailed from
present-day Zululand from where they were forced by the
tyrant Shaka who subsequently made several
unsuccessful attempts to bring them to heel.*

Chapter One

The Country

The word Transkei is composed of the Latin prefix 'trans', which means 'across' and 'Kei', a Hottentot word meaning 'clear' or 'shiny', a name given by the Hottentots to this particular river.

Transkei is located between 27° and 30° east and 30° and 33° south. Situated in the south-east of Southern Africa, it is bounded by the Indian Ocean in the south-east, the Kingdom of Lesotho in the north and by the Republic of South Africa: the province of Natal in the north-east and the Cape Province in the north and north-west. The boundaries are mostly clear and rigid physical features: the larger part of the Kei River in the west, mountain ranges, including the Drakensberg, to the north, the Umtamvuna River in the north-east and at least a 270-km shoreline of the Indian Ocean to the south-east (Fig 1).

Transkei has a total area of some 41 100 km². The exact area is difficult to ascertain in view of the intricate relief patterns. Almost 40 000 km² is one consolidated block of 26 districts while two outlying districts, Herschel and Umzimkulu, are in close proximity. The boundary of the new state measures approximately 1 700 km.

The country is larger than Lesotho (30 000 km²) and the Netherlands (34 000 km²) and more than twice the size of Swaziland (17 000 km²).

Typical Transkei country. Through fertile valleys the Umzimvubu River, largest in the country, finds its majestic way to the Indian Ocean. About one-quarter of the total rainfall of South Africa and Transkei falls in Transkei.

Geologically, Transkei is situated mainly on the Beaufort Series of the Karoo System, in the temperate to warm and humid subtropical climatic region.

Terrain features

The great escarpment, the outstanding relief feature of Southern Africa, sculptured in rocks of diverse nature and greatly varying age by the erosion of rivers cutting back into the plateau, constitutes the major part of the boundary between Transkei and Lesotho. Scenically, the most majestic of the mountain features, the Drakensberg, is a barrier to communication between Transkei and Lesotho, but an asset in promoting the hydrological cycle over the country.

The entire escarpment along the border with Lesotho is capped by Stormberg lava and because it overlies the cave sandstone it forms a continuous scarp, abrupt and rugged.

The highest peaks are situated in the north-west, viz. The Twins, Dragon's Peak (west of Matatiele) and Castle Rock with altitudes of more than 2 400 m above sea-level. Towards the south, the altitude of the escarp decreases gradually over a distance of some 370 km to about 1 700 m above sea-level in the vicinity of Xalanga.

A foothill zone connects the mountain area with the inland plateau and falls away in the direction of the Indian Ocean. This descent occurs over a relatively short distance of 160 km and has a profound effect on the incision of the drainage lines as well as the velocity of stream run-off.

The sandstone forms pediment spurs to the plateau edge, jutting out for many kilometres in some places between the headwaters of the east-flowing streams. The more important rivers from north to south are Umzimvubu, Umtata, Bashee and the Great Kei. Owing to river incision the entire landscape of Transkei has an undulating to broken character. In fact, only about twenty per cent of the total area is ploughed.

Because the great escarpment and smaller escarpments clearly give a terraced character to a cross profile of the Transkeian landscape, the latter may be divided into three relief regions (Fig 2).

It seems valid to use the terms the Drakensberg highland, the interior plateau and the coastal plain. The marked altitudinal differences between these three relief zones also have a profound effect on the climate, whilst differences of structure and rock formation have been so projected into the surface features as to produce distinct subregions. Often too, they are transmitted into differing soils and vegetation and account for differing opportunities for human occupation and endeavour.

The Drakensberg highland

The escarpment or Drakensberg highland is intimately related to rainfall distribution and communications. This highland varies in altitude from 1 350 m to 1 800 m above sea-level. It comprises

Fig. 1 Location of Transkei in Southern Africa

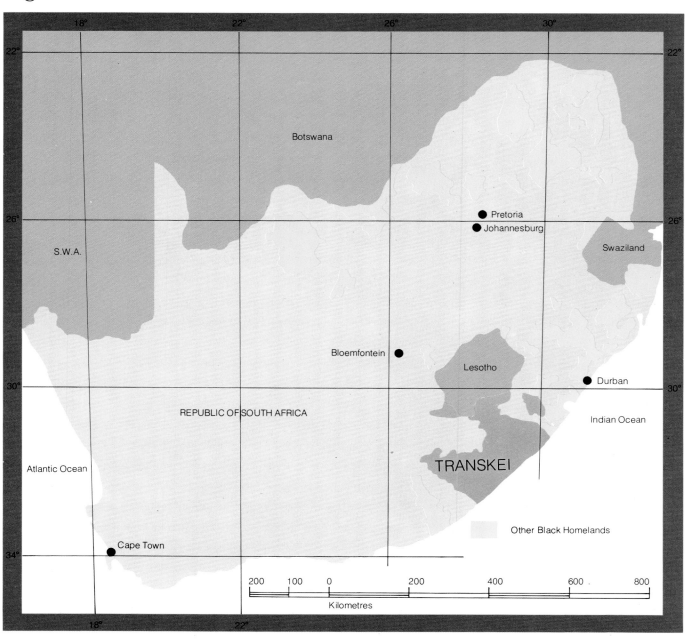

the mountain slopes and foothills of the Drakensberg: it is not only high-lying, but often has abrupt scarp faces. Valley plains finger into the mountains between great ridges where crest lines seldom fall below 1 800 m. Communication between isolated settlements near the head of the valley flats is therefore often difficult.

The entire region is a monument to river sculpturing directed from north-west to south-east, but intrusive conditions, however, are also abundant, for example where an isolated tumble of mountains – Mt. Currie and Bokberg – lies in advance of the mountain zone.

The exceptionally inclined surfaces and steep slopes result in shallow skeleton and immature soils: there are only small areas of really good agricultural soil. When the high rainfall is related to relief, it is obvious that surface erosion could be a distinct problem on cultivated lands. The vegetative cover is, fortunately, of such a nature that it can resist excessive and heavy grazing.

The eastern plateau slopes and the interior plateau midlands

The eastern uplands of Transkei lie between 300 to 900 m above sea-level. Their southerly location and proximity to the sea combine to produce a moderate climate.

Fig. 2   Relief Regions of Transkei

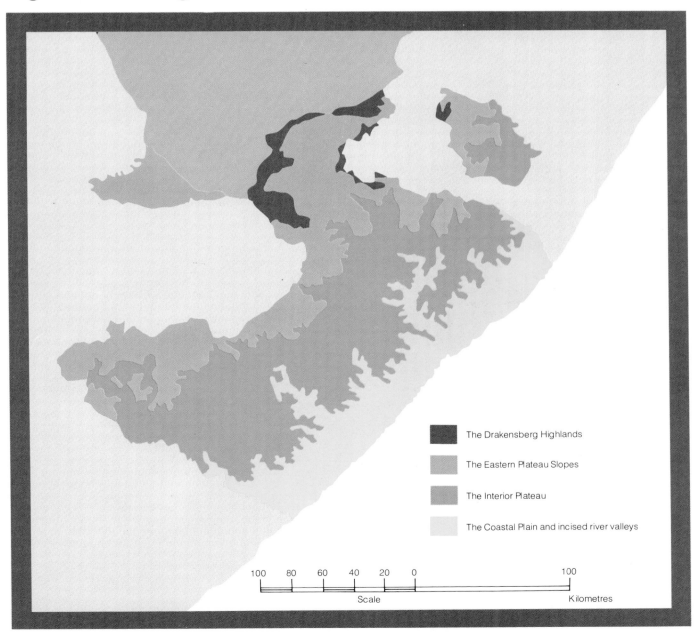

The Drakensberg Highlands

The Eastern Plateau Slopes

The Interior Plateau

The Coastal Plain and incised river valleys

100   80   60   40   20   0   100

Scale   Kilometres

The rivers rising in the mountain region are deeply incised, especially in the north. Towards the south the landscape opens up into a flat interior plateau of which the Unga plain is the most prominent feature. This is an old erosion surface lying between 1 200 m and 1 500 m. It is not continuous, however, but is broken up by the prominent Umsinga and Kranskop spurs.

The interior plateau embraces the districts of Gcuwa (formerly Butterworth), Idutywa, Nqamakwe, southern Cofimvaba, Engcobo, Umtata and portions of Tsolo and Libode as far north as the Umzimkulu River (See Fig 2).

Physically, the interior plateau of Transkei is one of the most favoured areas for mixed farming in Southern Africa. It consists of gently rolling hills, interspersed with a number of great valleys. Old sedimentary rocks are found over most of the area, but they are much intruded by dolerite which weathers into deep and fertile soils.

The river valleys are deeply incised. The larger rivers have cut relatively large and wide embayments or basins. The river profiles are relatively steep and fertile agricultural soils are found along some of the river courses. The river valleys have their own characteristic vegetation, consisting mainly of valley bushveld, while the vegetative cover of the remainder of the plateau is of a sour grassland type.

The coastal plain

The interior border of the coastal plain coincides approximately with the 300 – 450 metre contour line. This long but narrow coastal region is much lower than the interior plateau, but still has a steep slope along the cross profile to the ocean, although it is relatively flat along its longitudinal profile from north to south.

Between Port St.Johns and Port Shepstone (Natal), the Table Mountain sandstone accounts for the high cliffs which characterise the Wild Coast of Pondoland.

Scenically, the coast is at its most magnificent best where it is breached by the deep gorge of the Umzimvubu River at Port St. Johns.

A unique feature of the Transkeian landscape – Mlengana rock. The cultivated lands on the comparatively steep incline in the background are quite common in Transkei and in these conditions soil erosion is inevitable unless great care is taken.

Climate
Rainfall

A relatively high rainfall is one of the main assets of Transkei.

Position and location with regard to latitude, the rest of the subcontinent, the pressure zones and climatic regions imply a relatively high average annual rainfall. The spatial distribution of rainfall is, however, strongly influenced by the relief of the land, and three rainfall zones may be distinguished: the coastal area, the midlands and, thirdly, the great escarpment area where precipitation is possibly higher than in the coastal area.

A marked decrease in rainfall is apparent across Transkei from the coast (Port St. Johns) over the midlands (Mt. Frere) towards the mountainous highland (Mt. Fletcher). Thereafter precipitation increases again with the increase in altitude from the mountain foothills to the ridge of the east-facing escarpment. Between these two high rainfall zones (coast and escarp) there is a marked lower rainfall belt of varying width.

Average annual rainfall is relatively high throughout Transkei.

Compared with the Republic of South Africa, Transkei is in a most favourable situation: almost 90 per cent of South Africa – but only 10 per cent of Transkei – receives less than 750 mm a year. The annual rainfall ranges from 750 mm to 1 400 mm over the coastal plain and between 500 mm and 1 250 mm over the interior and the mountain areas. The long-term annual precipitation for Transkei is 815 mm (Fig 3).

The highest rainfall occurs during summer (October to March). At Port St. Johns and Willowvale (coastal area) between 69 and 73 per cent of the total annual rainfall occurs in summer, compared with a summer precipitation of between 76 and 82 per cent for Cofimvaba and Matatiele in the interior. Summer rainfall varies between 600 and 800 mm, with a maximum of rainy days during October and November. The distribution over the summer period is fairly even, except for March, the wettest month, and February, the driest. Another interesting feature of the seasonal rainfall distribution is the almost abrupt drop from March to April.

In a meteorological sense, Transkei is located in a convergence area. Frontal showers occur on nine days of every summer month and five of each winter month. In the northern coastal area frontal showers fall on up to 13 days every summer month.

Thunderstorms often occur on hot summer afternoons. There is no definite pattern and in one season, thunderstorms may produce enough precipitation to start planting in August, September and even October, but in another season they might appear late. A third type of precipitation is mist and drizzle – common in the mountains. This precipitation is not sufficient to commence the ploughing season but is of great value in afforestation.

In the coastal plain rainfall is of a showery nature and thunderstorms are quite frequent – about 20 to 30 a year. They are occasionally accompanied by hail especially towards the interior. In the midlands and mountain region rainfall is largely of the

thunderstorm type, sometimes of great intensity. From 60 to 90 thunderstorms are experienced in these regions every year.

Over the long term the coefficient of rainfall variation for Transkei in general ranges from 17 to 20 per cent. Furthermore, the difference in variation between the coastal area (Willowvale: 20,1 per cent) does not differ significantly from that over the interior (Umtata: 19,6 per cent).

An analysis of the seasonal variability of rainfall shows that planting crops too early in summer is risky, except along the coastal area. Over the interior mountain area (Cofimvaba and Mt. Fletcher) variability remains relatively high even

Fig. 3 Average Annual Rainfall

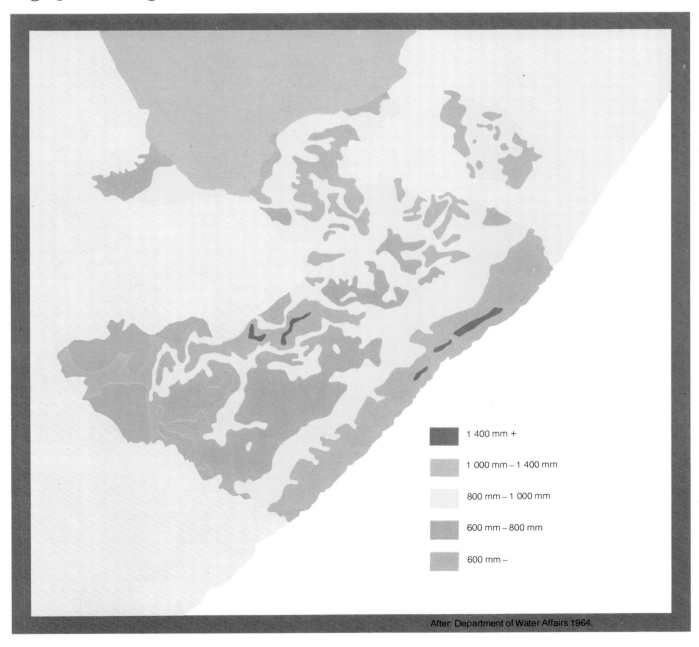

1 400 mm +

1 000 mm – 1 400 mm

800 mm – 1 000 mm

600 mm – 800 mm

600 mm –

After: Department of Water Affairs 1964.

13

during October. Considering the water requirements for dry-land agricultural crops, the best planting season seems to be October-November. In the interior the thermal growing season terminates fairly early in late summer and late planting is to be avoided.

Sunshine

Over the coastal region the sky is mostly clear in winter when the duration of sunshine is about 70 per cent of the maximum possible. In summer it is often cloudy to overcast resulting in only about 50 per cent of the possible sunshine duration. In the interior the actual duration of sunshine varies from 50 to 60 per cent of the possible maximum in summer, and from 70 to 80 per cent in winter. Sunshine intensity and degree of cloudiness are not growth-limiting factors in Transkei.

Snow

Snow is more frequent on the mountains than anywhere else in Transkei, probably on account of the great elevation of the Drakensberg. On average, snow falls about eight times a year, the peak of the snow season being July.

Usually the snow-cap melts within a day or two.

Temperature

Along the coast the average annual daily maximum temperature is 23,2°C, the average minimum 16,7°C, with an overall general range of 20°C. The relatively modest difference between the average maximum and minimum is due to the influence of the Indian Ocean. The northern coastal area is more tropical in climate and vegetation.

The average daily maximum temperatures of the coastal region are 28°C in January and 21°C in July, though extremes of 43°C and 34°C are recorded when hot winds blow. Average daily minima are 17°C in January and 8°C in July, but extremes of 12°C and 3°C respectively have been recorded on the coast and 5°C and −5°C in valleys in the interior.

The midlands experience higher maximum temperatures (Umtata: 25°C) and lower minimum temperatures (Umtata: 10,1°C) than the coastal area, with an annual mean of 17,6°C. The range

A watery winter sun is about to set in the valley, the last rays setting aflame the wall of the hut in the foreground. The harvest has been gathered and the grain stored in the pits. The scene is typical of the highlands of Transkei where much rain falls and the winters are pretty cold.

between maximum and minimum temperatures rises sharply to 15°C.

In the interior midland and Drakensberg regions the average daily maximum temperature is 27°C in January and 19°C in July, whilst extremes of 40°C and 30°C respectively have been recorded.

Average daily minima are 15°C in January and 3°C in July, whilst extremes may drop to 3°C and − 10°C respectively in summer and winter.

In the interior the frost period varies with altitude and is related to local relief and morphology. At Matatiele, for example, the average frost period is 61 days, whilst at Kokstad, only 60 km further inland in the Cape Province, it extends to 116 days. On average, the frost period over the coldest regions lasts 150 days, decreases across the mountain foothills to 120 days and drops to 90 days. Across the midlands it decreases from 90 to 30 days coastwards.

In the mountain highland region the average maximum temperature falls to 23°C and the average minimum temperature to 7,70°C.

Winds

Winds blow mainly parallel to the coast – north-easterly and south-westerly – and occasionally reach gale force. During north-easterly winds the sky is usually cloudless but hazy, and south-westerly winds bring cool cloudy weather and rain. Sometimes, mainly during late winter, very dry and hot 'berg winds' (foehn) are experienced.

Across the interior, winds are mainly southerly and northerly to north-westerly, the latter often very strong, especially in autumn. Further inland, wind direction changes again, but the most striking difference is the increase in calm periods, viz. 26,3 per cent, compared to 4,0 per cent for Idutywa. Inland, the average annual wind speed also decreases to five km per hour.

In Transkei wind has no or little effect on agricultural production. In the coastal region, however, local storms or gales may injure tea and coffee plantations, whilst dry 'berg winds', when they blow for days on end, increase evapotranspiration of natural vegetation and tend to scorch young crops, especially grain.

Agricultural implications

An average annual precipitation of between 500 and 625 mm is normally taken as the dividing line between livestock farming and cultivation farming areas. On this basis, 92 per cent of the arable area

of Transkei is suitable for agriculture (see Agriculture).

In the coastal region climatic conditions are favourable for the production of maize, sugarcane, tea, coffee, cotton, tobacco, tropical fruits, e.g. bananas, papaws, and a variety of vegetables.

Precipitation in the interior is suitable for a variety of agricultural crops but production is limited to the summer months owing to the occurrence of frost. Conditions are, however, favourable for maize, sorghum varieties, potatoes, dry beans and fodder crops. Cotton, groundnuts, wheat, lucerne, onions and potatoes will flourish under irrigation in the drier southern interior of Transkei. The wet mountain slopes are ideal for afforestation. Indeed, climate is no limiting factor in Transkeian agriculture.

Animal husbandry is directly and indirectly affected by climate. In the high rainfall region large-stock ranching is more successful than small-stock farming.

The cool moist climate of Transkei promotes vegetation and veld types suitable for meat and dairy cattle and swine. In the relatively drier midlands, and especially in the river valleys, the climate is suitable for sheep and cattle farming.

As far as climate is concerned, Transkei is potentially one of the best mixed farming regions in South Africa. The thornveld areas are especially suited to intensive cattle farming, crops and small stock, while the coastal region is suited to a wide variety of crops and bovine.

Geology and soil types

Rock formations of Transkei are mainly of the Karoo System, which covers by far the largest area, but Table Mountain sandstone and basalt also occur. The sentinels on either side of the Umzimvubu River mouth are fashioned in sandstone identical to the better known sandstone of the Western Cape Province. Quartzite-rich, quartzose-veined sandstone is also found in Pondoland, in northern Transkei, where it constitutes the coastal plateau.

Soil groups in Transkei include red and yellow

A glorious sight that repeats itself a hundred times over in the uplands of Transkei – a little mountain stream jumps its first hurdle on its course to the sea. The highest peaks are situated in the north-west of the country, with altitudes of more than 2 400 m above sea-level.

laterites, podsolic soils and, less frequently, solonetzic soils. Each main soil group is represented by a large number of soil types: variation is to be expected because of the extensive plateau and peneplains where the effects of topography would cause a wide variety of soil types even if the climate and parent material remained fairly constant.

Most Transkei soils fall in the sandy to sandy loam groups. Clay soils also occur, but heavy clays are the exception rather than the rule. The physical properties of all light-textured soils make for easy cultivation, good permeability but low water-holding capacity. Thus even short-term droughts tend to lower crop yields (Fig 4).

Erosion is a serious problem in Transkei. Most soils tend to erode fairly easily.

While soil depth is generally a limiting factor in Transkei, most soils have all the morphological characteristics ideal for field crop production. Alluvial-colluvial and podsolic soils are seldom too shallow for cultivating, however, except in mountain regions where immature soils are found. Two factors which may have a limiting effect in some areas are slope and impeded drainage owing to the presence of impermeable layers in the subsoil.

Only the doleritic and coastal soils contain moderate amounts of organic matter. Most soils are fairly rich in potassium, calcium and magnesium. All soil types, except doleritic soils, are low in phosphorous content.

The best crop soils are podsolic and doleritic soils. They are suitable for most grains, such as maize and sorghum, various legumes, perennial pastures, fodders and vegetables. Lateritic soils are especially suitable for various fodder crops and for afforestation. Coastal and semi-coastal soils – except those very rich in aluminium – are ideal for production of sugar-cane, coffee and tea, fibre plants, subtropical fruits and a great variety of vegetables.

Owing to the generally broken nature of the terrain and the location of the major rivers, irrigation possibilities in Transkei are somewhat limited. In fact, it has been estimated that only 22 000 hectares – or three per cent of the total arable area of the country – can be flood irrigated. On the other hand, it has been calculated that if this area could be brought under irrigation and properly cultivated, it would be sufficient to produce, for instance, enough maize – the staple food – to feed at least half the population of Transkei! (see Agriculture).

Nor is there ever likely to be insufficient water to

fill the dams providing the life-giving water for these irrigation schemes. It has been estimated that some 25 per cent of the total precipitation of South Africa falls on Transkei. Thus, the run-off of the rivers is considerable, especially in summer.

Solonetzic soils

Generally, the southern interior is relatively dry, compared with the rest of Transkei. With less leaching (rainfall between 500 and 600 mm), conditions are favourable for the formation of solonetzic soils.

Most Transkei solonetzic soils are shallow, ranging

from about 15 cm to alluvial soils along rivers and streams which are up to two metres in depth. Permeability of topsoil is fair to good, but drainage in lower layers is seldom better than moderate. The soils are low in organic matter content, fairly rich in phosphates and rich in potassium, calcium and magnesium.

Lateritic soils

Lateritic soils occur mainly in the higher mountain regions where the annual rainfall varies from 900 to 1 200 mm. Mist and rain often occur in the mountains and diurnal temperature fluctuations are wide. Under the influence of high rainfall,

Fig. 4 Soils

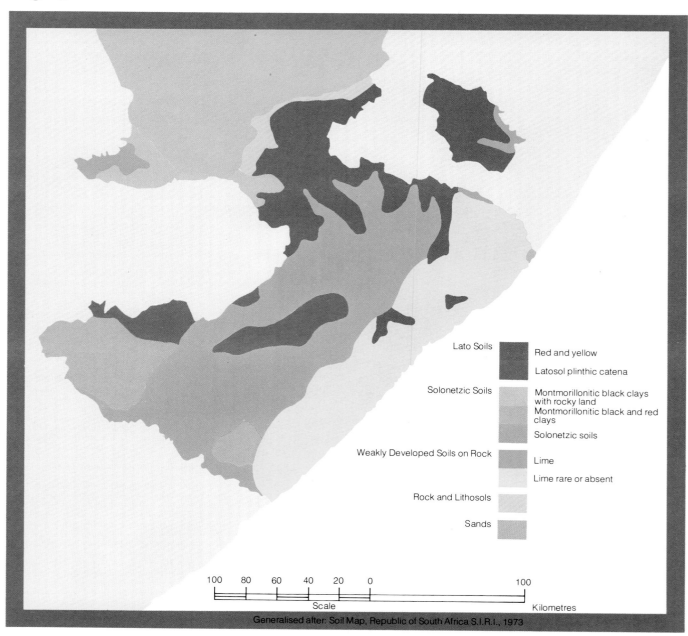

Lato Soils — Red and yellow
Latosol plinthic catena

Solonetzic Soils — Montmorillonitic black clays with rocky land
Montmorillonitic black and red clays
Solonetzic soils

Weakly Developed Soils on Rock — Lime
Lime rare or absent

Rock and Lithosols

Sands

Scale
100 80 60 40 20 0 100
Kilometres

Generalised after: Soil Map, Republic of South Africa S.I.R.I., 1973

alternate high and low temperatures and efficient internal and surface drainage, the geological formations weather to form lateritic soils. These brown and yellow earths are essentially sandy and clay soils from which soluble silica has been removed. They are easily cultivated but the crumbly clay structure is not very stable and the topsoil erodes easily, leaving the subsoil exposed so that donga-type erosion takes place.

Transverse movement of soil material by water and gravity leads to the formation of shallow immature soils on slopes and fairly deep soils in lower drainage lines. On slopes of four to ten per cent, the average depth of topsoil seldom exceeds 25 cm, while the subsoil varies from 40 cm to 120 cm in depth. Because lateritic soils support a dense cover of grass very little erosion occurs in virgin soils.

Most laterites are low in organic matter, calcium and potash.

Podsolic soils

Podsolic soils occur throughout Transkei where conditions are ideal for podsolisation. Mountain, midland and coastal podsols are found.

Topographically, relief conditions vary from undulating hills along the deeply incised coastal belt to very rugged foothill terrain along the eastern slopes of the Drakensberg range. The foothill region in particular is highly dissected to form intricate land surface patterns. In the midland region there are gigantic plateau spurs between deep valleys cut by the larger rivers.

Great variations in climate are found in podsolic regions. Rainfall varies from 1 400 mm a year along the coastal belt to 900 mm over the higher region near the mountains. Transkei podsolic soils consist of sandy loam layers, 40 cm to 50 cm deep, on yellowish brown clay horizons of varying depths.

Coastal region soils

True coastal soils are limited to a comparatively narrow belt along the coast of northern Pondoland. For all practical purposes, these soils are simply an extension of the sugar belt soils of Natal. The annual rainfall is high, varying from 1 200 to 1 400 mm.

The effective depth of these soils depends on the slope. In general, the topsoil depth is 20-25 cm and the subsoil depth 30-60 cm. Impermeable layers are very uncommon in these soils and drainage is always good.

Coastal sandy soils are poor in essential plant nutrients like phosphorous, nitrogen and potassium.

Intrazonal soils

Intrazonal soils occur throughout Transkei and are derived from dolerite intrusions. Basic igneous rocks – in this case Karoo dolerite – weather to form two main types of intrazonal soils – either less mature blackish brown clay soil or mature dark brown soil overlying deep reddish brown subsoil, depending on climatic and vegetational conditions.

Formative conditions vary from region to region, but the parent material seems to be the dominant factor in determining the soil type. Karoo dolerite invariably produces dark brown to black clay soil resting on lighter brown to yellow subsoil. Permeability is good in the topsoil but tends to moderate where textures are heavy. Intrazonal soils have excellent water-holding capacity, are relatively deep, except on steep mountain slopes and in more undulating coastal regions. The average topsoil depth ranges from 45-60 cm. Profiles of up to 250 cm are not uncommon in Transkei where doleritic soils are generally the most fertile soils for crop production.

Minor soil groups

There is also a number of minor soil groups. Basaltic soils occur in the mountain region between Lesotho and Transkei, and alluvial flood plains in a few isolated places. All alluvial deposits are of economic importance because the soils are deep, fertile and excellent for irrigation.

Veld types

Because of the temperate humid climate, natural vegetation varies from open grassy plains on the high-lying interior plateaux to dense forest growth along the coast and in the larger river valleys. In those areas where the natural vegetative cover has not been disturbed, vegetation stabilises to a climax of dense forest or tall grasses. In general however, the present vegetation is no longer the result of natural factors only, but more particularly of the veld utilisation pattern of the Black farmer over the past century or more. Over large areas there is no climax veld at all.

There are nine different veld types, grouped into three main categories for the purpose of this discussion: coastal forest and thorn veld, valley bushveld and Transkei grassveld proper. Owing to the uneven relief, one veld type may gradually merge into another or the change may be abrupt (Fig 5). The types are discussed below.

Coastal forest and thorn veld

The subtypes of this main group are the coastal forest and thorn veld, the Pondoland sour veld, 'Ngongoni veld and, to a lesser degree, the valley bushveld. The northern hot and humid coastal area is covered by dense and tangled trees and shrubs interspersed by grassy patches. Further southwards, where the climate tends to be drier, the forest is less dense and sour grassveld may reach down to the sea. Climax forest proper is found only in the many deeply incised river valleys and canyons. The remainder of the area is covered by more open grassveld, e.g. the 'Ngongoni and Pondoland sour veld.

The 'Ngongoni veld type has developed mainly through overgrazing and trampling of the veld, while the Pondoland sour veld has been established in the coastal area where Table Mountain sandstone occurs. These veld types are exceptionally dense and grow luxuriantly, but are very sour and supply good grazing only during the summer months.

The coastal forest consists mainly of evergreen trees and shrubs with a wide variety of undergrowth, mostly ferns and climbers. Along the coastline the forest is relatively short (five to ten metres) and very dense and tangled, but against the seaward-facing hills backing the coastal area it is taller and less tangled, about 18 metres high, sometimes more. The rainfall ranges between 875 mm to 1 500 mm a year and is, therefore, nowhere insufficient for forest. The vegetative cover is exceptionally dense and comprises 372 species on any two hectares. The most important trees in this forest are *Millettia caffra* (Transkei ironwood), *Vepris lanceolata* (White ironwood), *Combretum kraussii* (Vaderlandswilg), *Ficus natalensis* (Wild rubber), *Rhus legati* (Kieriewood). The dense mass of shrubs and climbers includes *Unvaria caffra, Dalbergia obovata, Tricalysia lanceolata* and *Entada spicata*. The more important grass species include *Themeda triandra, Hyparshenia filipendula, Heteropogon contortus* and *Tristachya hispida*.

The thorn veld appears inland from the coastal forest. This veld type contains patches of thorn trees and shrubs with wide open grassveld interspersed. The grass cover is dense and tall.

Pasture management of the coastal areas is dif-

Cattle grazing on a slope in central Transkei. During the day the animals are usually watched over by one or more herd-boys and by night they are herded into kraals (pens) close to the homestead. Sour veld predominates in the high mountain areas and provides good grazing.

ficult. The dense tree and shrub growth hampers veld utilisation, and often botanical composition changes so that trees and shrubs become dominant while weaker grasses invade.

Valley bushveld

As the name valley bushveld implies, this peculiar karroid veld type is found in the valleys of Transkeian rivers. On the whole the valleys are hot and receive less rain than the intervening ridges and towards the south they tend to become drier. Tree growth is less dense and of medium height. The most important trees are *Dombeya cymosa, Euphorbia tirucalli, Acacia arabica, Acacia karoo, Acacia ataxacantha, Ziziphus mucronata* and *Aloe spectablis*. Grasses grow between the trees. Generally the veld may be described as sweet but as much as 50 per cent may be sour veld.

Typical Eastern Province thorn veld is found on the ridges between river valleys. The term thorn veld is, however, misleading because the common sweet thorn-tree (*Acacia karoo*) is fairly rare. The veld is usually sour and the most common thorn-tree is *Cassia mimosoides*. The main grass sward is rather sour.

Valley bushveld provides excellent sweet grazing. The high degree of palatability leads to both overgrazing and selective grazing, with the result that these areas are trampled and in some cases badly eroded.

Transkei grassveld

The largest part of Transkei is covered by sour veld. Owing to variations in relief, rainfall and soil types there is a number of subtypes of which highland sour veld is the most important.

Between altitudes of 1 200 and 2 100 m above sea-level the eastern mountain slopes and foothills of the Drakensberg are covered by tall grass sour veld. These slopes receive orographic rain from the south-east and north-west and with an annual average rainfall of 750 to 1 250 mm this area is moist and humid. The winters are cold and dry and snow falls regularly. Tall grassveld occurs at various altitudes and along the higher slopes the *Themeda Festuca* veld type dominates. Various scrubs are also fairly common.

Patches of southern tall grassveld occur everywhere in the Transkeian highlands. These consist mainly of *Themeda triandra* and *Hyparrhenia hirta*. The most extensive areas are around Cala, in the Bashee-Xuka valley near Engcobo, in the Ixgu valley north of Tsolo and in the upper reaches of the Umzimvubu and Umzimhlava Rivers. Smaller areas are found south of Mt. Fletcher and in the Kinira valley directly north of Mt. Frere, as well as to the west of the town of Umzimkulu. In general, the vegetation is shorter than in the highlands due to lower precipitation. There are fewer shrubs but *Acacia caffra,* characteristic of the southern tall grassveld, is fairly common.

The 'Ngongoni veld is found in a narrow broken belt running from the Umtata River just above the coastal forest. Considering the climate, one would expect there to be a climax vegetation of forest and shrubs, but today by far the greater part of the area is dominated by *Aristida junciformis,* for which reason it has been named the 'Ngongoni veld. This thorn veld is generally very open, except at the edges of the bush-filled valleys. This veld type is

sour and provides the best grazing in spring.

In Herschel the *Themeda-Festuca* Alpine veld occurs at altitudes higher than 2 000 m where precipitation exceeds 575 mm a year. This short, dense grassveld varies from sweet to mixed and is dominated by *Themeda triandra,* with an admixture of the usual grassveld species, although it has a high proportion of less common grasses, especially at higher altitudes, as well as scrub forest in sheltered kloofs. The soil is generally black and turfy and extremely erodible. Mismanagement of the veld tends to favour the southern element of the flora.

Evaluation of veld types

Generally, the vegetation cover of Transkei is

Fig. 5 Veld Types

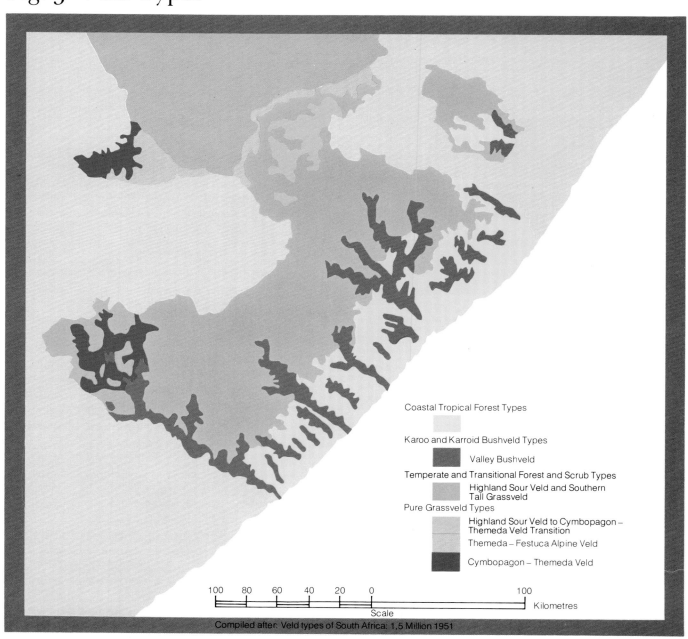

Coastal Tropical Forest Types

Karoo and Karroid Bushveld Types

Valley Bushveld

Temperate and Transitional Forest and Scrub Types

Highland Sour Veld and Southern Tall Grassveld

Pure Grassveld Types

Highland Sour Veld to Cymbopagon – Themeda Veld Transition

Themeda – Festuca Alpine Veld

Cymbopagon – Themeda Veld

100 80 60 40 20 0   100

Kilometres

Scale

Compiled after: Veld types of South Africa: 1,5 Million 1951

among the densest in South Africa and, where it has not been destroyed, secures good protection for the soil. The veld types have an amazing ability to recover; some climax grasses still occur even under heavy or severe grazing and after a period of rest they are fairly quickly restored to their former dense state.

The nutritive value of the natural vegetation follows the general pattern of the grassveld of the eastern coastal areas. In the high mountain areas sour veld predominates and provides good grazing in summer. Sweet veld, on the other hand, retains most of its nutritive value during autumn and winter. Like all grassveld areas of Southern Africa, these also manifest a mineral shortage throughout the year.

The grassveld flourishes under prevailing climatic conditions and a surplus often occurs in summer. This fact opens up the possibility of two land-use systems: cutting hay as additional winter fodder, or a grazing programme heavier than the accepted average but provided bovine are marketed at the end of summer to avoid overgrazing during the winter months.

Fauna

Much of the natural fauna of Transkei has been either driven away or destroyed: like all other Black peoples of South Africa, Transkeians have been hunters for centuries. Some areas have been denuded of indigenous species, such as blue buck and bush buck. Comparatively large numbers of these animals and of grey duiker, are, however, still found in the protected forests where hunting is prohibited and poaching efficiently controlled.

Some of the rarer species of waterfowl, such as white-backed duck, maccoa-duck and the African pochard, are appearing in ever increasing numbers on the Tsolo fish-breeding dams and many species of duck and goose have recently established themselves on new dams, such as Lubisi and Ncora. The numbers of partridges, on the other hand, have been severely decreased owing to the destruction of their habitat by overgrazing.

The Transkei government has ambitious plans for the resuscitation and conservation of the natural fauna of the territory. The first nature reserve in Transkei was established in 1974 on the Dwessa and Cwebe forest reserves. These are coastal forests on either side of the Bashee River (see section on Nature Conservation and chapter on Agriculture).

Freshwater fish

The trout streams of Transkei are inland, away from the warmer coastal region and in and near the mountain regions.

Some of the upper tributaries of the Great Kei and Bashee Rivers, as well as the Tsomo River, yield an abundance of rainbow trout. The Tsomo is muddy for a long period during the summer rainy season when fishing for large eels is a popular activity.

A number of upland streams of the Bashee River system – the Mgwali, Gqutyeni, Mnyolo and Qumanco – have also been stocked with rainbow trout. On several occasions since 1903 the upper tributaries of the Umtata River were unsuccessfully stocked with trout ova. Since 1954 new methods have been employed and reared rainbow fingerlings from the Pirie Hatchery near King William's Town have been released into the river.

Originally the Umzimvubu River system entering the sea at Port St. Johns was completely without indigenous freshwater fishes, with the exception of the minnow-sized gillieminkie (*Barbus anoplous* or *karkensis*) and migratory freshwater eels (*Anquilla mossombica* and *A. marmorata*). This habitat was subsequently stocked with rainbow trout and the Umzimvubu River system still provides some of the best trout fishing in Transkei – despite the deterioration of a promising environment caused by severe soil erosion in the upper reaches and the silting of river beds so evident in the estuary at Port St. Johns.

In the Matatiele area carp is found in the slower-flowing, willow-hung meandering stretches which also produce large trout at times. The border river, Umtamvuna, in the district of Bizana is also a good trout water.

The Great Kei River system is poor in indigenous freshwater species, originally holding only eels and gillieminkie minnows. Throughout Transkei the main freshwater prize is the eel. In some rivers, for instance the Umtata River, small-mouth bass has been introduced below the trout areas, with varying results.

The carp-populated stretches of the rivers attract many anglers and yield a considerable amount of fish of rather inferior quality. A number of storage dams in Transkei are also stocked with bass. (See the chapter on Agriculture, where this subject is also dealt with and the point is made that Transkei can build up an export market in fresh fish.)

Chapter Two

The People
Historical Survey

The people of Transkei, with those of the Ciskei, are the southernmost representatives of the Bantu-speaking peoples of Africa, speaking a virile and beautiful language called *isiXhosa* and inhabiting the corridor between the Drakensberg range and the Indian Ocean. They are famous in the annals of South African history for their strong national pride and conservatism, but also for the way in which they have responded to the challenges of change. Today we still see these apparently contradictory qualities. In the remoter areas traditional values and customs are jealously guarded and in others there is evidence of progressive farming and virtually full attendance at school. For fifty years the United Transkeian Territories General Council, or Bunga, set an example of responsible co-operation that cut across tribal groups. Who are these people, about to enter an exciting new era of national development?

They are generally referred to as the Xhosa, but this is not accurate. They are all Xhosa-speaking, for the dialect of the westernmost section was the first to be reduced to writing, but the people themselves are divided into a number of separate tribal clusters, each with its own history and culture. There are about ten of these clusters, including the Thembu, Mpondo, Mpondomise, Bhaca, Xesibe and the Xhosa proper, the distribution of which is shown on the accompanying map. In the

A Mpondo man and his wife have come to town for the day. The Mpondo tribes have occupied their present regions – the central midlands and seaboard – for centuries. The Mpondo are one of ten major tribal clusters (see map) of Transkei.

past there has often been conflict both between and within the tribal clusters but, as often, co-operation, and today, although the consciousness of tribal affiliation is still strong, there has grown up a strong sense of common Transkeian allegiance.

Neither in the old Bunga, nor in the political alignments since self-government in 1963, has tribalism or ethnicity been an important factor.

Transkeians (they are called Cape Nguni by anthropologists) were occupying the eastern half of their territory by at least the fourteenth century and, during the sixteenth century, slowly moved westward until in 1702 they met the eastward moving White pioneers in the region of the Fish River, a thousand kilometres from Cape Town. Here they also came into contact with the Gonaqua Khoi (Hottentots), whom they absorbed, and other Khoi groups with whom they fought and traded. In the early seventeenth century there was close contact between the westernmost Xhosa-speakers and the Khoi. Intermarriage between royal families occurred and there was an important trade in which Xhosa cannabis was exchanged for copper rings and beads. There was also prolonged contact with San (Bushman) bands. Sometimes, as among the Mpondomise, the San were employed as rain-makers. This close contact with the San hunters and Khoi pastoralists had a profound effect on the Xhosa language in that borrowing occurred of both words and sounds – the famous "clicks" which add so much to the vividness of the Xhosa language. The boundary between the Xhosa-speakers and the Khoisan can be seen in the names of rivers in the area. North of the Kei River

the names are Bantu, e.g. Qhora, Mbashe (Bashee) Mthatha, Mzimvubu, Mzimkhulu: south they are Khoi, e.g. Keiskama, Kariega, Kasouga and Gamtoos. Generally, the Bantu-speakers practised mixed hoe-culture and pastoralism and remained to the east of the 500 mm rainfall line.

Originally, the entry of the Xhosa-speakers into the area now known as Transkei must have been from the north-east. Traditions are very vague but there are legends referring to an origin 'in the east', i.e. Natal, and an entry route close under the Drakensberg or, possibly, along the coast from Natal. Archaeological evidence would appear to favour the latter. What is certain is that when the first of a series of shipwrecks on the Transkeian coast occurred, the survivors found the area occupied by people who were undoubtedly Cape Nguni.

The first of these was the *São João,* which went ashore just north of the Mzimvubu River in June 1552. This was followed by the *São Bento* in 1554, the *Santo Alberto* (1593), the *São João Baptista* (1622), the *Nossa Senhora de Belem* (1635) and the *Stavenisse* (1686). The survivors of these shipwrecks left some account of the people they met in their attempts to reach safety and it is quite clear from their reports that the east coast was occupied by Xhosa-speakers. It seems that, as is the case even today, the broken coastal strip with its sour veld was not as thickly settled as the interior, but in the undulating country of the corridor along which the national highway now runs 'the country was thickly populated and provided with cattle'. The recorder of the *Santo Alberto* describes the dress of the people as "a mantle of ox-hide, with the hair outwards, which they rub with grease to make it soft . . . their kings and chiefs wear, hanging from the left ear, a copper ornament made after their own fashion . . . they cultivate millet, which is white and the size of a peppercorn . . . ground between two stones or in wooden mortars . . . their cattle are very fat, tender, well-flavoured and large . . . they live in small villages, in huts made of reed mats . . . they obey chiefs whom they call Inkosis". The latter was the first recorded use of a Xhosa word. In June 1635, the survivors of the *Belem* spent six months with the Xhosa (who addressed the captain as *umlungu* and *unkulu*) and the report describes their way of life in some detail.

'The men of this country are very lean and

The Fingo or Mfengu tribe, of which this man is a member, is unique in one major respect. Unlike the names of all other major tribes, Mfengu is not derived from the name of an ancestor, but is a term applied to these people by the Gcaleka.

upright, tall of stature, and handsome. They can endure great labour, hunger and cold; they live two hundred years and even more in good health, and with all their teeth. They are so light that they can run over the rugged mountains as fleetly as stags. They are clothed in skins which hang over their shoulders to the knees; these are cow-hides, but they have the art of dressing them till they are as soft as velvet. There are rich and poor among them, but this is according to the number of their cattle. They all carry sticks in their hands about two spans in length, with a tail at the end like the brush of a fox, which serves them as a handkerchief and fan. They use sandals of elephant's hide, which they carry hanging from their hands, and I never saw them on their feet. Their arms are assegais with broad well-fashioned heads. Their shields are of elephant hide with handles like ours . . . They all have dogs with ears and tails cropped, with which they hunt wild pigs and stags, as well as buffaloes, elephants, tigers (leopards) and lions . . .

'The kings have four, five, and seven wives . . . cows are what they chiefly value: these are very fine and the tamest cattle I have ever seen in any country' (Theal *Records of South-Eastern Africa,* vol. VIII, pp. 204-5).

It is clear that the Xhosa-speakers have been in Transkei for many hundreds of years, that they were cattlemen and practised agriculture. But in those days the staple crop was millet, not maize. Milk was plentiful and, as sour milk, the main item in their diet. Cultivation was by means of a digging stick and the digger worked sitting down. It was only after the coming of the missionaries in the 1820s that the plough was introduced. Both polygamy and circumcision were recorded.

By 1686 and the wreck of the *Stavenisse,* the main tribal groups seem to have been in more or less their present territories. Search parties were dispatched from the Cape to seek for survivors and one reported that the peoples they had found along the coast were 'the Magosses (Xhosa), the Magrigas (Riligwa), the Matimbes (Thembu), Mapontes (Mpondo), Emboas (Mbo).' Inland the country was reported to be 'exceedingly fertile and incredibly populous, and full of cattle'. Chieftainship was in its full vigour. The people 'submit their disputes to the king', assaults were punished by the payment of a fine to the chief, and 'no one must presume to barter anything to a stranger without the king's consent'. And the famed Transkeian hospitality goes back a long way: the people were 'so hospitable that at every kraal there was a hut kept purposely for the accommodation of strangers', and so sociable that 'they never passed each other without stopping and conversing'. (Bird *Annals of Natal I,* pp. 42-7).

Exactly how the earlier Xhosa-speakers came into the area is difficult to reconstruct with any degree of certainty. The earliest traditions, recorded by writers such as J. H. Soga, A. T. Bryant, R. T. Kawa, T. B. Soga and Chief Victor Poto Ndamase, all locate the earliest remembered localities within the area now occupied by Nguni peoples. Thus the traditions of both the Xhosa and Mpondomise start at the "sources of the Mzimvubu (River) called the Dedesi", but all attempts to find the Dedesi have failed. Other groups speak of coming from *Eluhlangeni*, but this is probably a mythical reference. *Uhlanga*, from which the name is derived, may mean either a hole in the ground from which the original stock of these people is believed to have emerged, or a reed bed, in which case the

symbolism is that of various tribes and nations splitting off, just as the suckers of the reed split and form new plants. A similar tradition is recorded by Steedman – that the first Xhosa chief came from a cave called *uDaliwe* to the east. But the word merely means 'to be created' and obviously refers to an origin myth.

What is clear is that the earliest groups to inhabit Transkei were the tribal clusters of the Xhosa, Thembu, Mpondomise, Mpondo and Bomvana.

The Xhosa were the first to arrive. In the period 1600-1650 they were well established just east of the Kei River, with the Thembu east of them. That they had moved slowly from the east is shown by

Fig. 6 Distribution of Tribes

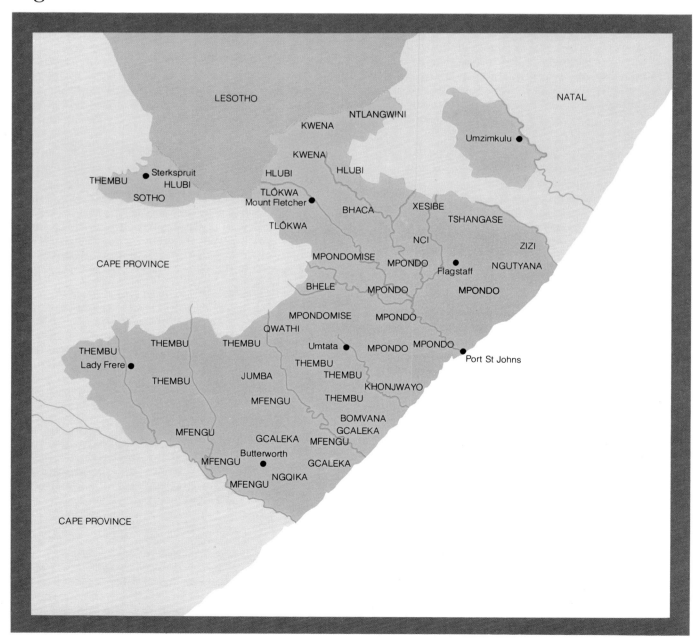

the graves of Xhosa chiefs east of the Mzimvubu. By 1650 they had crossed the Kei into what is now the Ciskei, and adventurous groups had proceeded even further west, so that in 1702 a fugitive group of Xhosa 'living in friendship with the Hottentots' was found near where Somerset East is today. In 1772 Thunberg met Xhosa on the Gamtoos and by the early 19th century there were groups of Xhosa on the Buffalo and Keiskama Rivers. One small group lived north of the Orange River, one in the Roggeveld, and the Gqunukhwebe, under Cungwa, lived for a time in the Long Kloof.

A striking feature of the Xhosa groups was the tendency to split and form new tribes. As we have seen, chiefs were polygamous and many had several wives who were ranked in 'houses', each forming a separate unit. Usually there were two main houses, a great house and a right-hand house, and all wives were allocated to either of these houses (see System of Justice). The senior wife in the great house was the mother of the heir to the chieftainship, but the heir in the right-hand house sometimes set up his own chieftainship, with his own followers. This often occurred when a chief died and his son in the great house was still a minor and an uncle was appointed as regent. When the boy came of age the regent was reluctant to give up office and hived off with his supporters. Thus an original group would split into a number of new chiefdoms. This has, in fact, happened to all major groups in Transkei. The Xhosa, for instance, now consist of the original chiefdom (now called the Gcaleka), the Ndlambe, Ngqika, Mdushane, Gasela, Gwali, Qhayi, Dange, Hleke and Gqunukhwebe (who absorbed the Gonaqua Hottentots). Legend relates that the chief Tshiwo had a chief executioner, Khwane, who hid those tribesmen accused of witchcraft and thus condemned to death. Later, when Tshiwo was beset by his enemies, Khwane produced an *impi* of these refugees, who turned the tide of battle. In gratitude Khwane was granted his own chieftainship, and the Gqunukhwebe came into being.

The prime necessity for any new chiefdom was to establish its own territory, and it was the westernmost Xhosa who first came into conflict with the expanding White pioneers. Most of the subsequent frontier wars, waged sporadically over a century from 1779, were between these chiefdoms, moving in a south-westerly direction, and the advancing Whites. The eastern border of the Cape Colony was the first of many frontiers to be established between Black and White. A major reason for the frontier wars and clashes was that both groups were cattle farmers and often desired the same grazing land. As their customs concerning land ownership were totally different, misunder-

standings inevitably occurred. Both groups were also hunters who sought game for meat and skins. For many years the numerically superior Xhosa effectively opposed the White pioneers, although the latter initially had a monopoly of fire-arms and a considerable advantage in that they fought on horseback. The immediate causes of the earliest armed clashes on the border (from 1779 onward) cannot easily be established. Generally, there seems to have been a chronic lack of control on both sides. Consequently, unruly elements sometimes succeeded in causing reactions which led to extensive military action.

On the Xhosa side there were uninhabited buffer zones between the chiefdoms. The survivors of the wreck of the *Grosvenor* reported them in 1790, as did the Reverend Bransby Key, fifty years later, among the Mpondomise.

He wrote that between the territory of the Mpondo and Mpondomise was 'a belt of unoccupied country some twenty miles across, waving with grass, intersected by no roads. There were only one or two little narrow footpaths, hardly visible in the long grass, worn by the few travellers who passed from tribe to tribe . . .'

This neutral zone was the haunt of game and said to be occupied by lion. Although these belts of unoccupied territory served primarily a defensive purpose, they were probably also hunting areas. The chief of the senior tribe in a tribal cluster was called the paramount and he was held in great respect as the head of the royal lineage, to which all the chiefs of the cluster belonged. They tended to consult him on matters of national importance, on royal marriages and on matters concerning the royal family, but in their own chiefdoms they were to a large extent independent. Appeals from the court of a chief did not normally go to that of the paramount and, indeed, there was occasionally armed conflict between a chief and his paramount.

Among the Xhosa the splitting process was perhaps more prominent than in other groups. The earliest recorded chiefs were Mnguni, Xhosa, Malangana, Nkosiyamntu and Tshawe (who gave his name to the royal lineage) but there is no information on them. Tentative dates have been fixed for Ngcwangu (1550-1580) and Sikomo (1580-1610). Both were buried near the Mzimvubu, in what is now Mpondoland. By the time of the next chief, Togu (1610-1640), the Xhosa were on the Kei River, in close contact with the Khoi (Hottentots) and John Knox Bokwe states that Togu took the daughter of Ngosini, chief of 'the Lawo', as one of his minor wives. The son of this union was Ntinde, who founded the Ntinde section of the Xhosa. Ntinde, with Gwali, was the first

chief's son to break away from the main Xhosa stem. But, before this occurred, Togu was succeeded by Ngconde (1640-1670). It was during Ngconde's reign that the small groups referred to earlier (those found in Somerset East and the Suurveld) broke away, but there is no evidence of permanent settlement west of the Fish River at this period.

Ngconde was followed by Tshiwo (1670-1702) who was buried at Nqcwanguba forest just west of the Mthatha River and was followed by Phalo (1702-1775), who had his great place near the Amathole Mountains in 1752. It was during Phalo's reign that the first break-away resulting in the formation of new chieftainships occurred. Mdange was regent during Phalo's minority, and when Gwali, right-hand son of Tshiwo attempted to usurp the chieftainship and was supported by Ntinde and his section, Mdange organised a punitive expedition which defeated Gwali's forces near the Fish River. Soga states that Mdange was so impressed by the country across the Kei that, on Phalo's succession, he obtained his permission to settle there with his section, the imiDange. Gwali and Ntinde both fled and established independent chiefdoms. The amaGwali and the amaNtinde today reside in the Ciskei. Later, in the early part of the eighteenth century, a section broke away under Hleke, a minor son of a supporting house of Ngconde.

The major split in the Xhosa tribal cluster occurred in a conflict between Phalo's heirs in the great house and right-hand house respectively, Gcaleka and Rarabe. Tradition relates that Gcaleka intrigued against his father, who was supported by Rarabe, his favourite son in the right-hand house. The majority of the tribe appears to have favoured Gcaleka, as Phalo was a weak chief, but in the ensuing trial of strength Gcaleka was defeated. Yet, Rarabe decided to move west after the death of Phalo in 1775 and settled on the Keiskama River. The amaGcaleka, under Gcaleka's descendants Khawutha, Hintsa, Sarili and Sigcawu, eventually returned to Transkei and today occupy most of the district of Gatyana (formerly Willowvale). They are the senior Xhosa tribe and their chief is paramount of all the Xhosa.

Rarabe did not bequeath his name to an independent group. His heir, Mlawu, predeceased his father, leaving an infant son, Ngqika. During Ngqika's minority Mlawu's younger brother, Ndlambe, was appointed regent and his personal-

Gcaleka tribal dancing. The Amagcaleka are the senior Xhosa tribe of Transkei and their chief is paramount chief of all the Xhosa. Gcaleka, originator of the tribe, intrigued against his father Phalo who was supported by Rarabe, his favourite son in the right-hand house.

ity and ability secured him a large following. In 1797 civil war broke out and, although Ndlambe was defeated, he was joined by many supporters, especially after Ngqika abducted Thuthula, one of his uncle's wives. Ndlambe's section finally achieved independence after defeating Ngqika at the Battle of Amalinda in 1818. The amaNdlambe now reside in the Ciskei, between King William's Town and East London, while the amaNgqika occupy the Transkeian district of Centane (formerly Kentani).

It was the Rarabe tribes (with the Ntinde, Dange and Gwali) who were mostly involved with the White pioneers during the frontier wars. The Gcaleka under Hintsa and, later, Sarili, tended to remain aloof in their territory east of the Kei River. This did not stop Hintsa being held responsible by the British authorities for the actions of these minor chiefs. In the 1834-35 war he was blamed by Colonel (later Sir) Harry Smith, governor of the Cape Colony, for the activities of the other Xhosa tribes in the 'neutral territory' between the Fish and Keiskama Rivers for, after all, was he not the paramount? It was not realised that the authority of a paramount was not political, and that the westernmost chiefs were acting as independent agents. It is highly probable, though, that Gcaleka territory was being used for secreting stolen cattle.

One occurrence affected nearly all the Xhosa chiefdoms and certainly involved the Gcaleka in a major way. This was the tragic episode of *Nongqawuse*, known also as the 'national suicide of the amaXhosa'. In late 1857 Nongqawuse, the niece of Mhlakaza, a Xhosa noble who lived at the Gxara stream in the Centane district, claimed that she had received visitations from the tribal ancestors, especially Ngqika, Hintsa and Maqoma, who instructed the Xhosa to destroy their cattle and crops. If this were done, on a certain day the sun would turn blood-red, the dead would arise, the grain pits would be full and the millennium would be ushered in. The Xhosa were under great pressure, both from the White pioneers and from the ravages of lung-sickness. Not all believed the prophecy – Sandile of the amaNgqika refused to slaughter his stock – but the Gcaleka laid waste their wealth. When the appointed day arrived and went, destitution stalked the land. Thousands died and many others crossed into the Cape Colony to find work. Gcaleka territory, which had extended towards Queenstown, shrank to little more than its present extent.

The next most populous tribal cluster after the Xhosa is that of the Thembu which today extends in a great arc from Mqanduli, through Umtata and Engcobo, to St. Mark's and Cala. They seem to have entered Transkei at about the same time as the Xhosa and they, too, were split into a number of chiefdoms. Between about 1650 and 1830, six new chiefdoms came into being. J. H. Soga could find no connection between the Thembu and the other Transkeian tribes. Certainly, there were a number of groups calling themselves Thembu in Natal and one of these moved south into Transkei. As has been pointed out, the survivors of the *Stavenisse* in 1686 found 'Matimbes', probably in the region of the Mthamvuna River, but there is evidence that others were further west. Still today in Natal, at the Qhudeni Mountains, is a group calling themselves *abaThembu baseQhudeni*.

The early chiefs were Thembu, Bomoyi, Ntongakazi, Ceduma, Toyi, Ntande and Mguti. Nothing is known of them. The next chief, Nxego, seems to have lived in the middle seventeenth century and was buried at Msana, on the Mbashe (Bashee River), so the main body of Thembu have been in their present locality since at least that time.

The Thembu split in about 1640 on a dispute between Nxego's two sons in the great house, Hlanga and Dlomo. Dlomo, the younger, was the favourite of the people and Nxego, noting this, sent Dlomo to the cattle posts where he collected a following and defied his father. Nxego and Hlanga attacked but Dlomo, assisted by Ndungwana, an elder son in a non-chiefly house, prevailed and the chieftainship passed to this line. For many years Hlanga and his followers remained between the Mbashe and Kei Rivers. Later other groups broke away and formed separate chieftaincies – the amaNdungwana, the amaTshatshu and the amaJumba. The main Dlomo line continued under the chiefs Hala, Madiba, Taro, Zondwa and Ndaba. Ndaba's son, Ngubengcuka or Vusani, was born towards the end of the eighteenth century. It was during his reign that a group of Xesibe, the amaQwathi, was accepted as tributary to the Thembu and still resides today in the district of Engcobo.

The year 1828 was an anxious one for the Thembu. A group of Natal Nguni, the Ngwane under their redoubtable leader Matiwane, was expelled from Natal by Shaka, builder of the Zulu empire and one of the greatest conquerors in African history. They invaded Thembu territory from the direction of the Caledon River. They first fell on the Qwathi, and Ngubengcuka called on the colonial authorities for help. A battle was fought at Mbolompo, near Umtata, on 28 August 1828 under the command of Col. Henry Somerset and, with Thembu assistance, the Ngwane were put to flight. The disturbances caused by the Ngwane incursion caused another secession. A part of the Thembu people, the so-called Emigrant Thembu,

moved from the neighbourhood of Umtata to the area of Glen Grey and Cofimvaba, under Mathanzima of the right-hand house of Mthikrakra, son of Ngubengcuka. They consisted of the Tshatshu under Bawana, the Hala under Mathanzima, the Ndungwana under Darala, and two non-Thembu tribes, the Gcina and the Qwathi, who recognised the Thembu paramount. Mathanzima's descendant, Paramount Chief Kaiser Matanzima, is the first Prime Minister of the independent Transkei.

The Ngwane were not the only invaders to trouble Transkei during this period. Shaka's Zulu also made sporadic incursions, as did the Hlubi under Mpangazitha. Often it was unclear just who the threatening groups were. They all tended to be called Mfecane. On 31 August 1827 the missionary William Shaw wrote in his *Journal*: "The country has been kept in a continual state of alarm, for some time past, in consequence of the near approach of a large marauding tribe from the interior . . . For several years past there have been continual wars among the interior tribes, both of Bootshuanas and Caffres, originating in the restless spirit of some powerful Chiefs, not far from Delagoa Bay. There are at present in Caffreland thousands of fugitives from the interior, of various nations, all of whom have been scattered or driven from their homes by these commotions. The tribe now approaching the Colony . . . is called by the Caffres Fikani (Mfecane)." In 1829, while in Mpondoland, Shaw wrote of the Zulu raids that had occurred the year before, probably the last Zulu raid before the death of Shaka. He recorded that the Zulu cooked and ate the dogs of the Mpondo: 'When some of the Amapondas enquired why they did not leave them their dogs for the purpose of hunting, seeing that they were carrying off their cattle, they answered: we eat them to render ourselves more fierce and powerful in battle'. More will be said of the *Mfecane* later.

The numerous Mpondo have also been in their present area for centuries. The earliest description we have is from the Journal of Jacob van Reenen, who led an expedition from Cape Town in 1790-1 in search of survivors of the *Grosvenor* which was wrecked on the Mpondoland coast on 4 August 1782. They describe how, on the banks of the Mbotyi River, 'the natives brought us many potatoes, sugar-reed, corn and beans and also gold and silver, which we bartered for beads'. Van Reenen was particularly impressed with the 'large and beautiful gardens planted with kaffir-corn, mealies, sugar-reed, bananas, black beans, etc', in the Mngazi valley. In July 1828, Major W. B. Dundas passed through Mpondoland on his way to see the Zulu chief Shaka and visited the great chief Faku. Because the Mpondo were in constant danger of Zulu raids they were living in broken

country. In 1830 Faku allowed the missionaries, Richard Tainton and William Boyce, to establish a mission station called Buntingville among his people. In 1849 Faku appointed Ndamase, his son in the right-hand house as chief over what is now Western Mpondoland (Nyandeni), and Faku's descendant, Paramount Chief Botha Sigcawu of Eastern Mpondoland (Qaukeni), is to be President of the independent Transkei.

According to tradition Mpondo and Mpondomise, sons of Nyanja, son of Sibiside, were twins. A dispute arose in connection with their ranking and the two sections became independent tribes. The line of chiefs goes back to Malangana (c. 1465), so that the Mpondomise were very early settlers. From a stay at the Dedesi it seems that the tribe moved to the Mzimvubu where they remained until Mgabisa (c.1765) moved into the Tsitsa and Tsolo River basins. This coincided with a split within the tribe. Mgabisa was a son in a minor house of Chief Phalo and became the founder of the junior section under Mditshwa and his descendants. There are thus two tribes of Mpondomise. The senior occupies territory extending from the Qanqu to the Tsitsa Rivers in the Qumbu district and the junior occupies land west of the Tsitsa, in the Tsolo district.

The history of the Mpondomise has in the main been tranquil, but in 1880 occurred the tragic episode in which the magistrate of Qumbu, Hamilton Hope, and two of his assistants were murdered by Chief Mhlontlo, who had come out on the side of the Basuto in the so-called Gun War. J. R. Thomson, magistrate of Maclear, was besieged in his residency, but was assisted by the Tlôkwa under Lehana. At the same time the other section of the Mpondomise under Mditshwa, attacked the Tsolo residency and magistrate Welsh and the residents of the village were besieged for a week in the gaol. The rebellion of 1880 affected the districts of Matatiele, Qumbu, Tsolo and Maclear. After the war a commission was appointed to re-allocate the land. A large part of the Qumbu district was given to the Mfengu from Matatiele, Mount Frere (Ludidi's Hlubi) and from the Izeli valley in the Ciskeian district of King William's Town. The Mpondomise area was placed under Mzantsi, brother of Mhlontlo and a piece of land was given to a section of the Sotho, under Sophonia Moshesh. Mfengu were also settled in Tsolo, as were the Tola under Bikwe, who had migrated from Mpondoland in 1882.

The most populous tribal cluster after the Xhosa is that of the Thembu. They seem to have entered Transkei at about the same time as the Xhosa and they, too, were split into a number of chiefdoms. Our picture shows a young Thembu woman smoking her long-stemmed pipe.

According to Soga, the earliest known home of the Bomvana was in the country around the Mkomanzi River in southern Natal. In about 1650 Chief Dibandlela quarrelled with his grandfather Njilo over some cattle and fled into Mpondoland. Later the rest of the tribe migrated to Mpondoland and remained there until the early years of the nineteenth century.

Tradition relates that in c. 1806 a split occurred in the Bomvana tribe. The great son and heir of Jalamba, third son of the great house of Tshezi, was Mbili. When Mbili died his heir, Ngezana, was a minor and the tribe was placed under the regency of his uncle Gambushe, a man of fine character and qualities. Many of the people supported Gambushe and Ngezana accused him of trying to usurp the chieftainship. The crisis came when Khawutla, the Xhosa chief, sent his daughter as bride for Ntshunqe, Gambushe's son, instead of Ngezana. Fighting broke out in which Ngezana was assisted by his father-in-law, the Mpondo chief Ngqungqushe. Ngqungqushe was killed and Gambushe and his section were forced to flee from Mpondoland. He appealed to Khawutha who, for 20 head of cattle, gave them a tail of land between the Mthatha and Mbashe Rivers, in what is now the Mqanduli district. The Tshezi, under Makunzi, were not involved in the quarrel and remained in Mpondoland until c. 1825, when they were forced to move to Tembuland where Chief Ngangelizwe allowed them to settle.

In 1837 Gambushe's followers were driven across the Bashee by the Mpondo and sought refuge among the Gcaleka. They settled between the Nqabwa and Shixini Rivers in what is now the Gatyana district and lived there for 20 years until the Nongqawuse (cattle killing) of 1857. The Bomvana refused to kill their cattle and, seeing the devastation around them, moved back across the Mbashe to the territory they occupy at present.

Reference has been made to the *Mfecane* and the incursion of Zulu *impis* into Transkei. The term *Mfecane* refers to the violent upheaval among the Bantu-speaking peoples of South, Central and East Africa in the nineteenth century which followed the sudden emergence of the Zulu state in Zululand. From a number of small chiefdoms there arose, under Shaka, an extreme example of military despotism. The young men were organised into regiments and concentrated in barracks; the throwing assegai was replaced by the stabbing spear; military tactics were transformed and a policy of expansion initiated. These wars of conquest transformed the tribal picture of Southern Africa. New kingdoms were established, sometimes far from Zululand and the fugitives sent shock waves north, west and south. Thus a whole

new group, the Ndebele, was formed under one of Shaka's captains, Mzilikazi. After laying waste what is now the southern Transvaal, Mzilikazi led his regiments across the Limpopo and built the Ndebele kingdom, largely on Zulu lines, in Rhodesia. Another group under Soshangane left Zululand in 1820-1 and founded the empire of Kwa-Gasa in Gasaland, Mozambique. A third body of Zulu-speakers was led north by Zwangendaba. They attempted to settle in Gasaland, but clashed with Soshangane and, after an extraordinary career, finally settled as Ngoni in the neighbourhood of Lake Nyasa. After 1822 the effects of these developments began to be felt on the South African highveld. A succession of invaders, Nguni, Sotho, Kora and Griqua began to prey on the small Sotho kingdoms in the area. These wars, called *Difaqane* in Sotho and *Mfecane* in Xhosa, caused such devastation that the White pioneers advancing from the south found the land vacant. Theal states that 28 chiefdoms 'disappeared, leaving not so much as a trace of their former existence'. The main culprits were the Ndebele, the Tlôkwa, under their redoubtable chieftainess MaNthatisi; the Taung under Moletsane and the Phuting under Tshane. Two other Nguni groups that embarked on expeditions of plunder were the Ngwane under Matiwane, who, as we have shown, were defeated near Umtata, and a Hlubi group under Mpangazita.

While the main influence of the *Mfecane* was on the Sotho-speaking highveld, in the Trans-Orange and Trans-Vaal, its repercussions were also felt in Transkei. In fact, a number of important Transkei tribes owe their genesis to Shaka's rise to power, fleeing into the area from the Zulu tyrant.

The best-known of these is the group called the Mfengu or Fingo. The term 'Mfengu' is not a tribal name, but is a term applied to them by the Gcaleka, among whom they sought refuge. It means 'homeless wanderer', and refers to a group of tribal fragments that were either defeated by the Zulu or by the chain reaction that caused tribes fleeing from the Zulu to cannon into them. Most of these tribes were related to one another, e.g. the Hlubi, Bhele, Zizi, Tolo, Khuze, Reledwane and Ntlangwini, while others were not so related, e.g. the Miya, Shwawu and Maduma. The Mfengu first entered the Cape in c. 1829 and sought refuge with Hintsa's Gcaleka. Capt. J. E. Alexander described them in 1835, just before they were moved out of Gcalekaland by Sir Benjamin D'Urban, governor

A Thembu boy in full regalia for the dance. In the early nineteenth century part of the Thembu tribe, the so-called Emigrant Thembu under Mathanzima moved from Umtata to the area of Glen Grey (today the district of Cacadu) and Cofimvaba.

of the Cape Colony, in a document of some historical interest (his spelling of names has been modernised):

* Mhlambiso of the amaHlubi, who were living at a place called Esixwonxwani. They originally lived on the Mzinyati River, Natal, and had been attached by Matiwane's amaNgwane in c. 1825.
* Matomela of the amaReledwane, also at Esixwonxwani. They had first been defeated by Bungane, the Hlubi chief, and later scattered by the amaNgwane in c. 1821.
* Njokweni of the amaZizi. They were living near Butterworth in 1835 and had originally lived on the Tugela River, north of Durban.
* Nkwenkwezi of the amaBhele also lived near Butterworth and is described as the only Christian chief. The Bhele had been living on the left bank of the Tugela, but had been scattered by the amaNgwane in c. 1817.
* Cwane and his amaGobizembe lived on the Kei River. They had come from the Nkunzi River, north of Durban, and had been practically destroyed by the Hlubi in c. 1815.
* Hliso of the amaSekunene lived near Butterworth. The tribe had been practically destroyed by the amaNgwane.
* Mkwali and his abaShwawu also lived near Butterworth. They had been dispersed by the Bhaca chief Madzikane in c. 1815.
* Nomtshato with his abakwaNtozakhe lived at the Shixini, Gatyana. Formerly they had resided in northern Natal, but were broken up by Shaka in c. 1815.
* Finally, the abaYimani under Mkuzengwe lived at the Thuthura River, Centane. Formerly they had lived on the Mzinyati River, Natal, and were dispersed by the Ngwane.

It is clear from this that the main cause of the Mfengu flight from Natal was the Ngwane raids, not the Zulu themselves, although the Ngwane depredations were a reaction to Shaka's reign.

The Mfengu remained among the Gcaleka for about seven years (1828-35). There is much controversy as to the way in which they were treated. Alexander maintains that they were 'living in a state of abject slavery under the AmaKosa chief' and that 'when a Kaffir wanted a kaross or mantle, he waited until he saw a Fingo making one for himself, and when he was ready, seized it'. On the other hand, J. H. Soga (part-Xhosa himself) denies that the Mfengu were ever slaves. He points out that during the seven years that they lived among the Gcaleka they rose from destitute paupers to wealthy cattle owners. This was supported in 1835 by a missionary, a Mr McDiarmid, who described as nonsense what was said of the slavery of the Fingoes. 'They were only under the same laws as

the Caffirs. But perhaps the laws in respect of them . . . were more rigidly put in force. They were received kindly into Caffreland, having scarcely any property. They now left it (1835) with 20 000 head of cattle. They had the free use of the country to sow corn etc., and their time was their own. They were allowed to accumulate property, but according to the law, could not remove it without permission of the chiefs under whom they resorted'. It is impossible now to get to the truth of the matter. Certainly, 'slavery' as such was unkown in Cape Nguni society. It is unlikely that the Mfengu were treated badly as a whole, although there were undoubted cases of individuals being oppressed.

Be this as it may, when Hintsa's Gcaleka were defeated by Col. (later Sir) Harry Smith in 1835, the Mfengu asked to be 'liberated' and sought the protection of the government. Under the direction of the Wesleyan missionary John Ayliff some 16 000 were moved to the Peddie district of the Ciskei. On 9 May 1835 the emigration commenced. As Ayliff and Whiteside record it, 'the day broke misty, with occasional showers of rain, but nothing could lessen the imposing character of the scene. A column, a mile and a half in breadth, and eight miles in length, containing 2 000 men, 5 600 women, 9 200 children, with probably not less than 15 000 cattle, moved slowly over the veld. Col. Somerset and a body of burghers on horseback led the way. The Rev. J. Ayliff and his family in a Trekker wagon followed with the transport wagons, after which came the Fingoes. The cattle were driven in small herds of fifty for greater convenience, and each herd was under the care of men armed with assegais and shields'. This was necessary as the rear of the column was attacked by Gcaleka while it was crossing the Kei, but the attack was repulsed by the Cape Mounted Rifles and a hundred burghers.

On 14 May the Mfengu crossed the Keiskama into the district of Peddie. Later a mass meeting was held by Ayliff at Emqwashwini, halfway between Peddie and Breakfast Vlei, near a large milkwood tree (umqwashu) at which the Mfengu pledged themselves 'to be faithful to God, to be loyal to the British King, and to do all in their power to support the missionaries and educate their children'. This promise has been kept and the Mfengu today are a progressive and go-ahead section of the Transkei population. For many years they considered themselves British subjects and early reports

The sheer joy of being young, alive and near the sea is superbly expressed in this solo dance. Note the elaborate headdress and the intricate beadwork. Generally girls before marriage leave their breasts uncovered. Beautifully fashioned beadwork is made by all groups.

by the British army describe how well-trained and impressive the Mfengu soldiers were. On the other hand, their loyalty did not endear them to the Gcaleka and today there is still evidence of hostility between these two groups, which is, however, slowly fading.

Fort Peddie was built to protect the new-settled Mfengu and J. M. Bowker was appointed magistrate among them. Soon it was decided to form a second settlement at the Gaga River, near the present town of Alice, but many Mfengu entered the Colony and obtained employment as farm labourers or settled in the developing frontier towns. Unfortunateiy, the surrounding Xhosa resented the Peddie and Gaga settlements and 'skirmishes among them were an almost daily occurrence' (Ayliff and Whiteside p. 38). Those at the Gaga were attacked by Matwa, a son of Ngqika, and were relocated at the Tsitsikama.

The period 1835 to 1857 was troublesome for the Mfengu. Despite the 1844 treaty in terms of which the Peddie chiefs were to be protected, they were called to fight in the War of the Axe (1846) and the War of Mlangeni (1851-3). In the latter war a further group of 7 000 under the Rev. F. Gladwin was removed from among the Gcaleka at the Butterworth mission and land was allocated to them in the valleys of the Tyume and Upper Keiskama Rivers. Then, after the Nongqawuse cattle killing in 1857-8, when a large part of the Gcaleka territory had been denuded of people, Sir Philip Wodehouse, governor of the Cape Colony, offered them land in what is now Fingoland. In about 1866 there was a general move back into Transkei from the Mfengu 'locations' at Fort Beaufort, Annshaw, Peddie and Mount Coke, and nearly 40 000 were settled in the districts of Nqamakwe, Tsomo and Gcuwa (formerly Butterworth).

But this major return was not to be the only Mfengu resettlement in Transkei. After the Gcaleka under Chief Sarili were defeated in the Ngcayechibi War of 1877-8, Mfengu were settled as a buffer in the north-eastern portion of Gatyana where today there are eight non-Gcaleka administrative units. The other major resettlement in Transkei occurred after the Mpondomise rebellion in 1880. We have already shown that a large part of the Tsolo and Qumbu districts was allocated to various Mfengu groups, particularly Bhele and Zizi. Today Mfengu are widespread in Transkei and their chieftainships have been reinstated. Examples are the Bhele chieftaincy of Mabandla in Tsolo and the Hlubi, Zizi and Bhele chieftaincies in Tsomo.

The Hlubi originated in Natal and in the second

decade of the nineteenth century were one of the largest and most powerful tribes in that area. Mpangazita, head of Chief Bungane's right-hand house, was practically independent of his half-brother, Mthimkhulu II. Legend has it that Matiwane of the Ngwane placed his tribal cattle in the care of Mthimkhulu during a time of war, but that the latter refused to give them up. The Ngwane attacked, Mthimkhulu was killed and the Hlubi fled over the Drakensberg where they settled temporarily in Basutoland (today Lesotho). Later the Hlubi again encountered the Ngwane and were badly defeated at the Caledon River. Mpangazita's heir, Sidinane, escaped with a number of followers, but eventually sought refuge with Matiwane, who had him put to death. His brother, Mehlomakhulu, first attached himself to Mzilikazi's Ndebele and, after many vicissitudes, settled in the Herschel district. His descendants are still to be found there, and in the Ncomo and Kinira areas of Kwabhaca (formerly Mount Frere). There are also Hlubi chiefs in Matatiele.

The Mfengu of today might be interested to read the description of their forefathers by Capt J. E. Alexander in 1835:

'The men of the Fingos have . . . straight and muscular limbs, and average five feet eight inches in height. Their dress consists of dressed ox-hide, worn with the hair inwards, rude sandals on their feet and a skin (penis) sheath like the other tribes; their ornaments are bead earrings, tufts of jackal's tails on their heads, bead necklaces, generally blue and white, brass rings on their arms, and a belt of small brass rings, strung on leather, round their waist. The women wear a small turban of skins or cloth . . . a petticoat of hide, a skin breast cover, ornamented with beads. They also wear bead necklaces and brass bracelets . . . the men labour in the fields as well as the women . . . the huts . . . are hemispheres of boughs covered with grass – their food curdled milk and millet'.

Another important group that fled from Natal during the *Mfecane* were the Bhaca. It seems that the original home of the Bhaca was below the Lebombo Mountains, and their dialect of Xhosa shows some resemblance to Swazi, especially in the use of 't' for 'z' and 'dz' for 'd', a phenomenon called *thsefula*. Like the term Mfengu, the tribal name is not that of an early chief, but comes from a Zulu word meaning 'to hide oneself, to take shelter, to lie low', given to them, it is said, by Shaka

A well turned-out gentleman from the country takes an afternoon stroll. Formerly all tribes dressed in skins, with slight difference of style. Men of most tribes went naked except for a sheath and a cloak thrown over the shoulder. These days there are distinctive cloth styles.

himself. According to tradition, the earliest chief was Lufulwenja, of the abakwaZelemu. Sometime during the period 1734-1800 the Zelemu trekked south with their herds and settled near the powerful tribe of the Wushe. All was peaceful until the expansion of the Zulu might. At first the Zelemu-Wushe were immune but soon they were attacked by fleeing tribes, attempting to escape Shaka's wrath. First the Cunu, and then a confederacy of Bhele, Dunge, Mafunze and Ntlangwini, smashed through them, practically destroying the Wushe and dismembering the Zelemu in the process. The Wushe ceased to exist as a separate entity and the remnants were gathered together under Madzikane, son of the great Zelemu chief, Kalimeshe.

Nothing now stood between the Zelemu and Shaka, but it was only in 1820 that the inevitable clash occurred. When Zulu regiments were sent out, Madzikane and his people fled south along the route taken by the other fleeing tribes.

The fleeing Bhaca crossed the Mkomanzi River and entered into an alliance with the Cunu. The two tribes commenced a reign of terror throughout southern Natal. The Vundle and Ntunzela were raided and a party under Nondzaba attacked the Mpondomise at Rode. The Mpondomise were driven south, but Nondzaba was killed near Tsolo on the hill which still bears his name.

Madzikane returned to the Mkomanzi River, but soon settled his people between Rode and the Mgano Mountains, in the present district of Kwabhaca. Here he built his Mbondzeni kraal. The following years saw almost continuous raids by the Bhaca – against Xhosa and Thembu, against the Mpondomise at Nqadu, the seizing of cattle from the Sotho chief Hluwe and the looting of various small tribes in the Mzimkhulu area. Even Matiwane's Ngwane were taken on and defeated.

In the late twenties Shaka made a final attempt to bring the Bhaca to heel. He sent a punitive *impi*, but Madzikane learnt of this and sent the tribe to safety in the Mgano and Liyengweni ranges. The army readied itself at Lutateni. The advancing Zulu crossed the precipitous Nunge range and during the night were overtaken by a severe snowstorm. Large numbers died of exposure and thereafter the range was called Intsizwe ('young men'). This miraculous victory was attributed to the magic of Madzikane. It is said that the thick smoke rising from his ritual fire turned into the lowering clouds that brought the snow and sleet. It was probably at this time that the Bhaca received their tribal name.

Within four years the redoubtable Madzikane was

dead, killed by a force of Thembu and Qwathi at the Gqutywini forest while on a raid into Tembuland. As Mdutyana, his heir, was still a minor, his uncle Ncaphayi, of the right-hand house, became regent (c. 1833-4). Capt. Allen Gardiner describes the condition of the Bhaca at the time as follows:

'At present (1835) their whole force is computed at about three thousand fighting men – a small army indeed, when compared with that of some of the neighbouring states: but from the peculiar wariness of their attacks – generally at night – their acknowledged courage and indiscriminate carnage . . . they have long been the terror of this part of the country; and under the present enterprising chief (Ncaphayi), were their population more numerous, would rival Charka himself in rapine and war. They are frequently receiving accessions from other tribes . . . and it is not improbable that they may eventually rise to be a powerful nation.' (A. Gardiner: *Narrative of a Journey to the Zoolu Country in South Africa*, 1836, p. 277). As for Ncaphayi, Gardiner describes him as follows:

'He was seated before the fire . . . attended by eight or nine men . . . He seemed amused by my asking, as I entered, which was Tpai; but although the light was not favourable to a narrow inspection, it was soon evident that I was in the presence of one of the shrewdest and most desperate characters in this part of Africa. His figure is slight and active, of middle stature; but the searching quickness of his eye, the point of his questions, and the extreme caution of his replies, stamped him at once as a man capable of ruling the wild and sanguinary spirits by which he is surrounded'. (*Narrative*, p. 280-1).

Under Ncaphayi the Bhaca became much feared. He was known to the Whites as a 'notorious freebooter' and both the Bhaca and the Ntlangwini felt the weight of his impis. For some reason or other, the tribe later moved into Mpondoland, where they became tributary to the Mpondo chief Faku and were settled at the Ntafufu, near the present Port St Johns. From here they raided their old enemies, the Mpondomise, and attacked the Gcina and Qwathi. In alliance with the Mpondo they invaded Tembuland on three occasions, and practically denuded Thembu country of cattle.

Soon, however, the Mpondo and Bhaca quarrelled. Battles were fought at Lusikisiki and Mkatha and the Bhaca withdrew into what is now Cweraland. Later, in c. 1844, Ncaphayi attacked Faku and was killed at Mkatha.

After Ncaphayi's death the tribe split into two sections and the great house, under Mdutyana, moved back to Mzimkhulu. Ncaphayi's son, Makhaula, was still a minor and Diko acted as regent. When Makhaula assumed the chieftainship, peace was made with the Mpondo and he became a British subject in 1875.

For a number of years the great house section remained at Mzimkhulu, which at that time was part of the Griqua state of Adam Kok, but Chief Nomtsheketshe fell foul of the Griqua authorities and eventually joined Makhaula in Kwabhaca. There are still Bhaca in Mzimkhulu under Chief Msingaphantsi.

Until recently Bhaca women were distinctive in their traditional dress, especially the headdress *(unyaba)*. The hair was smeared with red ochre and fat and pushed through a wool-padded headring so that ringlets hung down all round the head. Practically all Bhaca practise face-incision *(chaza)* and, until recently, they were the only Cape Nguni people to perform the spectacular *ingcubhe* ritual of the feast of the first fruits and the doctoring of the army.

Another important group who fled from Natal as a result of the *Mfecane* was the Xesibe, although they are reputed to be closely related to the Mpondo and Mpondomise. The ancient residence of the Xesibe was in the vicinity of the sources of the Mpanza River in Natal. Although a fairly powerful tribe, they fled from Shaka and allied themselves to the Funze, but they were attacked by Shaka and moved south to their cousins, the Mpondo. Quarrels soon broke out however, especially when the Xesibe sided with the Bhaca against Faku. Faku approached the governor of the Cape Colony, Sir Peregrine Maitland, who declared the entire territory between the Mthamvuna and Mtsikaba Rivers (including the area of the Xesibe) part of Mpondoland. Thus the left-hand house under Jojo, son of Mjoli, son of Sinama, came under the Mpondo chief.

The right-hand section under Mgubudzeli moved through Mpondoland and sought refuge with the Thembu. They now live in Mqanduli. Jojo's Xesibe settled in Maxesibeni (Mount Ayliff) and were taken under the authority of the colonial government in 1874.

One other important group that came into Transkei because of the Shaka wars is the Ntlangwini. Originally descended from Sibalukulu, the right-hand son of the Hlubi chief Dlamini, they fled

A Gcaleka matron in the doorway of her hut. The size of the largest homesteads is usually determined by both polygamy and the practice of sons to make their homes in their father's settlement. Today, some very large homesteads are still found, but polygamy is on the decline.

from Natal after being shaken by the southward-moving Thembu of Qhudeni and thereafter, as pointed out earlier, joined in a confederacy with the Bhele, Dunge and Funze which smashed through the Bhaca. Nombewu, the more important of the two Ntlangwini chiefs, proceeded to the Mzimkhulu River and settled there, but was attacked and killed by the Bhaca chief Ncaphayi. He was succeeded by Fodo, who assisted the Voortrekkers under Andries Pretorius on their expedition against the Bhaca in 1840. Later, in 1880, Chief Sidoyi assisted the Whites during the Gun War, preventing the Basuto from overrunning the Kokstad and Maxesibeni (Mount Ayliff) districts. Today Ntlangwini live in Matatiele and Umzimkulu.

A description of the people of Transkei would be incomplete without some reference to the Sotho groups, who are an integral part of the new state. They are the Kwena of Chief Moshesh and Lebenya, the Hlakwana of Zibi and the Tlôkwa of Lehana. Although these tribes are small, they have made an important contribution to the development of Transkei. In 1858 the Sotho Chief Moshesh sent Nehemiah Sekhonyana Moshesh, his only son in the third house, with a large following to settle in what is now the district of Matatiele. This was the first large Sotho settlement in what was then known as No man's land – the present East Griqualand – and it was soon followed by the arrival of the Hlakwana under Lepheana Phamotse. In 1867, after the Free State-Basuto War, other Sotho-speaking sections came into Transkei. The Monaheng clan of Kwena, under Lebenya, descended the Drakensberg, followed by another section under Chief Makuzi. The Tlôkwa under Lehana, son of the famous Sekhonyela, came over from the Herschel district and today Mount Fletcher is almost entirely Sotho-speaking.

These, then are the people of Transkei. The great majority speak Xhosa (except for the Sotho) but they are divided into a number of cultural groups based on historical and genealogical criteria. Some of these groups have been in the area for half a millennium at least; even the relative newcomers have been there for one and a half centuries.

Transkei as we know it today came into existence as a result of a series of British annexations which began with the incorporation of Fingoland and Griqualand East into the Cape Colony in 1879 and ended with the annexation of Pondoland in 1894.

The word has gone out that there will be a dance today so these two Thembu men have donned all the finery demanded by the occasion. Tribal dancing is enjoyed by young and old and the youngsters will burst into song at the drop of a hat.

Prior to this, the various Xhosa tribes in what is now Ciskei had been incorporated into the Cape Colony. A succession of boundaries sought to define the respective areas of White and Black. In 1743 the boundary was fixed at the Great Brak River, but by then some White frontiersmen were already near the Gamtoos. In 1770 the Gamtoos became the eastern boundary of the Colony and then, in 1774, Bruyntjieshoogte. In 1775 the government again moved the frontier to the Fish River, and in 1835 Sir Benjamin D'Urban proclaimed the annexation of the land between the Keiskama and Kei Rivers which was rescinded in 1836. It was not until 1847 that the Kei finally became the boundary between the Cape Colony and Transkei.

In 1875 both Fingoland (the districts of Tsomo, Mqamakwe and Gcuwa) and the so-called Idutywa Reserve were annexed to the Colony, as was No man's land, and the area between the Mthatha River and the Natal border and Mpondoland and the Drakensberg. The area depopulated by the cattle killing in 1857 and restored to the Gcaleka chief Sarili in 1864 was not immediately annexed to the Colony. The Gcaleka desired to remain independent, government being represented amongst them by an agent who had no power to interfere in tribal matters. But this arrangement was not to last. In August 1877 war broke out between the Xhosa and Thembu. Colonial troops supported Thembu Chief Ngangelizwe and, at the Battle of Kentani, Sarili and his warriors were decisively beaten. In September 1877 this newly conquered territory (Gcalekaland, the district of Gatyana and Centane) was added to Idutywa and Fingoland, thus forming what became known as 'Transkei Proper', under Captain Matthew Blyth as chief magistrate. The Bomvana of Xhora, under the aged Chief Moni, also came in. 'East Griqualand', comprising the districts of Elliot, Maclear, Mount Fletcher, Qumbu, Tsolo, Matatiele, Kokstad, Umzimkulu and Kwabhaca (Mount Frere), in December 1878 also became a chief magistracy under Charles Brownlee. Elliot, Maclear and, recently, Kokstad, have since been excised from Transkei.

The annexation of Tembuland was soon to follow. Ngangelizwe had had trouble both with the Gcaleka Chief Sarili and with the Emigrant Thembu and eventually asked for protection from the British government. Terms of cession were drawn up by the Rev. P. Hargreaves, missionary at Clarkebury, and in June 1876 an Annexation Bill was passed. The new chief magistracy included Mqanduli, Umtata, Engcobo and the Emigrant Thembu districts of Cofimvaba and Xalanga.

By 1877 a very large proportion of what is now

Transkei was under colonial rule. In 1878 Xesibe in Maxesibeni were attached to East Griqualand and formally annexed in 1886. Mpondoland followed suit in 1894. Major Henry Elliot, British resident in Western Mpondoland, met Chief Sigcawu with a small party on 8 March 1894 and a deed of submission was signed on 17 March. Two days later Nqwiliso, the Western Mpondo chief, signed a similar document. In September 1894 both Eastern and Western Mpondoland were annexed to the Cape Colony.

At that time the area known as Transkei consisted of the chief magistracies of Transkei Proper (capital Butterworth), Tembuland (Umtata) and East Griqualand (Kokstad) with Mpondoland, which never had a chief magistrate. In 1903 all four were united as the United Transkeian Territories under a chief magistrate in Umtata. Each of the 27 districts was under the control of a magistrate, directly responsible to Umtata.

During the early years of the twentieth century the administrative pattern was extended. The districts were divided into locations, each under a government-appointed headman who himself appointed sub-headmen over smaller areas. Usually traditional headmen were appointed to these positions but in some areas, notably Fingoland, they were interpreters, clerks, policemen and others, singled out for their leadership qualities or loyalty. A Transkeian Appeal Court was instituted and a Transkeian penal code, based on the Indian penal code, came into force on 1 January 1887. Proclamations governing control of stock disease, noxious weeds, conservation of thatching grass, magistrate's court procedure and a host of other matters were introduced.

But perhaps the most important step, in the light of later developments, was the introduction of a system of district councils – the so-called Bunga system. Rhodes decided to extend to Transkei the council system which was first introduced in his Glen Grey Act of 1894. By Proclamation 352 of 1894 provision was made for the establishment of councils in the southern Transkeian districts of Gcuwa, Idutywa, Nqamakwe and Tsomo, all mainly Mfengu. The Transkeian Council came into operation at the beginning of 1895 and consisted of six members, of whom two were appointed by the magistrate who acted as chairman. Meetings were held quarterly. In 1899 the system was extended to the district of Centane, and

An Emigrant Thembu woman in traditional costume. Thembu usually wear heavily ochred blankets edged with black braid, and married women always wear turbans of some dark colour. In all tribal societies in Transkei the woman's place is inferior to that of the man.

later to Tembuland and East Griqualand. Each year two members were nominated to attend the Transkeian Territories General Council (Bunga) which met under the chairmanship of the chief magistrate. The magistrates of constituent districts were also present *ex officio.* In 1911, councils were introduced into Mpondoland and in 1927 the Mpondoland General Council was formed. Finally, on 1 January 1931 the two general councils were amalgamated into the United Transkeian Territories General Council which consisted of the 26 magistrates, the Paramount Chiefs of Tembuland, Eastern Mpondoland and Western Mpondoland, and three representatives from each district council – 108 in all. Revenues for this central body were derived from the rent for quit-rent land and from the proceeds of the ten shillings hut tax. The General Council operated engineering and agricultural departments, made a *pro rata* contribution to the cost of treating patients in state-aided and mission hospitals, and spent considerable sums on soil and water conservation, road-building and fencing. Resolutions were reviewed by a conference of official members before being submitted to the Governor-General of the Union of South Africa for his information.

As the first stage in the election of the district council the magistrate called a meeting, usually at a trading store, of all registered tax-payers in each of the electoral wards into which the district was divided. Nominations were called for and voting took place by show of hands. The three candidates polling most votes were elected. Elected men met at the magistrate's office and, from among themselves, chose four to serve on the local district council. The magistrate appointed two members. In Mpondoland, two were appointed by the Paramount Chief, two by the magistrate and two by elected members.

The *Proceedings* of the Bunga give evidence over the years of the high standard of debate and responsible involvement of members in the work of this body. While in the 1930s and 1940s a large number of commoners – teachers, interpreters, and others – were elected, gradually more chiefs and headmen were elected.

The Bunga system gave valuable training in the problems and conduct of local government and provided a forum for Transkeian opinion which transcended tribal differences and went a long way to inculcate a sense of Transkeian citizenship. Generally speaking, Bunga members approached problems in a magisterial way and did not allow tribal affiliation to prejudice their decisions. There can be no doubt that the present system of Transkeian government owes a debt to the initial, if stumbling, steps of the Bunga.

Chapter Three

The People
Way of Life and Culture

The great majority of Transkeians belong to a cultural category called by scientists the 'Cape Nguni' and all speak dialects of a language called *isiXhosa*. The dialect of the Ngqika tribe (part of the Xhosa tribal cluster) was the first to be committed to writing and have its grammatical structure determined by the publication in 1834 of W. B. Boyce's *Grammar of the Kafir Language*. And here the role of the missionaries must not be forgotten.

The first attempt to evangelise the Xhosa was made in 1799 by Dr J. T. van der Kemp of the London Missionary Society, but his mission was abandoned after eighteen months because of the antagonism of Chief Ngqika. Later, in 1816, the Rev. J. Williams of the same society founded a station at the Kat River, about fifteen miles from Ngqika's great place, but he died after two years and the site was abandoned. In 1820 the Rev. John Brownlee was appointed government missionary with the Ngqika and a station was founded on the Tyume River, near the present town of Alice. Thus, mission work has been under way for over 150 years and its effects on Transkei have been dramatic.

In 1820 the remarkable missionary-statesman William Shaw arrived in South Africa and commenced establishing a chain of mission stations throughout

A Mpondo herd-boy somewhere in the rolling hills of central Transkei. There are thousands more like him and they play a most important role in the agriculture of Transkei. It is their function to see that the tribe's herd grazes in the pastures assigned to it.

Transkei. First, Wesleyville was founded in 1823 among the Gqunukhwebe of Chief Phato; then Mount Coke in 1825 among the Ndlambe; then Butterworth (1827) among Hintsa's Gcaleka; then Morley (1829) among the Bomvana. In 1830 two more stations were established – Clarkebury among Ngubengcuka's Thembu and Buntingville among Faku's Mpondo. Later Shawbury was founded by the Rev. W. H. Garner among the Bhaca of Chief Ncaphayi, and, after a section of the Mpondo had moved to the Natal side of the Umzimvubu, Palmerton was established among them by the Rev. Thomas Jenkins. These were Wesleyan-Methodist stations, but other denominations also entered the field. The Glasgow Missionary Society founded Lovedale in 1824. In 1826, John Brownlee of the London Missionary Society, founded the Buffalo station among the Ntinde and in 1830 the Pirie Mission was established by the Rev. John Ross of the Glasgow Missionary Society. The Berlin Missionary Society commenced work among the Gasela at the Bethel Mission (afterwards Dohne), followed by Emmaus near Toise River (1840), Liefeldt Mission (1856), Mdizeni (1864) and Entembeni (1868). The first Anglican mission was that of St Luke's on the Xinira River, established at the request of the Ndlambe Chief Mhala. Others were established at St Mark's among the Emigrant Thembu, Umtata (Thembu), St Cuthberts (Mpondomise), All Saints (Thembu) and Holy Cross (Mpondo). Each mission had a number of outstations and by the mid-nineteenth century there was hardly a place where the gospel was not preached.

The response to this missionary activity has been mixed. Significantly, those groups who, scattered

by the Mfecane, sought refuge in Transkei, have been most receptive to the new religion. The Mfengu, especially, joined the mission (notably at Butterworth), as did the Bhaca and Ntlangwini. The great majority in Fingoland are Christians. Some of the older-established tribal clusters resisted to a greater or lesser degree. This is particularly true of the Xhosa, who tend to wear their conservatism as a badge. Yet, it is probably true to say that well over half the people of Transkei are today members of a Christian church. The percentage of adherents tends to drop the further one moves from the central corridor towards the broken coastal strip.

The work of the missions has not been confined to evangelism. Medical work has been important, especially among the Anglican, Roman Catholic and Church of Scotland missions. The Dutch Reformed Churches commenced active mission work in Transkei in the late nineteenth century. Activities were on a modest scale until the 'fifties of this century and by the early 'sixties the DRC had established ten hospitals. Education has also been a major contribution of the missions, with the Methodists in the forefront. They have established secondary institutions at Clarkebury, Shawbury, Buntingville and Palmerton. The Anglican Church has a seminary in Umtata (St Bede's), as has the Dutch Reformed Church (Decoligny).

The social effect of this missionary activity has been fundamental. It has meant a division between the 'believers' (amakholwa) and the traditionalists (amaqaba) which is far-reaching in its implications. The missionaries insisted on their converts forsaking 'heathen' ways. Church members are forbidden to attend traditional rituals and, except among Catholics and Anglicans, traditional beer is forbidden. The missions frown on marriage between their members (the 'School People') and the 'Reds' (a reference to the red blanket worn by the more primitive Transkeians). Thus, the social life of the two sections tends to operate on different and seldom overlapping planes. But this must not be overstressed. Christians have traditionalist relatives and co-operate amicably with traditionalist neighbours in agricultural activities and in deliberations of the headman's court. Christians are usually the most progressive section of the community. Most send their children to school, but in the last few years the 'Reds' too have been doing so to an ever increasing extent.

A Roman Catholic Church on a hill near Mount Ayliff. Most Transkeian Christians are members of one or other of the main denominations of Southern Africa and the Independent Church movement is not as active in Transkei as elsewhere.

The Christians tend to have their own social life. Apart from church services, Bible classes and prayer meetings there are also concerts and dances at which the young people gather. Although some local communities are either wholly Christian or wholly Red, in most areas the two sections are intermingled – with a remarkable degree of co-operation and lack of tension.

The traditional culture of the Cape Nguni is of great interest and, with the language, has considerable vitality. There are today groups in Lesotho who were originally Cape Nguni and still retain their distinctive culture.

From the beginning, the Cape Nguni were cattle-keepers par excellence. The cattle described by the Portuguese as large and 'very tame', often without horns, were markedly different from the Sanga breed kept by the Zulu. There is a very special relationship between a Xhosa and his cattle. Great care is lavished on them and there are names for the various colours and horn shapes. Particularly in the past, each man had his favourite ox. The riding of oxen seems to have been learned from the Khoi (Hottentots) and cattle racing was indulged in by Xhosa, Mpondo and Bhaca – among the last mentioned especially at the first fruit ritual (ingcubhe). Cattle are the main index of wealth among the traditionalists, the appropriate elements in the *lobola* marriage transactions and also the most acceptable offerings to the ancestral spirits. The Bomvana are unique in having a sacred herd of (Bolowane) cattle, associated with the chief and descended in the maternal line.

The other traditional animals are the dog and goat. Woolled sheep are a comparatively new introduction and large numbers are found today in the inland districts. Large numbers of horses, pigs and the European goat (ibhokhwe) and poultry are also kept. Even today traditional Transkeian women will not touch eggs (see Health Services).

John Brownlee describes the hoe-cultural techniques practised by the Xhosa at the beginning of the nineteenth century. He states that the chief crops were millet (*Holcus sorghum*), maize, kidney beans, pumpkins and watermelons. The only implement used was a 'sort of spade, made of the *nieshout* tree (sneezewood: *Pteroxylon utile*), in shape not unlike the broad end of an oar'. This digging stick was about two feet long and the cultivator had to work in a sitting position. The grain was scattered on the ground and the soil turned to a depth of about three inches. Weeds and grass roots were spread over as a protection, and removed after the shoots had appeared.

William Paterson noted in February 1779 that they

also '. . . cultivate several vegetables, which are not indigenous to their country, such as tobacco, watermelons . . . and hemp, none of which I found growing spontaneously' (*A Narrative of Four Journeys into the Country of the Hottentots and Caffres in the years 1777-8-9, London, 1789, p. 94*). But the Cape Nguni were not really interested in crops. H. Lichtenstein comments on the predominantly pastoral life of the Xhosa: 'They live chiefly upon flesh, and grow very little corn . . . Milk is the principal article of diet with them'.

Today the position has changed. Despite the considerable overstocking in some areas, meat is not always in adequate supply and maize is the staple diet. On the other hand, the plough and other advanced agricultural implements are being used to an ever increasing extent.

Traditional agriculture in Transkei is *communal* only in the sense that all land is held in trust for the tribe by the chief or headman and cannot be alienated. It does not mean that individuals do not enjoy a form of ownership. Every married man is entitled to a piece of land for his wife to cultivate and rights in the land and its products rest entirely in him (or rather in her) as long as the land continues to be cultivated. Only if it is neglected will it revert to the community. But after harvest, these rights lapse temporarily: the fields of all must be thrown open for stubble-grazing for the cattle of the entire community. This is one of the reasons for the widespread resistance to the fencing of fields: in the light of this custom it would be an anti-social act. Pasturage is common to all and the cattle are herded by herdboys, sometimes at some distance away at cattle-posts (see Agriculture).

Traditionally hunting was a source of some food and clothing, but it was more a sport, except for the hunting of elephant for the lucrative ivory trade. John Brownlee described the Xhosa hunt: 'They generally go out to hunt in large parties, and when they find game in the open fields, they endeavour to surround the animals or drive them to some narrow pass, which is previously occupied by long files of hunters, stationed on either side, who, as the herd rushes through between, pierce them with a shower of assegais'. The end of the mourning period for a chief was always marked by a great hunt, organised like a military expedition. Formerly Transkei abounded in antelope, elephant, rhino, buffalo and lion. Today most of the game

has been wiped out, but hunts are still organised for jackal, small buck and other small animals. Herding and hunting were men's work, whereas cultivation of the land, apart from the heavy work of clearing bush, was the work of women, and it is tempting to relate the present lack of real interest in agricultural pursuits to this fact (see Agriculture).

Unlike some other Bantu-speaking peoples, the Cape Nguni do not live in closely-settled villages but in homesteads scattered over the tribal territory. In the past each consisted of from two to forty huts, grouped round a circular cattle kraal. The size of the largest homesteads was determined by both polygamy and the practice of sons to make their home in the same settlement as their father. Today some very large homesteads (*imizi*) are still found, but polygamy is on the decline, probably down to six per cent of the population. The homesteads of chiefs tended to be larger than those of commoners and the capitals of Xhosa chiefs were distinguished by an elephant's tail suspended from a pole at the entrance to the cattle kraal. William Shaw comments in his *Journal* that 'the Amapondo kraals are each on average three times as large and populous as the Caffre (Xhosa) kraals'. Today most homesteads have a small garden in which early maize and pumpkins are planted. In many parts of Transkei huts are painted with a white band and, especially among the Hlubi, walls are decorated with intricate finger patterns. All tend to face eastwards, away from the prevailing rain.

The homesteads are not uniformly scattered over the land, but tend to be concentrated into certain areas, usually along a ridge or against a mountain. These neighbourhoods are named and tend to be inhabited by descendants of a common grandfather or great-grandfather in the male line, but there are usually a number of unrelated families present as well. The neighbourhood today is under the general control of a sub-headman (*ibhodi*) appointed by the headman to look after its affairs. The fields of a neighbourhood tend to lie together in a nearby river valley and all members co-operate in tilling and other chores. It is the nearest Transkeian approximation to the true village.

Four or five neighbourhoods make up an administrative unit under a headman who usually inherits his position. Normally, there are twenty to thirty administrative units to a district, which is controlled by a magistrate and his staff at the central village. In addition, administrative units of the same tribal cluster have been grouped into tribal and regional authorities (see System of Government).

Several homesteads along a fertile river valley. Note the heart-shaped decoration on the walls of the huts.
Transkeians on the whole do not live in villages, but in homesteads scattered over the tribal territory. Until recently each consisted of from two to forty huts.

Each tribe is headed by a chief (*inkosi*). Today the chief receives a government stipend and no longer the *isizi* (death dues), part of the harvest, and the spoils from cattle raiding, as formerly. Early travellers report that certain spoils of the chase were the prerogative of the chief. Alberti (1810) states that the tusks, ears and tail of an elephant were the chief's due and both Brownlee (1827) and Rose (1829) mention 'the breast of the hippopotamus being his right'. Rose also mentions that 'the chief is generally distinguished from his followers by a karosse of tiger's (leopard's) skin, and by a narrow tasteful beaded band worn round the head . . .'. J. H. Soga refers to a necklace of red beads (*ubuhlala*) being the only insignia of Xhosa royalty and Alberti comments that only chiefs could wear the leopard skin. The death of a chief was followed by a mourning period of about a year and Sir Walter Currie mentions that, on the death of a Gcaleka chief, one or two kraals were destroyed 'to go with him'. He states that this was still the custom in 1861, 'unless the chief just before his death gives out what they call 'a word' . . . stating that no one is the cause of his death, but that he is dying of natural causes, and that no one is to suffer for it'. This is a reference to witchcraft, to be discussed below.

Chiefs were, and are, granted great respect. They are considered the father of their people, the custodians of the tribal territory, and to the traditionalist they are the living mediators between tribesmen and the august spirits of the royal ancestors. But, despite this, Cape Nguni chiefs were seldom despots. Unlike some of those of the Zulu, the chieftaincies were, in effect, constitutional monarchies in which the chief *reigned* but the actual *ruling* was a subtle process of interaction between chiefs and people.

An eminent Mpondomise describes this balance of power in the following way:

'Even strong chiefs like Mhlontlo never made laws that went against the wishes of the people. Even in the past a chief always had his councillors. These men were his advisers on matters of law and order. Even in times of crisis a chief would have to listen to their advice on what action to take. They would refuse to sanction tactics which they regarded as dangerous.

'In making a new law a chief had to consult his close advisers and discuss the intended law with them.

A young Mpondo woman photographed in her best tribal finery. Note the styling of the hair and the earrings.
More than 90 per cent of the population of Transkei live in rural areas and the vast majority of these still adhere to the customs and modes of dress of their forebears.

Then a meeting of the whole tribe would be called and the matter laid before them. Influential men would have the chance of airing their views and, after thorough discussion, the chief and his advisers would have the feeling of the meeting. Opponents of the plan were encouraged to speak out because people should not be like a stream that flows only in one direction. After full discussion, the chief and his councillors would withdraw so that the councillors could voice their opinion as to whether they felt that the majority were in favour of the matter or not, and whether modifications should not perhaps be made.

'A chief would then return to the *ibandla* with his advisers, and formally pronounce the new law. If the people were obviously unhappy about it, it was withdrawn. A chief who dared to go against the wishes of his people ran the risk of losing their support, and perhaps his chieftainship' (W. D. Hammond-Tooke, *Command or Consensus*, 1974, p. 67).

The position of councillors (*amaphakathi*) was all-important. By virtue of their intelligence, personality and loyalty, they were the chief's closest advisers. One or two may have been councillors of the late chief; and others boyhood friends of the current chief. They were sometimes called 'sifters', because they sifted and evaluated evidence. Formerly, they tasted the chief's food to guard against poisoning. Around this semi-permanent core of close councillors there was a fluctuating group consisting of the more prominent tribesmen who spent much of their time at the great place. Theoretically, anyone could become a councillor, and ideally the tribal council consisted of all adult members of the chiefdom.

Among the councillors was one who held a special position: the chief councillor, or 'prime minister', who was the chief's mouthpiece. As the Ngqika councillors, giving evidence before the Cape Native Laws and Customs Commission of 1883, stated: 'Yes, a chief can do wrong, and it often happens that when a chief does wrong he is interfered with, and punished, by having his favourite councillor, or prime minister, eaten up . . . The prime minister is the chief's mouthpiece, and the other councillors say, as a reason for eating him up, that it must have been by his advice that the chief did wrong'. The chieftainship is sacred and must be protected from criticism. This is done by placing the blame on the true decision makers.

As symbolic head of the tribe, the chief's person was sacred and protected by magico-religious precautions. It was necessary that he be periodically doctored with strong medicines to renew the aura of office, his *isithunzi* or shadow. These medicines

included the powdered bone of lion, leopard or elephant, 'to make him strong and fearless'. Typically, he was doctored by a foreign herbalist. Among the Bhaca an important part of the first fruit ritual (ingcubhe) was the strengthening of the chieftainship.

But the greatest chiefly quality was generosity. The chief was bound by tradition to use his wealth for the good of the people. For instance, a poor man could go to the great place and ask for 'a beast to feed his family' and to be given a few cows 'to milk'. In time of famine a chief's grain pits were used to feed the destitute: all visitors, and those gathered at the great place for court cases, were provided with food and drink. Old informants state that it was rare for a chief to impose specific levies on his people. Rather, it was the duty of the people to see that their chief was not reduced to having to beg. Occasionally tribesmen were forced to work in the chief's fields for a few days. The relationship between subject and chief was, and is, described as *khonza.* To the Cape Nguni the chieftainship was the centre of their social life, the subject of their deepest loyalties.

Tribal membership was expressed by details in dress and certain markings. Formerly, all groups dressed in skins, with slight differences of style, but with the introduction of cloth, distinctive styles have become traditional. The Xhosa, Thembu, Mpondomise and Khonjwayo wear heavily ochred blankets edged with black braid, and married women wear turbans of some dark colour. Mfengu ochre is a deeper red and clothing is typically decorated with beads and mother-of-pearl buttons. Men of most tribes formerly went naked except for a penis sheath and a cloak thrown over the shoulder for warmth. Mpondo men, however, wore loin cloths and claimed to be shocked at those who did not. Bhaca and Xesibe women do not use ochre and dress in goat-skin or cotton skirts, heavily smeared with fat, and they wear their hair ringletted in a distinctive coiffure. Mpondo women wear white blankets, except for the *amadikazi* (associations of unattached women) who dye their blankets a pale blue. Generally, girls before marriage leave the breasts uncovered and wear short skirts. Beautifully fashioned beadwork is made by all groups and worn by young people of both sexes. Tattooing is practised by some Thembu and Bhaca; Xesibe and some Mfengu scarify the face (chaza). The custom of ingqithi (amputation of one or more joints of the little finger) is still fairly common

Three very young maidens in a spontaneous dance by the sea. On the whole, those tribes living close to the sea are the most conservative of all, because in a sense they are the furthest removed from the centres of development – Umtata and Butterworth, in particular.

among the Xhosa and is probably of San (Bushman) origin.

The kinship system of all groups is strongly patrilineal. A group of men descended from a common father or grandfather constitute a lineage, and tend to live together in the same area, but this is not always so. Lineage members are expected to assist one another and together they worship the deceased forefathers of the lineage. Each man also belongs to a clan. Both lineages and clans are exogamous in that intermarriage between clan members is strictly forbidden and regarded as incest. It is also forbidden to drink sour milk (amasi) in any but your own clan (among the Mpondo, your own lineage). The exogamy rules mean that brides are always strangers and marriage means the loss of a daughter to another group. This loss of a valued member must be made good, and this is done through the system of bridewealth (ikhazi) exchange which lies at the heart of Cape Nguni marriage. By the giving of bridewealth (formerly in cattle and small stock, but today often in cash and other goods as well) the bride's group is enabled to use the cattle to marry a wife for a son, and brothers and sisters are often linked together for this purpose. The passage of cattle transfers two types of rights from the woman's group to the man's – rights over the woman herself and rights over any children of the marriage. In a very definite sense, therefore, marriage is between the two families and the groom's family is concerned that children shall be raised up to it. Thus if the wife dies or is barren, the custom of the sororate is initiated whereby her sister will be sent to support her. In the same way, if the husband dies, a younger brother will 'go into' the widow and raise issue for the dead man. This custom, called the levirate, is found among all groups except Xhosa and Thembu to whom it is anathema, but among whom it is expected that widows will 'pick up' children for the lineage by strangers.

In a system such as this, divorce tends to be rare. This is directly due to the institution of bridewealth which gives both parties to the marriage transaction a very definite interest in its continuance.

Before boys or girls may marry, they must first undergo important rituals, which, in fact, make them fully adult men and women. Before these are performed they are regarded as irresponsible children. Afterwards they take on the full responsibilities of citizenship although women, for the whole of their lives, are jural minors subject to the guardianship of husband or father. The Mpondo, Xesibe and Bhaca no longer circumcise.

Among the Sotho peoples initiation is performed

on a tribal basis, under the control of the chief. Young men among the Cape Nguni, however, undergo a local ceremony with other young men of their neighbourhood. One of the fathers will take the initiative and arrange with other men who have boys of the right age to build a lodge, some distance from the settlement. The services of a professional circumciser are engaged. For a week or two before the ritual, the boys are allowed a period of license, and, dressed in fantastic garb, they roam the countryside, making a thorough nuisance of themselves. On the night before the ceremony a ritual killing is made to inform the ancestors, and early the next morning the mothers thatch the lodge which has been built by the men. The boys are then circumcised, smeared with white clay to symbolise their special status, and secluded in the lodge for three or four months. After about a week, a special ritual is performed, called *ukojiswa*, to free them from the rigid food taboos of the first few days. Among the Xhosa, Bomvana and Thembu, especially, spectacular *tshilo* dances are held at which the initiates dance dressed in twenty-foot long grass skirts and masks, to the drumming of a stretched cow-hide *(igqong-qo)*. At the end of the period of seclusion, the initiates run down to the nearest stream and wash off the white clay and then walk slowly back to the lodge, accompanied by the men and the all-important cattle. The blankets and all things used during the seclusion period are thrown on top of the lodge which is set alight. Thus, everything associated with boyhood is consumed by fire. The initiates are smeared with fat to counteract the dryness of the white clay and are given new blankets and sticks. They are smeared with red ochre, to symbolise their reincorporation into society, and are then called *amakrwala*.

Girls' initiation is called *intonjane*. Because it is usually closely associated with her first menstruation, it is done individually for each girl. The ritual lasts from a few weeks to a month, during which time the girl is secluded behind a screen in a hut. One or two goats are slaughtered and the married women perform a ritual dance every morning and evening during the whole period of the *intonjane's* seclusion. During the whole period, neither the father nor the mother may enter the seclusion hut. In fact, all men are excluded. Special roots are chewed. A few days before the 'coming-out' ceremony a beast is killed and the gall-bladder worn by the *intonjane* on her wrist. The ritual ends with a special washing at the river. The missionaries have

A scene during the initiation ceremony for young Transkeian boys, which is described in full in the text. In most tribes, with the exception of the Mpondo, Xesibe and Bhaca, boys are circumcised before they take on the full responsibilities of adult citizenship.

strenuously opposed *intonjane*. No Christian girls undergo it but they are also secluded before marriage.

But the social life of the Cape Nguni is not confined to relationship of descent and marriage. Because these people live together in little communities with similar interests and problems, they tend to co-operate as neighbours and friends. Indeed, there is evidence that good neighbourliness is valued even higher than kinship. Thus people co-operate in hoeing parties *(amalima)*, in mutual benefit societies *(iitimiti)* and in social 'clubs', such as the *amatshawe* organisations of Mpondo men and women. Age plays an important part in community associations. Among all groups there are associations of young people of about the same age, usually from the same locality, who go to dances together. Leadership in the boys' groups is usually based on physical prowess, especially in stick fighting, but it is striking how young people, especially among the traditionalists, continue to respect age and seniority. Perhaps the main social occasions for adults are the frequent beer-drinks at which Transkeian hospitality is seen at its most typical. Often these are accompanied by a killing, either for sacrifice or 'just for meat', and at such times the beer and meat are allocated in a special way, all participants sitting in groups according to their localities *(izithebe)*.

Religion

The peoples of Transkei, like people everywhere, are concerned with the fundamental questions of existence. Where do we come from? How was the world created? What happens after death? Perhaps most important of all, what are the causes of evil and misfortune?

The Cape Nguni believe the world was created by a Supreme Being called *Mdali* or *Qamatha*, but he no longer concerns himself, to any great extent, with the details of his creation and no prayers or rituals are directed to him. The origin of men themselves is ascribed to the myth of the *Eluhlangeni* reed-bed (previous chapter) or they are believed to have emerged from holes in the ground. Alberti, who visited the Xhosa in 1807 and wrote the first full account of their way of life, could glean no more of their cosmological ideas than a myth which he quotes: 'In the land where the sun rises there was a cavern from which the Xhosa and, in fact, all peoples, as also the stock of every kind of animal, came forth. At the same time, the sun and moon came into being to shed their light, and trees, grass and other plants to provide food for man and cattle'. When the missionaries commenced work among the Xhosa, they hesitated to equate *Mdali* or *Qamatha* with the God of the Bible and used a Khoi word, *Thixo*, to refer to him. Today *uThixo* is the general term for God, used by both Christians and traditionalists.

The beings from whom the people actively seek assistance are the ancestors *(iminyanya, izinyanya, amathongo)*, the dead members of the lineage. These are believed to continue to take a close interest in their descendants and to brood over the homestead. Ancestors like their names to be remembered and to be kept informed of all important events, such as births, initiations, marriages and deaths. If they are neglected they may send misfortune and even sickness to their descendants. They often appear in dreams and indicate the beast that should be slaughtered for them. The important ancestors tend to be men, the deceased fathers, grandfathers and great-grandfathers, although some say that women also become ancestors. A special ritual, performed about a year after death, formally transforms the spirit of the dead father into an ancestor and thereafter his name is included in the praises intoned at the rituals. Responsibility for officiating at a sacrifice is vested in the *inkulu*, the lineage head, who must sometimes make long journeys to the homesteads of scattered lineage members to discharge this office. The sacrificial goats and oxen are slaughtered in the cattle kraal which is sacred to the ancestors. Formerly a deceased homestead head was buried at the gate of the cattle kraal, but among the Xhosa of the early 1800s it was apparently the custom to leave the body of a commoner out in the veld to be eaten by hyenas. Alberti also records mourning customs for widows. On the death of her husband, the widow would take an ember from the fire and kindle a new fire out in the veld. She remained in 'her lonely place in the veld' for a month, living on herbs and wild vegetables. After this period she discarded her clothes, washed her entire body, put on a grass skirt and returned to her home at sundown. Here she was given an ember with which to start a new fire and drank sweet milk ritually to end her period of impurity. The cow from which the milk was taken was never milked again or killed: it was impure and allowed to die a natural death. A widower did the same, but remained a fortnight in the veld. He took some hairs from the tail of an ox, threaded on them some copper rings and wore this necklace until the hair perished.

The ancestors are not the only cause of misfortune, however, nor are they the most feared in this respect. It is believed that most illness and trouble is sent by individuals called witches or sorcerers *(abathakathi)*. Witches are ordinary tribesmen who, through malice, envy and greed, send misfortune to their fellows. They do this either by leaving the body sleeping in the hut and going out to meet other witches in the veld, or, more usually, they use

familiars to work their infamous purposes. The best-known of these familiars is perhaps *uthikoloshe*, a little man often kept in a store-hut by his owner, but there is also *ichanti, mamlambo, impundulu* or lightning bird, and the dreaded *isithunzela*, or resurrected corpse, dug up by witches and used to do their bidding.

Witches are believed to have sexual intercourse with their familiars and frigidity in women is sometimes attributed to this. But the really frightening thing about witches is that they attack their nearest and dearest. They typically harm neighbours or close kin, and this reversal of normal morality is symbolised in the belief that witches walk backwards, or ride backwards on the backs of baboons.

With this belief in the mystical causation of misfortune, the first question that arises when someone gets sick is: who is bewitching me? Is the illness caused by witches, or are the ancestors angry and punishing me for some neglect of custom? To ascertain this, it is necessary to consult a diviner *(igqirha, isangoma)*. Diviners are called to their profession by the ancestors themselves, who send a special illness called *thwasa*. Someone diagnosed as ill with *thwasa* must apprentice herself (most diviners are women) to an established diviner and learn the art of divining and healing from her. Diviners commune with the ancestors who indicate to them the exact cause of the 'illness'.

In the past, reaction to the discovered witch was swift and violent. She was killed, with all her family, for witchcraft may be inherited and all would be tainted. Sometimes the witch was tortured to make her confess. Today the accusation of witchcraft is a criminal offence but accused witches often leave the district to escape public disapproval.

Another important specialist is the herbalist *(ixhwele, inyanga)*. Rather like a pharmacist, he is a specialist in medicines which are used for a wide variety of purposes – promoting fertility in fields and stock, protection against lightning and thieves, and to ensure success in uncertain enterprises. Sometimes the professions of diviner and herbalist are combined in the same person.

It is probably true to say that most Transkeians still believe in the reality of witchcraft and magic, and that even Christians feel the closeness and loving care of their ancestors. In many ways the system of belief described above is more satisfying than the rather cold explanation in terms of scientific laws, which explain only *how* things happen, not why.

The Christian community tends to refrain from making ritual killings to the ancestors, but points to

the Christian doctrine of the communion of saints as a justification for their continuing reverence for their forefathers. Most Transkeian Christians are members of one or other of the main churches in South Africa and the Independent Church movement is not as active in Transkei as it is in other parts of the country. Christians are the main agents for social change. Sunday is widely observed by Christian and traditionalist alike.

The religious rituals described so far are all related to the immediate family and lineage. In the past there were other rituals, on a tribal scale, involving all tribesmen. Some were essentially religious, in that they invoked the ancestors of the chief, while others seem to have been more magical in nature. The main communal rituals were for rain-making, securing fertility of lands and crops, protecting the country against lightning and hail and strengthening the chief and army.

Responsibility for rain-making was vested in the chief who employed a special rain doctor to perform the ceremonies which, as a central rite, included the killing of a black-coloured animal. Sometimes, if rain did not fall, special prayers were offered to the chief's ancestors.

Mpondomise chiefs relied for rain-making on certain San (Bushman) families who lived in the Tsolo area until 1910 and subsisted on tribal charity in recognition of their services.

Among the Bhaca no one could begin to plant before the chief had used his medicine to secure a good crop. At the end of winter the chief sent word that on a certain day representatives of all families should gather at the great place, each bringing with him a small basket containing choice seeds of millet and maize. On their arrival, all seeds were put into large baskets together with seed from the chief's fields, and the whole doctored with medicines. The baskets were then refilled and the representatives returned home with 'the blessed seed of the great place'. Protection of the country against lightning and hail was achieved by placing on the boundaries of the tribal territory medicated pegs smeared with 'dark medicines' from the great place, while the maize crop was protected from blight by a ritual, again initiated by the chief, called *abagijimisi bokudla* ('the runners of the food'). Unmarried girls ran through the fields of maize, plucking the dwarfed cobs rotten with blight. They slept that night at the great place, and the follow-

A young man at the door of the hut in which the young initiates are secluded for three or four months.
Afterwards everything used during their stay in the hut, including their blankets and the hut itself, is burnt. This signifies their final graduation from boyhood to manhood.

ing day ceremoniously threw the cobs into the river.

By far the most important communal ritual was the annual feast of the first fruits, called *ulibo* by all groups except the Bhaca and Mpondo. No one could partake of the new harvest ripening in the fields before it had been ritually 'tasted' by the chief at a ceremony held at the great place, with a ritual eating also in each homestead. Among Mpondo and Bhaca this was combined with a doctoring of the army and, among the Bhaca, of the chieftainship itself. Among the Mpondo the ritual was called *ingxwala* and among the Bhaca, *ingcubhe*.

The Bhaca *ingcubhe* always took place at the end of summer, usually during February or March, when the maize, millet and pumpkins were ripening. Some time before, the tribal herbalist (*inyanga yempi*) and his assistants collected medicines in the forests. These were stored in a special hut in the royal homestead, in which the sacra of chiefship were also kept. Men were sent by the chief to build a special cattle kraal in which the ritual was to be performed, while the people practised cattle racing and prepared their festive costumes. Also, certain men went secretly to the fields of surrounding peoples, bringing back cobs of green maize, sweet reed and green calabash.

On the day of *ingcubhe* the army concentrated at the great place and, in a remarkable ritual manoeuvred beforehand by the chief, sang songs which appeared to insult him and accuse him of misgovernment. Later, the chief ritually tasted the medicated greenstuffs and spat (*khafula*) strong medicines to the four points of the compass to strengthen the tribe against enemy attack. Finally, the army went to the river and washed themselves in protective medicines. Performed annually in the old days, *ingcubhe* was the most important ritual of the Bhaca, symbolically bringing together the whole tribe and strengthening the all-important chieftainship.

These religious and magical rituals expressed symbolically the importance of certain basic institutions in Cape Nguni society. What is their value system, their conception of morality? How did, and do, the people of Transkei conceive the 'good man' and correct behaviour between man and man?

One very basic value is the health, fertility and well-being of man, cattle and crops. Another, equally important, is the attainment of harmonious social life and co-operation and good will between kin and neighbours, and the elimination of discord. These values are interrelated, for, as we

have seen, failure in health and fortune is attributed to failure in social relations. Illness and misfortune are thus explained in moral terms.

There are also other basic values. Cape Nguni society is not egalitarian, but divided on the basis of rank and age. The chief's lineage is superior to that of commoners. There is also a class of nobles – those belonging to minor lineages of the chief's clan. Lineages themselves are stratified into genealogically more senior and less senior lines. Strict respect is enjoined between members of one generation and those above it. Perhaps the most important moral rule is that respect should be shown to lineage seniors. Children are taught obedience to parents: they must not interrupt adult conversations and they must always address them formally. Parents whose children fail to behave well are said to feel shame (intloni). Younger brothers must respect elder brothers, and lineage members their lineage head. Respectful behaviour to seniors is a moral good in itself but, as has been seen, it is also a factor in religious practices. Every time a killing is made for the ancestors, human dependence on the supernatural is acknowledged. Respect is due to all seniors, whether related or not.

At beer-drinks and other feasts, members of various age groups sit separately, and young men do not eat from the same dish as their seniors. A junior may not sit on something while a senior sits on the ground. Women respect men and it is not considered right for a woman to join a man's group unless asked.

A good man not only respects seniors and shows loyalty to his kin group. He is also a good neighbour. The Mpondomise say that in time of trouble one can expect assistance from neighbours rather than from kinsmen. Neighbours assist one another working the fields, bringing home the harvest, and in times of sickness. Generosity is the virtue par excellence of chiefs, and every man tries to act like a chief. Of course, people sometimes need to be forced to behave morally. If a man refuses help, he may be refused help when his time comes to need assistance. The extreme condemnation of the witch (who attacks her neighbours) shows the high moral value placed on neighbourly co-operation. A good man is one free of the least taint of witchcraft.

Perhaps the greatest virtue in Cape Nguni society

Most Transkeians still believe in the reality of witchcraft and magic. Many believe that illness is caused by witchcraft and their first step is to consult a diviner (isangoma), usually female (like the one on the left in the photograph) who communes with the ancestors.

is the willingness to die for a chief. Loyalty to a chief and his subordinate political officers was a supreme good in the past, and there are many stirring accounts in tribal histories of deeds of incredible valour. Linked with this is the prohibition of manslaughter within the chiefdom, for this involves killing the chief's man. To this day chiefs enjoy considerable loyalty, especially among their more conservative followers.

Traditional arts and crafts are not highly developed. The potter's art was formerly practised fairly widely, but there was not much wood-carving, probably due to the scarcity of large trees. Iron-working was known, but, as iron is not found in Transkei, it had to be obtained through barter. The preparation of skins had reached a high state of development. The main weapons were various types of throwing spears, clubs and large, oval cow-hide shields. The bow was unknown as a weapon. Grasswork, in the form of mats, beer-strainers and baskets, is well established. Beadwork has been developed into a highly artistic tradition, though there does not seem to be a symbolic 'language' in the beadwork as among the Zulu. The only musical instruments were the musical bow and, in Mpondoland, the friction drum. Percussion drums were not used but a rolled ox-hide is used as a drum at diviners' seances and shields were beaten before the army went into battle. Ox-horn trumpets were recorded among the Bomvana and Xhosa. The main type of musical expression is vocal, usually accompanied by clapping and dancing. The easternmost groups, e.g. the Bhaca and Mpondo, perform a stamping dance, similar to that of the Zulu and differing markedly from the 'shaking' dance of the Xhosa, Thembu and Bomvana of western Transkei where the emphasis is on control of the muscles of the chest.

This was essentially an oral culture in which ideas, traditions and disputations, couched in the musical cadences of *isiXhosa*, or in music itself, were more important than material objects. One of the most valued characteristics of a councillor was his ability closely to analyse the complex points in a law case, or to swing an argument through logic and rhetoric. Another valued achievement is the ability to recount the events of the past, hence the glorious tradition of story-telling that has given pleasure to generations of Transkeians. Recently an American scholar, Harold Scheub, produced a study based on his witnessing of over 4 000 performances of Xhosa story-tellers *(iintsomi)* and even the non-Xhosa reader can now share in the adventures of 'Little Red Stomach' or Umkuywana and the activities of *Imbulu* and *uZimu,* and to this day it is an exhilirating experience to listen to a Xhosa story-teller.

Literature

Probably the first 'literary' composition was the famous and well-loved hymn, *Ntsikana's Bell,* composed by an early convert of the Rev. Joseph Williams at Gwali ('Old Lovedale') and recorded by Dr J. Philip and the Rev. J. K. Bokwe in the 1890s. From that time there has been a steadily increasing flow of compositions from Transkeian authors.

The first book ever to be printed in Xhosa was the *Incwadi yokuqala ekuteteni ngokwamaXosa eTyume,* printed in 1824 by the Rev. John Bennie at the printing press at Tyume. It was followed by *A Systematic vocabulary of the Kaffrarian Language in two parts* (1826) and a number of translations from the Bible. Two Wesleyan missionaries, William Boyce and Barnabas Shaw, printed a translation of St Luke's gospel in 1830. The translation of the Bible and a large number of hymns into Xhosa was the result of the dedicated labour of the Revs. J. Bennie, H. H. Dugmore, J. W. Appleyard, A. Kropf, W. B. Boyce and, later, Tiyo Soga. Tiyo Soga was a remarkable man. Trained at Lovedale and in Scotland, he served on many committees for the translation of the Bible, but it was his translation of John Bunyan's *Pilgrim's Progress* (1886) for which he is perhaps best remembered. B. E. N. Mahlasela writes: 'For some who know the language the Soga version is an even more impressive allegorical narrative, and among the Xhosa-speaking people it has had an influence almost equal to the Bible itself'. Other Xhosa translations followed, among them the first biographies: Sinxo's *Abraham Lincoln,* Jolobe's *Up From Slavery* and Mqhayi's *Aggrey of Africa.* Then there are the plays, *Julius Caesar, Macbeth* and *Twelfth Night* by Mdledle; *Khwane* by Lupuwana, *Maya* by Jolobe, *uAdonisi wase Nthlango* by Mqhayi, and many others.

A number of articles, stories and comments were published in Xhosa magazines and newspapers which soon began to appear. In 1834 the Lovedale Press launched a magazine called *Ikwezi.* In 1850 the monthly *Isitunywa senyanga* and in 1862 *Iindaba* were established, but none lasted for more than a few numbers. More successful was *Imvo,* a bilingual Xhosa-English paper under the editorship of John Tengo Jabavu, but up to now Xhosa newspapers have found it difficult to survive.

Newspaper articles paved the way for more creative and scholarly writings. In 1906 W. B. Rubusana published an anthology of Xhosa folk-

Traditionalists believe that the world was created by a Supreme Being called Mdali *whom the missionaries hesitated to equate with the God of the Bible for whom another word,* uThixo, *is used today by both Christians and traditionalists.*

lore called *Zemk' iinkomo mgwala ndini* and also a *History of South Africa from the Native Point of View,* for which he was awarded an honorary doctorate by McKinley University. Other historical works by Xhosa writers were *Ibali lamaMpondo namaBhaca, maXesibe namaMpondomise* (1927) and *Ibali lamaThembu* (1925) by W. D. Cingo. At about the same time chief Victor Poto wrote his own *Ibali lamaMpondo.* Important biographies were J. K. Bokwe's *Ubomi bukaNtsikani* (1914) T. B. Soga's biography of Tiyo Soga (1923) and S. E. K. Mqhayi's *uBomi bomfundisi uJ. K. Bokwe.*

The first Xhosa novel appears to be *uTandiwe wakwaGcaleka,* by a woman, Laetitia Kakaza, and published in 1912. Then appeared S. E. Krune Mqhayi with his novels *uSamson* and the famous *Ityala lamaWele* ('The Lawsuit of the Twins'). As Mahlasela puts it, '(Mqhayi) is a master of the Xhosa language. In this respect he has few equals . . .' Mqhayi was followed by J. J. R. Jolobe and G. B. Sinxo, but the outstanding Xhosa novelist is undoubtedly the late Prof A. C. Jordan of the University of Wisconsin, whose *Ingqumbo yeminyanya* ('The Wrath of the Ancestors') remains unchallenged in its complexity of construction as a work of real merit in Xhosa literature.

Finally, it should be mentioned that in traditional society there are hardly any organised recreational activities in the Western sense of the word. Tribal dancing is the main form of relaxation and amusement for both sexes of all ages. Nor do traditionalists play any organised sports. In the urban areas, however, organised sport, particularly football, has made rapid strides.

In conclusion it is fitting to quote the comments of Professor Monica Wilson on the impression made on earlier writers by the people of the Transkei. 'The values of Nguni society were vividly realised by some of the survivors of the *Stavenisse* in 1686. They speak of the hospitality and courtesy of the Xhosa among whom they lived: of their respect for chiefs and for the rule of law. The concern for kinship and seniority, and the preoccupation with cattle, have also been described. One traveller after another mentions the gaiety and good humour of the women and the good manners of the men . . . and there is mention . . . of the reputation of men for their powers as orators in chiefs' courts'.

These are the qualities of character and intelligence, which will stand the people of Transkei in good stead in the years that lie ahead. For centuries they have tended their herds and crops on the rolling uplands and in the broken coastal strip of their lovely country. Here progressives and traditionalists together have reached an historic landmark in their history.

Chapter Four

The Capital – Umtata

The capital city of the Republic of Transkei is Umtata, approximately 100 years old. It straddles the Umtata River, from which it derives its name. Few towns of its size – or even Black African capitals – can rival its growth rate of the past few years. In a period of ten years buildings of more than $17,3 million were erected and the total valuation increased by more than 400 per cent, consumption of electricity more than doubled and water consumption rose by more than 300 per cent. In 1976 alone buildings worth $18,4 million will be completed.

Expansion projects recently completed, or about to be completed in the near future, include the following: the new high-rise administrative block for the Transkeian government; the presidential residence and a new suburb of luxury homes for Cabinet Ministers; large extensions to several existing residential areas; a new industrial township designed to attract more industries to Umtata; the new campus at Umtata of the University of Fort Hare headquartered at Alice some 200 km away to the south; the KD Matanzima Airport, Transkei's new international airport; the new headquarters of the Transkeian Defence Force; a large new sports stadium; a large new hotel which will virtually double hotel accommodation in Umtata, and a new in-service training centre for teachers.

Housing is in short supply and new houses are

An old sea cannon has been mounted on the lawns of the Umtata city hall (background). The city hall was completed in 1908 but the municipality of Umtata is about 100 years old. Total population of the town at independence was estimated at 30 000.

being built as fast as bricks and mortar can be supplied and handled. At independence, the population of Umtata was estimated at 30 000, of whom 5 500 were Whites. In fact, the increase in recent years of the White population of Umtata is one of the noteworthy features of the town's development. In the years leading up to independence several hundred of the White citizens of Umtata moved from the town into the Republic of South Africa after they had sold their properties to Blacks through the agency of the Transkei Development Corporation or the South African Bantu Trust. But they were far outnumbered by those who stayed and in the past year or so the ranks of the latter have been substantially reinforced by new arrivals.

Today Umtata is the venue for a meeting of abiding fascination between the old and the new. The newly installed automatic telephone exchange instantly links the town with the Republic of South Africa's telephone system and – through that system – with the world at large. Meanwhile, on a busy street intersection red-blanketed Xhosa men and women, up from tribal lands for a day's shopping, pass the time of day in elaborate ritual greetings and a leisurely conversation pattern laid down by centuries of tradition.

At the end of the working day hundreds of Black and White clerks and industrial workers rush home and on their way they brush shoulders with men, young and old, wearing nothing but a blanket, loin-cloth and a cap at a jaunty angle. Some might even pause a while at the sidewalk display of intricate beadwork offered for sale by a Xhosa matron, resplendent in her flowing robes and

peaked headdress, quietly puffing away at her long-stemmed pipe.

Umtata, youngest of the world's capitals, looks to the future with confidence, secure in the human and material infrastructure that has been fashioned over a century of constructive contact between Black and White.

History

Umtata – the name of the river eventually given to the town – was probably derived from the burial custom of the Amangcengana, a Tembu tribe who lived in this area long before the first White man reached this far into the interior. They committed the corpses of their departed ones to the river with the prayer: 'mThathe, Bawo!' ('Take him, father!'). The first part – 'mThathe' – was later corrupted into Umtata. Tradition has it that even today, as a mark of respect to the dead, women of the area do not lift their skirts while wading through drifts in the Umtata River. For the same reason, some men refuse to drink water from the river.

It was in the late 1860s that Tembu Chief Ngangelizwe began to offer land to White settlers on the south bank of the river. The annual quit-rent was the princely sum of £6, payable to the Chief himself. The first White settler to have availed himself of this offer is generally agreed to have been Richard W. Calverley. In 1870 he was granted 'Mission Bend' on which he built his home. Subsequently he sold his property to the Church of the Province for £300 and was granted another site by Chief Ngangelizwe.

At about the same time a small group of Voortrekkers (Dutch pioneer farmers from the eastern Cape Province) began to settle in the fertile valleys of Cicira, a little higher up on the river. Meanwhile, Pondo Chief Nqwiliso decided to establish a buffer settlement of White farmers on the northern banks of the river. Soon several farmers accepted land grants there on similar conditions as those on the southern bank.

The magistracy of Umtata was created in 1876 – a hundred years ago. From that year the farmers were required to pay their annual rental to the Cape government instead of to Chief Ngangelizwe. Later Bishop Callaway reported that when he first came to Umtata – in 1877 – the White

A panoramic view of the city hall gardens, with one of the new government buildings in the background.
Umtata has grown very rapidly in recent years. During the past ten years the municipal valuation increased by more than 400 per cent.

settlers were living in scattered homesteads, 'and there was nothing like a disposition to gather into a village'. He opened the first school in the same year.

On 5 January 1879 the magistrate reported that the village of Umtata had made rapid strides. A survey had been completed, erven marked off and several shops and houses erected.

On 27 March of the same year a group of some 50 pioneer settlers petitioned the colonial secretary of the time that a site be selected and surveyed for the *township* of Umtata Tembuland.

The newly constituted management board of Umtata met for the first time on 28 March 1882. By this time Umtata was a flourishing if still scattered village. Dr T. R. Craister was elected chairman of the board which had hardly assumed office when the citizens petitioned the colonial government to have Umtata proclaimed a municipality. This was done on 10 November 1882 and the same Dr Craister became Umtata's first mayor.

In those days the town's only reliable communication with the outside world was the telegraph. There was no railway and the roads were generally in a bad state of repair. Often during the wet season they were quite impassable and no mail cart or ox-wagon could get through to Umtata.

The town's first valuation roll was compiled in 1883. The total valuation of buildings in the town was put at £17 000 and the rate of taxation – two pennies in the pound – gave the municipality the sum of £142 a year to finance its current development expenditure! In these circumstances, with the town growing as fast as it did, the council found itself under great pressure from the very outset. To ease the pressure a little, the colonial government from time to time granted the municipality some land to sell in order to swell its funds. Nevertheless, in those days the municipal banking account was often overdrawn and when this happened the bank manager insisted on collateral in the form of a promissory note signed by every member of the council.

Two events of great importance took place during the last decade of the nineteenth century. In 1894 a bridge was constructed over the Umtata River eventually to become one of the major links in road communication between the Cape Colony and Natal. More immediately, it also meant that the two halves of the town were finally joined together by a reliable link.

During the early months of the same year Pondoland was annexed to the Cape Colony after the

Pondos had for years plundered Tembuland and conducted endless internecine wars among themselves.

This addition to the British Empire naturally enhanced the status of Umtata which by 1899 had become the commercial centre of a comparatively large region, as well as the headquarters of government, the military and the church. The town had been considerably enlarged by portions of the annexed Pondo territory.

In the beginning the council had no proper building in which to meet or conduct municipal business. The first meetings were held in an old hut lent by the government. Later the venue shifted to the public library and thereafter to a small chapel. In the year 1900 the council found a haven in the old court house where it remained until the completion in 1908 of the town hall of today. The original estimate of construction costs was £18 000 but, owing to a series of fortunate circumstances, the building was actually completed for £4 000 less! Even then, there was voluble criticism of the council's extravagance but this was silenced when, within a few years, all the offices in the building were occupied and on certain gala occasions the hall was filled to capacity.

Transportation

Gone are the days of the ox-wagon, mail cart and impassable roads. The first motor-car reached Umtata in October 1903 – a Lorraine Deidrich, complete with canvas hood and curtains, narrow mudguards, crank starter, oil head-lamps and gear-levers on the running-board.

The first train reached Umtata on 18 September 1916. Long before the appointed time a crowd of several thousand had gathered at the station. They had come from the valleys in carts, ox-wagons, on horseback and even in motor-cars. The first Prime Minister of South Africa, General Louis Botha, performed the opening ceremony by tightening up the last bolt on the track.

Today Umtata is still the railhead of the line from East London which will presumably continue to be Transkei's link with the sea-lanes of the world until such time as the new state builds its own port somewhere on the Wild Coast. The railway line is also one of the two most important links between Transkei and its markets and sources of supply in the Republic of South Africa and the rest of Southern Africa. The other is the national highway from Durban in Natal to East London and Port Elizabeth in the Cape Province, which runs through Umtata and is the main artery of overland communication between the various regions of the country, all interconnected with a network of secondary roads.

Till recently Umtata's – and therefore Transkei's – only air link with the outside world was via the small municipal aerodrome whose grass runways could accommodate only small aircraft. When the KD Matanzima international airport at Umtata is commissioned, modern aircraft will be used directly to link the capital with South Africa and the rest of the world.

Water supply

In the infant days of their town the citizens had to rely on private wells, rain-water tanks or the river itself. After considering and rejecting a number of water supply schemes for the town, the council in 1906 decided to adopt a scheme which would supply water from a perennial stream about 20 km away in the Kambi mountain forest.

Difficulties were encountered in raising the capital of £20 000, however. Eventually the mother city came to the rescue. The Cape Town Corporation decided to lend Umtata £20 000 for 34 years at an interest rate of 5,5 per cent. The scheme was duly completed but soon proved quite inadequate to meet the town's growing demands. The obvious source for supplementing the water supplies of the town was the Umtata River and a pumping station was duly constructed.

Two new reservoirs were recently completed at Owen Dam and one at Ncambedlana – with a total capacity of 5,5 million litres, while plans are ready for a large new dam in the Umtata River to be constructed by the Transkeian Department of Agriculture and Forestry. It will take at least three years to complete this dam and in order to augment water supplies in the interim the Department of Agriculture and Forestry is building a dam on the Mabeleni stream.

Electricity

The first electricity supply scheme was commissioned in 1921. Direct current was generated by a set of diesel motors to be supplied to consumers from dusk to midnight only. In response to the heavy demand the council was soon supplying current for virtually 24 hours a day!

The scheme was run at a substantial loss: the price of diesel fuel in Umtata was almost prohibitive and, in addition, there was the burden of the annual interest payments on the capital invested in the scheme. Charges were already high and could not be raised any further: consumers could not be expected to carry the burden.

To circumvent these difficulties and to augment supplies, the council in June 1928 inaugurated the Umtata Hydro-Electricity Scheme of 100 kw and at the same time changed from direct to alternating current.

This new facility enabled the council to reduce tariffs. For some time supply exceeded demand, but soon the demand for electricity began to exceed all expectations. In 1933, a second hydro-electric plant of 400 kw was installed at the second falls on Umtata River. The demand for electric power continued to increase at such a rate, however, that additional diesel generating units of 400 kw had to be installed as stand-by plant. In 1949 a third hydro-electric plant of 150 kw was commissioned at the first falls on the river.

After the Second World War development in the town proceeded at such a pace that the generating plant had to be continuously augmented and eventually the capacity of the diesel and hydro-electric plant together was raised to 2 000 kw. Finally the council decided that the cost of fuel had rendered the diesel plant uneconomical and in 1952 a thermal power station with a capacity of 1 500 kw was commissioned.

In 1965 two 1 000 kw steam generating sets were added to the thermal station, but these extensions were hardly completed when the council found it necessary to install another two sets of 3 000 kw each. On this occasion the council had to turn to the government of the Republic of South Africa for financial assistance to finance these extensions. During these negotiations the government decided to request the Electricity Supply Commission (ESCOM) to supply power to Umtata.

April 1975 was a red-letter day for Umtata when the town was finally linked with the national grid of ESCOM. Even in that first year ESCOM supplied more than half of the town's requirements – 14 million of the 22,5 million kwh sold. No sooner had Umtata been connected to ESCOM's grid than the council had to approach the Commission with the request that the implementation of the long-term agreement for the supply of power be accelerated so that maximum supplies could be delivered much sooner than originally planned. Negotiations have reached an advanced stage and current indications are that ESCOM will be able to meet the council's request.

In 1976 buildings worth more than $18 million will be completed in Umtata. Large construction projects either recently completed or about to be completed include a presidential residence, a new industrial township, a university campus, and an international airport.

Table 1 – Umtata capital expenditure, 1966 to 1975

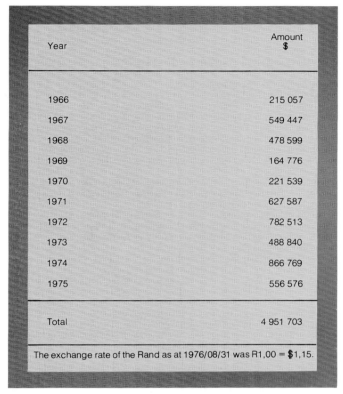

Year	Amount $
1966	215 057
1967	549 447
1968	478 599
1969	164 776
1970	221 539
1971	627 587
1972	782 513
1973	488 840
1974	866 769
1975	556 576
Total	4 951 703

The exchange rate of the Rand as at 1976/08/31 was R1,00 = $1,15.

Table 2 – Umtata revenue expenditure 1966 to 1975

Year	General Fund $	Bantu Revenue Fund $	Total $
1966	589 282	39 919	629 201
1967	690 298	49 486	739 784
1968	762 176	52 061	814 237
1969	847 248	80 827	928 075
1970	936 839	75 774	1 012 613
1971	1 081 194	86 383	1 167 576
1972	1 172 715	107 277	1 279 992
1973	1 407 128	107 458	1 514 586
1974	1 647 174	113 963	1 761 137
1975	2 256 678	159 587	2 416 265
Total	11 390 732	872 735	12 263 466

The exchange rate of the Rand as at 1976/08/31 was R1,00 = $1,15.

Chapter Five

Education and Vocational Training

There is a long tradition of education in Transkei, stretching over a period of about 150 years. Shortly after the arrival of the British Settlers in the Eastern Cape in 1820, the Wesleyan Methodist Missionary Society (WMMS), pioneers in the development of education in what is today Transkei, started to establish a chain of mission stations throughout the territory. Between 1827 and 1865, institutions such as Lamplough, Clarkebury, Shawbury and Emfundisweni, now household names in Transkei, came into being. The WMMS was followed by the missionaries of the Church of Scotland, the Moravians, the Anglican, Roman Catholic and Dutch Reformed Churches, to name only some.

For these early missionaries education was a tool of evangelisation. Reading was taught as a key to the treasures of the Bible. In those early days prominence was given to English, but it was these very missionaries who were responsible for the development of Xhosa as a written language and medium of communication. By 1833 the Rev. W. B. Boyce of the WMMS had completed a grammar of the Xhosa language, in which the principle of the euphonic concord was first established as basic to the structure of the Bantu languages.

The schools set up on these mission stations are older than all but a few White schools in South

A young boy doing an I Q test. The Transkeian Department of Education is responsible for over 500 000 pupils, about 2 000 schools and 10 000 teachers. These figures compare favourably with those of most Black African countries.

Africa. They have served generations of Transkeians and are held in affectionate regard by the people.

Until 1910 the missions continued to carry the major financial burden of providing education facilities for Transkeians. After 1854 some limited grants were paid by the government of the Cape Colony to the mission schools. These were continued after the Education Department of the Cape Colony first took over limited responsibility for Black education in 1865. It was only after the Union of South Africa was formed in 1910 that the subsidies paid to the missionary societies were substantially increased to indicate that the State, through the Cape Education Department, had begun to accept that Black education was a matter of national importance and concern.

Until 1955 the schools in Transkei remained under the dual control of the Cape Education Department and the missions. From 1925, when state funds were made available to the Cape Province through the Department of Native Affairs of the Union of South Africa, education began to expand rapidly and by 1932 there were 1 149 schools, 2 302 teachers and 65 898 pupils in Transkei. Eight years later the number of pupils had increased to 120 798, and the school had become one of the major agencies of social change in the territory.

Following on the Eiselen Commission of Inquiry into Native Education of 1949 – 1951, the Bantu Education Act was passed in 1953. The implementation of this was of critical importance in the history of education in Transkei and in establishing

the broad principles on which educational development was to take place in the pre-independence era. In terms of this Act control of education passed from the four provinces of the Union of South Africa to a central state department, which was in a position to establish a national education policy linked to the general development programme envisaged for territories such as Transkei.

At the local level, the control and administration of education passed from the churches into the hands of local communities, which were able to exert influence through representation on school committees and school boards.

In Transkei thousands of parents and local leaders, through their involvement in these bodies, gained invaluable experience in basic administration which was to stand them in good stead as their country prepared for independence.

Thus, two basic purposes of the 'new deal' in education were to involve the Transkeian people, both as parents and professional educators, more deeply in education; and to link education closely with the broad development programmes devised for greater self-realisation for Transkei.

When Transkei was granted a substantial degree of self-government by the central government of the Republic of South Africa, it was natural that among the first departments to be set up was the Transkeian Department of Education: in terms of homeland development it was clearly a key department. By 1966 the Transkei administration had passed its own Education Act and thereafter was able to develop independently of the 'mother' Department of Bantu Education of South Africa.

The newly formed Department of Education was particularly fortunate in that it could draw upon a reserve of Black education personnel – inspectors, teachers, clerks, hostel staff – who had had years of training and experience with the Department of Bantu Education. Thus, from the beginning it could operate with a minimum of White officials. In fact, only the head of the department (the Secretary for Education), and a few professional advisers and senior administrative officers were White. Recently, however, this was the first Transkei department of state to appoint a Black secretary, Mr G. Kakana, who has now been succeeded by Mr M. B. Potelwa. He is typical of many Trans-

A typical classroom in Transkei. In 1975, one of every six pupils who had entered secondary school four years earlier, reached Form V, the final school year. Since 1966 there has been a steady average annual increase of 25 per cent in Form V.

keian educationists. He is a product of one of the old missionary institutions and has come up the hard way by private study at the University of South Africa. No one is better prepared or more enthusiastic for the new responsibilities which independence will bring.

The Transkei Department of Education moves into the independence era with responsibility for over 500 000 pupils, about 2 000 schools and 10 000 teachers, only about 70 of whom are White. Its development since it came into being in 1963 is summed up in the statistics given in Table 1.

Primary education

If one accepts the UNESCO definition of minimum literacy as four years of schooling, the importance of primary education, now defined in Transkei as those classes from Substandard A to Standard 4 (the first six years), needs no stressing. It is of particular importance for rural communities where, in general, children tend to leave school after this stage is completed. Rather than being merely preparatory to secondary education, it is imperative that in this typical Third World situation the primary school course should be a 'rounded whole' in its own right. Thus, Transkei has given considerable attention to the content of primary school curricula, and has developed its own syllabuses to meet the needs of its own people and situation.

In the first four years the basic core consists of the elementary skills of speech, reading, writing and numeracy, together with health education and practical activities. In these years the pupil's mother-tongue (Xhosa or South-Sotho) is used as medium of instruction. In making this decision, Transkei drew on the conclusions of the Cingo Report of 1962, backed up by the reports of various conferences in Africa at which the importance had been highlighted of 'easing' the child into the school situation with the minimum of disruption. In a more recent Transkei education report (the K-N-N Commission of Inquiry) it is stated: 'His mother-tongue conjures up in him all sorts of pleasant associations; it is an embodiment of his culture and attitude to life, interests and ambitions, the family past and present, his successes and social status'.

In the later years of the primary school – from Std. 3 upwards – more attention is given to history, geography and general science, although the languages and mathematics still constitute the core. At the same time English is introduced as medium of instruction, although Xhosa continues to be an important subject throughout the school system. English was introduced as medium "in order to

79

Table 1. Education in Transkei, 1963 — 1975

Year	Schools	Teachers	Pupils
1963	1 618	4 711	276 942
1964	1 627	5 071	289 098
1965	1 588	5 351	302 401
1966	1 585	5 722	334 310
1967	1 588	6 126	352 431
1968	1 617	6 531	375 728
1969	1 650	6 781	400 642
1970	1 688	7 262	418 406
1971	1 724	7 667	441 507
1972	1 769	8 091	455 715
1973	1 820	8 452	477 338
1974	1 854	8 728	488 326
1975	1 946	9 944	517 975

The exchange rate of the Rand as at 1976/08/31 was R1,00 = $1,15.

ensure mainly a smoother system of communication with the larger world and Transkeians' ability to make their livelihood" (K-N-N report 1973).

Two-thirds of all teachers in primary schools are women who, despite grave misgivings on the part of the more conservative traditionalists in the early days, have come to be completely accepted by the local communities. As was to be expected, they have been particularly successful in creating a happy atmosphere in the classes for the younger children. Now that the school entrance age has been reduced from 7 to 5½ years, this is a factor of particular importance.

Play-time at a school in the country. Since 1972/73 the amount allocated to education by the Transkeian government has doubled and the unit cost per pupil has increased from $27,95 to $49,68. Education has always been one of the largest budget votes.

Table 2 briefly indicates development in the primary schools from 1963 – 1975 and also identifies certain problems which remain to be solved. The table shows that the first four years account for about two-thirds of total primary school enrolment and that even here there is a considerable drop-out problem. For instance, the 106 268 pupils in Sub-standard A in 1972 had decreased to 58 156 in Std. 2 in 1975. Transkei regards this as its major educational problem, both in terms of investment of funds and in the lack of realisation of potential, particularly in rural communities. The K-N-N Commission devoted much attention to this problem, spelt out the causes in considerable detail and made practical suggestions to improve the situation.

In the long term, even allowing for improved parental motivation and stronger 'holding power' on the part of schools, the drop-out problem will not be completely solved until some form of compulsory attendance is introduced. Indeed, the Transkei Education Act of 1966 makes provision for administrative regions to apply for the introduction of compulsory school attendance when they feel competent to apply it. The final decision, however, rests with the government. For rural communities the implications of compulsory education are radical, as they will affect long-established traditions and life-styles and demand new attitudes to child-bearing and upbringing, to the rearing of animals and use of the soil. Progress therefore will be gradual but in preparing for this ultimate ideal, Transkei's immediate targets are combating the drop-out rate, reducing the teacher-pupil ratio (1 to 52 at present) and improving the quality of teaching in primary schools. In all these areas some ground has been won and progress is perhaps best reflected in the increasing number of primary school pupils proceeding to some form of secondary education.

Secondary education

While the growth rate in primary education has been maintained at a steady average of five to six per cent a year, that in secondary education has reached an average of about 16 per cent a year, with the sudden boost in 1975 which will be referred to later. Whereas in 1968 only one of every 12 pupils who had entered secondary school four years earlier reached Form V, by 1975 this figure was better than one in six. The Department of Education plans to maintain this improvement and to broaden the apex of the educational pyramid, a basic need in all developing communities.

From 1966 onwards there has been a steady average increase of about 25 per cent a year in

Table 2. Primary education, 1963 — 1975

Year	Sub A	Sub B	Std. 1	Std. 2	Total Lower Primary	Std. 3	Std. 4	Std. 5	Std. 6	Total Higher Primary	Total Primary
1963	X	X	X	X	194 212	X	X	X	X	73 215	267 427
1966	96 997	54 830	48 019	36 326	236 172	30 984	22 177	16 979	14 598	84 738	320 910
1969	103 283	66 183	61 171	47 584	278 221	39 038	25 933	19 930	17 729	102 630	380 851
1972	106 268	70 883	67 135	54 595	298 881	47 646	34 070	24 954	21 251	127 921	426 802
1975	122 505	75 938	72 377	58 156	328 976	52 722	38 608	28 854	—	120 184	449 160

Notes:

X Not available

— No Std. 6 classes 1975: education structure reduced to 12 years.

Form V (final year of the secondary school), while successes in the final school examination (Senior Certificate/Matriculation) increased from 135 in 1966 to 646 in 1975.

These statistics reflect positive planning over the past ten years to give priority to secondary education which will supply the trained manpower, the recruits for tertiary education and the leaders at all levels that Transkei urgently requires. At the same time, the statistics also point to rising parental expectations for their children and stronger motivation in the pupils themselves. It is clear, for example, that the great majority of those who pass Form III (Junior Certificate) go on to some type of further education or training – Form IV, teacher training or nursing, in the main.

Until recently the secondary school offered a five-year course from Form I to Form V (from the ninth to the 13th school year) culminating in the Senior Certificate/Matriculation examination. Recently, however, the educational structure was reduced to 12 instead of 13 years, by the elimination of the Std. 6 year in the primary school. Std. 5 in the primary school is now regarded as the first year of the junior secondary course. At the beginning of 1975, therefore, Transkei upgraded about 600 of its primary schools which previously had had Std. 6, so that pupils could continue in the same school as far as Form I and Form II (renamed Std. 6 and 7). This move accounts for the vastly increased numbers in Form I and II in 1975 (see Table 3) and has brought junior secondary education within the reach of hundreds of pupils

who, under the old system because of distance or expense, would have left school after Std. 5.

The new senior secondary school will comprise Forms III to V (Stds. 8 to 10), the tenth to twelfth school years.

The syllabuses followed from Std. 5 to Form III are at present those of the Department of Bantu Education of the Republic of South Africa, while in Forms IV and V they are those of the Department of National Education or the Joint Matriculation Board of the Republic of South Africa. These syllabuses are basically those of all schools in South Africa, as they are drawn up by national syllabus committees representative of all examining bodies. The final Senior Certificate/Matriculation examination requirements are the same for all schools in South Africa and Transkei and are controlled by the Joint Matriculation Board, a statutory body charged with the maintenance of university entrance standards.

The basic curriculum up to Form II (Std. 7) comprises the mother-tongue, English, Afrikaans, mathematics, social studies and general science. Five of these subjects, including the three languages, are compulsory. Seven subjects have to be taken in all and additional subjects are chosen from the following: agricultural science, woodwork, home economics, needlework, art, music, accountancy, typewriting, etc.

From Form III upwards the only three compulsory subjects are the Bantu language, English and

Table 3. Secondary education, 1963 — 1975

Year	Form I	Form II	Form III	Form IV	Form V	Total
1963	X	X	X	X	X	8 077
1966	5 386	3 879	2 207	400	233	12 105
1969	6 979	5 964	3 957	892	407	18 199
1972	10 044	8 348	5 431	2 013	972	26 808
1975	25 279†	27 567†	8 073	3 462	1 672	66 053

Notes:

X Details not available

† New education structure: Pupils in Standards 5 and 6 in 1974 promoted to Forms I and II respectively in 1975.

Afrikaans. For the rest, a choice of three or four subjects is made from the following five groupings:

* Mathematics, functional mathematics;
* Physical science, biology, physiology;
* Accountancy, business economics, mercantile law, typing;
* German, Latin, history, geography, economics, Biblical studies;
* Home economics, housecraft, needlework, art, woodwork and metalwork, agricultural science.

Most of the subjects listed above may be offered at either of two levels – standard grade and higher grade. Syllabuses on the higher grade have an enriched content, and in teaching and examination the emphasis is on interpretation and insight. Pupils who wish to gain a Matriculation Certificate to qualify for university entrance must pass on the higher grade in at least three of these subjects, one of which must be the home language. No such requirements are prescribed for the school-leaving qualification (Senior Certificate) in which the choice of subjects is much freer.

With the large increase in secondary school numbers, Transkei is also experiencing the basic tension between the demands of quantity and quality, familiar to all developing countries. In the final instance, the quality of education rests firmly in the hands of the teacher, and this is where the problem lies. For there is a shortage of highly qualified secondary school teachers, and many teachers in secondary schools are teaching at a level beyond their qualifications and experience. As a result, the standard of work, particularly in the senior classes of the secondary school, is not what it should be.

There is no short-term solution to this. Apart from improving teacher supply and training (which will be discussed later), much could be done by introducing effective guidance services to assist parents and pupils in directing talent in the right direction. Considerable attention was given to this aspect in the recent K-N-N Commission report and a start has been made with the establishment of such services. As far as selection is concerned, the report stated that 'tests should be designed to assess each child's ability and aptitude and lead to a decision as to which type of secondary education is most suited to him'.

In 1975 there were 61 White teachers allocated by the Republic of South Africa to the Transkei Department of Education. They are all teaching in secondary schools or in teacher-training institutions where they not only offer academic subjects but also play a major role in technical education. This kind of assistance in the senior secondary school, particularly in subjects such as English, mathematics and science, will continue to be of great importance to Transkei after independence.

Most secondary schools have quite extensive extramural programmes. In addition to the popular sports such as football and athletics, and the choral groups, which are a feature of most schools, youth movements such as Boy Scouts, Girl Guides

Organised sports and other outdoor activities are part of the curriculum of most Transkeian schools. The Transkeian Department of Education firmly believes in the old adage, 'A healthy mind in a healthy body', and applies it in practice.

and Red Cross are to be found at many. The establishment of the Department of Education provides for a planner for cultural affairs and sport, as well as a sports organiser. Forty-eight of Transkei's post-primary schools have hostels accommodating some 11 000 pupils, and the richest variety of extramural activities is to be found in these boarding schools.

Technical and vocational education

Vital as agriculture may be to the future development of Transkei, there is general agreement that industrial expansion is imperative if sufficient work opportunities are to be provided for all those entering the labour market each year and the country is to become economically viable. Without the skilled manpower required at all levels, however, this development will be hampered. For the future of Transkei, therefore, skills training for a diversified economy is a matter of the greatest national importance.

To date, development in the field of technical education in Transkei has been limited, not so much in the courses offered, but in the number of trainees availing themselves of these facilities. In South Africa as a whole, the Black man has only in the past two to three years begun to take full advantage of this kind of training, largely owing to the previously limited employment opportunities in this field. In general, this has been the position in Transkei, too, where at present only between 500 and 600 pupils are in technical and vocational schools.

There are two trade schools, Ngqungqushe and Teko, at which the following courses are offered: concreting, bricklaying and plastering, plumbing, drain-laying and sheet metalwork, carpentry, joinery and cabinet-making, motor mechanics and tailoring.

The entrance qualification for these courses is Std. 7, except in the case of motor mechanics, for which trainees must have obtained a Junior (Form III) Certificate.

Trainees who have completed their two or three years at trade school are required to do further on-the-job training until a five-year span of experience (including the years in trade school) has been completed. At the end of this period they

The enrolment at technical and vocational schools at present is between 500 and 600. There are two trade schools which offer a wide variety of courses, ranging from bricklaying to motor mechanics. Much expansion in this branch of education is envisaged.

may apply to undergo a standardised trade test to qualify for artisan status.

In addition to the expansion of these facilities, what is now needed is the establishment of a statutory national apprenticeship system so that the status, wages and conditions of service of the qualified artisan may be defined and protected. Such a step would do much to stimulate interest in trade schools and the growth of the skilled artisan class which in many ways is the backbone of an industrial society.

The major technical institution in Transkei is the Umtata Technical College which at the moment is used for a number of purposes. One strong component is the commercial high school which not only accepts full-time pupils up to commercial Senior Certificate level (accountancy, business economics and typewriting), but has also developed part-time classes in these commercial subjects. In addition, it offers trade courses in carpentry, joinery and cabinet-making, motor mechanics, leatherwork, welding and metalwork.

A 'block-release' system of training has been introduced in various trades. In carpentry, the two-year course leads to the National Technical Certificate I of the South African Department of National Education, while in other trades a three-year course leads to the National Technical Certificate 2. In the mornings theoretical training is given in mathematics, applied science, trade theory and drawing, while in the afternoon the workshops are used for practical training.

For girls, vocational courses in homecraft and dressmaking are available at five institutions, while most secondary schools offer home economics and/or needlework as part of the normal school curriculum.

The expansion of trade and technical training facilities as part of the conventional school programmes will be an important segment of future development, but of even greater moment will be less conventional and more flexible programmes outside the school system. Industrialists moving into Transkei will require both semi-skilled operatives and skilled operators – men and women – often from a rural background. Because they have experienced some form of industrial orientation, many are highly responsive to training in the industrial situation, which is quite different from the long-term training of skilled craftsmen in trade schools: what will be needed are short-term, intensive, 'crash-course' programmes.

Useful precedents for this type of training have been developed in recent years in South Africa.

These comprise both 'in-factory' training through subsidies and tax concessions and 'crash-course' centres serving a group of factories with similar basic needs. A Transkei prototype of this kind of centre is being planned for the Butterworth industrial complex. This is an approach which holds considerable promise for a country with the particular needs of Transkei and is also a very practical way of 'rescuing' the school drop-out and making him or her a productive and efficient citizen.

The benefits of this kind of training were commented on in the K-N-N report of 1973: 'Transkei has a large labour force of illiterate and semi-literate able-bodied men who seek work within or outside its borders in the labour centres in the larger Republic of South Africa. Any labour-training scheme devised for such people will pay big dividends. Through it the labourer receives a form of adult education, of guidance and counselling, of preparation and re-orientation. Thus the possibility of trial and error as well as demoralising frustration may be reduced to a minimum in the output of the worker, who is enabled instead to plunge usefully into his job with heart and soul right from the start. Such a scheme is a double blessing . . . It blesses the employer and the employee, the State and the citizen'.

All this does not mean that the strategic place occupied by agriculture is not recognised. In fact, its importance has been stressed over and over again in recent months. Much is being done at the Tsolo Agricultural College where future officials of the Department of Agriculture are trained in up-to-date methods and techniques. While agricultural science is a well-supported subject in secondary schools, some educationists have asked whether in this respect the ordinary rural primary school is exerting its influence in the community as it should.

This is a daunting problem in all developing communities: to change attitudes is the most difficult educational task of all. It is generally accepted that changes in the school will have to be accompanied by adult education programmes; otherwise, if the experience of other countries is anything to go by, the prospects of making any fundamental impact are poor. Educationists agree that what is required is a willingness to experiment and to work outside the constraints of the normal school system, and to apply to this problem the resources recently recruited for industrial training.

The Efata School for the Deaf, sponsored by the Dutch Reformed Church, admitted its first 18 pupils in 1960. Plans are well advanced to increase the number to 300 in the near future. School syllabuses have been adapted to the needs of the deaf.

A respected retired Transkei educationist has said: 'There is an urgency about agriculture being made a powerful contributor to the economy of Transkei, and that can only be achieved when a national campaign has been organised in which all are involved, from the herd-boy to the national leader, from the student to the most senior agricultural officer. A conscious combined effort is essential'.

Special education

There are three special schools in Transkei, one for blind children, one for the deaf and the third for cerebral-palsied and crippled children. All three came into being as a result of initiatives by the Dutch Reformed Church in Africa and the Roman Catholic Church. Subsidies from the South African and Transkei governments amount to about 90 per cent of total expenditure.

The Efata School for the Blind admitted its first pupil in July 1958 in temporary accommodation in a disused cheese factory. The permanent buildings were opened in 1960 on land about 8 km from Umtata, which as far back as 1952 had been bought by the Dutch Reformed Church for this purpose. The school now caters for 100 blind pupils all of whom live in hostels on the grounds. The syllabuses used are the same as those followed in other schools in Transkei. Teaching is done through braille for which a standardised system has been evolved in Xhosa. The school uses the most modern braille writing machines and other special aids, such as the thermoform copier, devised for use in blind schools.

The Efata School for the Deaf, also sponsored by the Dutch Reformed Church, admitted its first 18 pupils in 1960. It was first housed in an old farmhouse, then in the cheese factory when that was vacated by the blind pupils, and finally it moved into its own buildings which now accommodate 200 pupils.

Plans are well advanced to increase the number to 300 in the near future. The syllabuses have been specially adapted to the needs of deaf children. The 'combined' system of communication is employed in order to develop the language ability of the deaf pupil as quickly as possible. Systematic signs in the Xhosa language, finger spelling, speech, speech reading, reading and writing are all part of this 'combined' approach. Audiometers and modern electronic hearing-aids are used extensively, together with special readers and a variety of projectors.

The Ikwezi Lokusa School for cerebral-palsied and orthopaedically handicapped children traces its history to 1958 when the first child was admitted

to the Roman Catholic mission at Glen Avent. To begin with, the children were transported to a nearby primary school at Ngangelizwe, but in 1964 new buildings were opened with accommodation for 100 pupils. These were later extended to take 175 children.

At Ikwezi Lokusa the pupils follow the ordinary school syllabuses, but there are a number of special classes for cerebral-palsied children with extreme learning problems.

All three schools provide adequate medical services (nursing and physiotherapy) and can call upon a wide variety of hospitals for corrective and remedial treatment. In addition, they do much to help pupils to earn a living and live useful, productive lives when they leave school. At Efata, for example, blind pupils are trained as telephonists and in various forms of handwork such as beadwork, knitting and mohair spinning. In the school for the deaf the girls are taught sewing, while the boys do building, carpentry and welding. At Ikwezi Lokusa a very fine ceramics section has been developed.

In 1968 a welfare organisation and after-care services were established to provide sheltered employment. In the fields of spinning, carpentry and building these services have shown that they can compete in the open market and thereby make a valuable contribution to the economic development of Transkei (see chapter on Welfare Services).

Black teachers at these schools all have a primary teacher's certificate and receive their specialist training on an in-service basis. Theoretical and practical work is supplemented by a correspondence course provided by the central Department of Bantu Education. The course lasts two years, comprises the history of special education, physiology, psychology, orthodidactics and practical teaching and leads to a diploma in special education. Several highly qualified White teachers have also been allocated to these schools.

Teacher training

First priority in the development of any educational programme is an adequate supply of teachers. In the field of primary education, Transkei is in a strong position: of 9 883 Black primary teachers in 1975, only 53 had no professional qualifications and of these only about 20 were in prim-

A science class in progress in a Transkeian high school. At present, secondary syllabuses are basically those of all schools in South Africa and are drawn up by national syllabus committees which represent all examining bodies.

ary schools. This happy position can be attributed to Transkei's long tradition of teacher training which dates back to the middle of the nineteenth century when the missions started their educational work.

Until the 1930s the only primary teacher qualification available was the Lower Primary Teachers Certificate, obtained after a three-year professional course following on the completion of an eight-year primary school education. This qualification is held by 2 430 of the older Transkei primary school teachers. Despite their modest academic background, the majority of these teachers are highly competent and have played a major role in laying the sound foundations on which the current educational system has been built. Many professional leaders in Transkei started their teaching careers with this professional certificate and thereafter added to their academic qualifications through years of private study.

By the middle 'sixties this training had been completely superseded by the (Higher) Primary Teachers Certificate, a two-year professional course following on Junior Certificate (11 years of schooling). This qualification is now held by very nearly 7 000 Transkei teachers. In 1975, seven colleges in Transkei – Clarkebury, Shawbury, Arthur Tsengiwe, Maluti, Cicira, Butterworth and Sigcau – offered this training and their total enrolment was 2 130. In future they should be able to produce at least 1 000 primary school teachers a year.

The two-year primary teachers certificate course has four basic components:

* Professional subjects, such as practical teaching, general method, theory of education and school management
* Teaching of basic subjects: languages and mathematics
* Teaching of other primary school subjects, such as general science, history and geography
* Limited specialisation in one practical subject, such as needlework, music or art and crafts.

The course was recently revised in order to reduce the extent of external examining and to increase the scope of the training colleges themselves to determine whether student teachers may be certificated. An external examination is now taken only in general method, languages and mathematics. More emphasis is also placed on practical teaching experience under normal classroom conditions.

As far as the supply of secondary school teachers is concerned, the position is less favourable. The

problem is not one of professional qualifications but rather of academic background. In 1975 there were 193 Black teachers with degrees, 103 with partially completed degrees and 970 with Senior Certificate/Matriculation qualifications. As far back as 1967, when it became apparent that the Faculty of Education at the University of Fort Hare would not be able to supply more than a limited number of graduates for the senior secondary classes, a special one-year course following on the Primary Teachers Certificate was instituted at Shawbury to produce teachers to teach Form I only. In 1970 this was superseded by the Junior Secondary Teachers Certificate, a two-year professional course following on Senior Certificate/Matriculation, for which 133 students had enrolled in 1975 at Cicira and Bethel Training Colleges. This training course is designed to equip teachers for Forms I to III (Stds 6 to 8) and has three basic components:

* The usual professional subjects, such as theory of education, practical teaching, educational psychology are taken by all students.
* Secondly, for 20 periods per week the student specialises in one of the following directions: languages, history and geography; mathematics and science; commercial subjects; or home economics.
* Thirdly, all students take certain background subjects, such as religious education, book education, organisation of sport and the use of English as medium of instruction.

As enrolments increase, this course should be able to produce enough teachers for junior secondary school, but the shortage of graduate teachers for senior secondary work is likely to continue for some time. At present graduate teachers are trained at the University of Fort Hare, but the competition for Black graduate manpower is such that comparatively few enter the teaching profession. The new university campus at Umtata (see University Education) should improve the situation since it is likely that a faculty of education will be among the first to be established on that campus.

Meanwhile, it will not be possible to replace underqualified teachers in the secondary schools. Many are doing competent work despite the limitations of their qualifications. It would seem that what Transkei needs at this point to help solve this problem is an effective, intensive system of in-service

On the way home after a day at school. As in South Africa, school hours are much shorter in Transkei than in European countries. Most children are home early in the afternoon and have the rest of the day for themselves – and their homework.

teacher training which will upgrade these underqualified teachers. If such a project were launched, the experience gained by South Africa's Department of Bantu Education at its in-service training centre at Mamelodi, would naturally be at the disposal of the Transkei Department of Education.

In-service training, however, is not merely a matter of upgrading underqualified teachers. However good a teacher's qualifications may be, he will be working in an age in which constant retraining is in any event imperative if he is to cope effectively with his task. In a new nation all education programmes, and particularly teacher training, must always be responsive to new needs, changing situations, modern methods and techniques. Educationists of Transkei realise that in-service training is not a temporary expedient to meet passing problems but an inherent and permanent part of the on-going training of the teacher.

Adult education

In any developing country such as Transkei where the growth rate of educational facilities is increasing rapidly, there is always the danger that the older generation may be neglected and a communication gap opened up between them and the younger people who have enjoyed the benefits of schooling. This is particularly true of rural communities where conservative attitudes and resistance to change may become a grave obstacle in the way of national development.

In the past there has been a tendency for adult education programmes to be centred on industry and the urban township, in disregard of the fact that agriculture is in the greatest need of change and that rural life in particular needs enriching. Transkei realises this and has launched a campaign against illiteracy as part of the programme of the Transkei Cultural Society. This is backed up by the resources of the Department of Education which has appointed an organiser to superintend this work. In each of the 28 districts a small number of literacy schools has been set up. The 'teachers', who are drawn from many walks of life, attend intensive courses in the techniques of literacy training and then work part-time at schools in their own communities.

In urban and industrial areas there will be an increasing demand for both the more formal type of night school and the kind of education offered at the Umtata Technical College in its part-time classes. Many educationists argue that if the new university campus in Umtata is to serve the nation in the way it should, extramural and part-time study would have to become an important part of its activities.

Important as the education of the child may be, it nevertheless has to be regarded as a long-term investment for the nation. Upgrading the adult, either in skills or in knowledge, produces immediate returns, particularly if his new competency is fully utilised. As a worker he becomes more productive, as a citizen more understanding. Educationists of Transkei realise this; hence their efforts to expand as far as possible facilities for adult education.

University education

The Alma Mater of many of Transkei's leaders is the University of Fort Hare at Alice in Ciskei, about 300 km from Umtata. This university dates back to 1916 when as the result of missionary initiative it was established as the South African Native College. It became a constituent college of the University of South Africa in 1923 when it was renamed the University College of Fort Hare. In 1970 it became a full-fledged autonomous university with its own charter and serving primarily the Xhosa peoples of Ciskei and Transkei. At present more than 400 of its students come from Transkei and over the years it has produced a steady stream of graduates who have taken up service in Transkei, particularly in the Department of Education.

For some years it has been the wish of the Transkeian government to set up a university for Transkei at Umtata. With the approach of independence this became a matter of some urgency and, as a first step, agreement was reached to establish a campus of Fort Hare at Umtata. The campus was commissioned in February 1976 in the grounds of the Technical College and under the guidance of Professor B. de V. van der Merwe, appointed by the Rector of Fort Hare as his representative in Umtata. Four professors, two of them Transkeians, and twelve lecturing staff have already been appointed, and the enrolment at the beginning of 1976 was 131. Teaching is offered in the following disciplines: Xhosa, South-Sotho, English and Afrikaans; history, geography and economics, politics, public administration, private law, mathematics and psychology.

In due course the Umtata campus will be developed into a full-fledged, autonomous, national university for Transkei.

Meanwhile, Transkei will still be able to send its young men and women to Fort Hare, to the medical university being established near Pretoria, and to other university institutions in South Africa and elsewhere which offer those directions of study which Umtata is not yet able to provide. In addition, there is the University of South Africa, that unique institution which teaches by correspon-

dence and draws its students from all over the world, Africa in particular. As before, those Transkeian adults who because of circumstances were unable to attend university as full-time students, will be able to enrol for the course of their choice at the University of South Africa.

Finance

Table 5 indicates the amounts budgeted for education in Transkei in the past 12 years. Since 1972-3 the amount allocated to education has doubled and the unit cost per pupil has risen from $27,95 to $49,68. It should be noted that no capital costs are included in these budgets which reflect only current expenditure. The cost of school buildings, extensions and maintenance is included in the budget of the Department of Works. Local communities and tribal and regional authorities also continue to build out of their own resources large

Table 4. Teacher training 1963 — 1975

Year	Total* students in Training	Production of Certificated Teachers	Additional Teaching Posts created at beginning of year
1963	879	331	
1964	848	327	360
1965	880	385	280
1966	934	360	371
1967	1 114	420	404
1968	1 218	512	405
1969	1 257	540	250
1970	1 432	572	481
1971	1 523	615	405
1972	1 624	700	424
1973	1 764	717	361
1974	1 933	795	276
1975	2 263	717	1 216

* Two-year courses of training

numbers of classrooms which are not reflected in these budget figures either.

The future

Transkei faces the challenges and opportunities not only of its own changed status but also of the last quarter of the twentieth century. The children at school today will be in the prime of their lives in the year 2000. This is both an exciting and a sobering thought. What will be needed most of all, perhaps, will be flexible and imaginative approaches to education, a readiness for change and a willingness to jettison conventional attitudes.

Many as the problems may be, Transkei has a sound foundation of education on which to build. Matters claiming immediate attention are the wastage of pupils in the early years of the primary school, the training of adequate numbers of secondary school teachers and the establishment of an effective system of on-going in-service training to

ensure quality teaching in the classroom at all times. These may be of even more fundamental importance at the present time than compulsory education.

With a view to economic development, both industrial and agricultural, Transkei now must turn its attention not only to vocational and technical education within the school system, but more importantly to more flexible, short-term training schemes directed at the adult. In this, the Department of Education has an important part to play through 'priming the pump', professional assistance and evaluation, but industrial and agricultural agencies, employers and communities, will all make their contribution. In fact, it is even possible that while the schools consolidate their position in the first few years of independence, some of the major advances in training will take place outside the school. This will be to the advantage of Transkei, because there is no doubt that experience in Africa in the past twenty years has shown that too much has been expected of the school as such in achieving economic development.

Education is a long-term investment and must be maintained, for it has social, political and human objectives as well as economic. The immediate challenge, however, will be to obtain the most effective 'mix' of educational programmes which the resources of Transkei will permit. Certain typical tensions will have to be resolved – between priorities for primary education (compulsory education, for example) on the one hand, and the expansion of a differentiated secondary school system on the other; between demands of quality and quantity; between in-school and out-of-school programmes; between the child and the adult.

There are no easy answers or magical recipes, but there is a fund of experience in Transkei itself and among its neighbours of whose goodwill the new country is assured. What is certain is that certain ingredients of the recipe are basic: hard work, the willingness to make mistakes and to learn from them and, above all, the will to succeed. There is nothing in the past history of education in Transkei, from the early pioneering work of the missionaries to its present leadership, to suggest that it cannot meet this challenge.

The Transkeian government has always looked upon education in all its ramifications as being of the highest priority and the education vote has always been of the highest in the national budget. If the pattern prior to independence is anything to go by, one can safely say that the government will never be found wanting when it comes to the provision of the funds for schools, teacher training, equipment, and whatever else may be necessary.

Table 5. Current education budgets, 1964 — 1976

Financial Year	Amount	Percentage Increase on Previous Year
1964-5	$ 4 802 400	
1965-6	$ 4 992 200	3,95
1966-7	$ 5 425 700	8,68
1967-8	$ 6 387 100	17,72
1968-9	$ 6 925 300	8,43
1969-70	$ 7 621 100	10,05
1970-1	$ 8 950 000	17,44
1971-2	$11 070 000	23,68
1972-3	$12 717 000	14,88
1973-4	$15 106 000	18,79
1974-5	$23 041 000	52,53
1975-6	$25 728 900	11,66

The exchange rate of the Rand as at 1976/08/31 was R1,00 = $1,15.

NOTE: Capital costs of buildings *not* included. These are provided in the budgets of the Transkeian Department of Works.

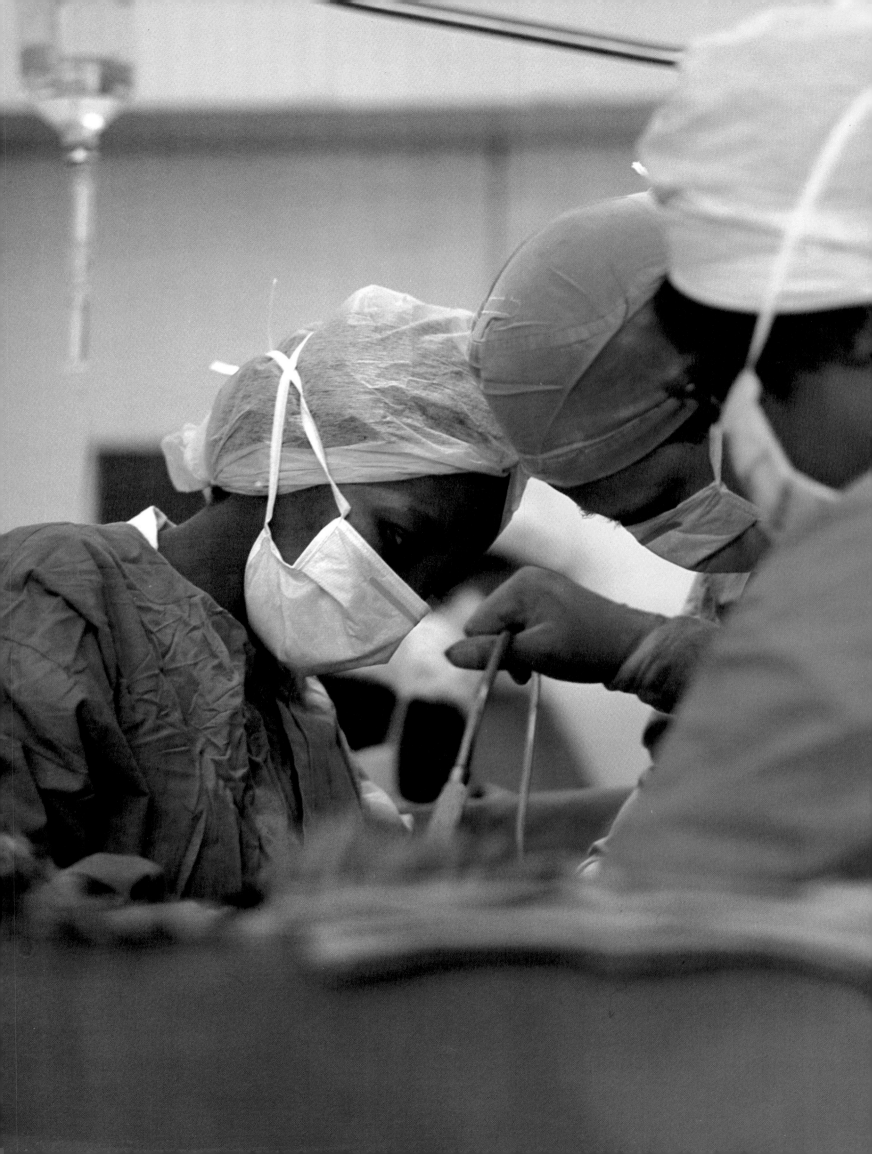

Chapter Six

Health Services

The newly independent Republic of Transkei can boast a sound and comprehensive infrastructure of health services. These are not confined to the large hospitals situated in urban concentrations where the most sophisticated treatment is available virtually free of charge. In fact, the linch-pin of the entire health programme is the rural clinic where highly qualified nurses not only administer modern medicine to the tribesmen and their families but also educate them in the basic concepts of nutrition and family health care.

Funds voted by the Transkeian Parliament for health services have increased markedly in recent years. For the year which ended on 31 March 1976 (the last year before independence) the appropriation amounted to $1 490 000. For the year ending on 31 March 1977 an amount of $1 989 000 has been allocated – an increase of 33,5 per cent.

There are 31 hospitals in Transkei with a total of 7 561 beds. This means one hospital bed for every 225 of the population. There are also 131 district clinics and 32 mobile teams in the field. In addition, a new hospital of $27,6 million is being planned for Umtata, the capital.

Health services in both hospital and clinic are provided at a nominal fee. Full-time patients in hospitals pay either $1,15 or $2,30 per day, depending on

An operation in progress in the operating theatre of Umtata hospital, the central referral hospital of Transkei. There are 31 hospitals in Transkei with a combined total of 7 561 beds, which means there is one bed for every 225 citizens.

income. These fees include all investigations, treatment, medications and operations. Out-patients at hospitals pay only 57,5 cents per call. Clinics charge 23 cents per call and $1,15 for a confinement, including all ante-natal visits.

All school-children are immunised against smallpox, tuberculosis, poliomyelitis, diphtheria, whooping cough, tetanus and measles. All schools are regularly visited by nurses who examine every child and apply immediate treatment or refer serious cases to a medical practitioner. These services are free of charge.

At least as important as these services provided in loco for the people of Transkei, is the continued co-operation between the Department of Health of Transkei and similar authorities and institutions in South Africa. In fact, the entire product of medical research and achievement in the Republic of South Africa will always be at the disposal of the people of Transkei. This is no mean back-up facility by world standards since, among other things, the first heart-transplant operation was performed in South Africa and South African medical scientists in many fields are renowned the world over.

Health services in Transkei, as in many other parts of the world, were initiated by various missionary societies. The activities varied from road-side itinerant clinics to the building of substantial hospitals. The missionaries still play a major role and to this day many hospitals, although they have been taken over by the government, are supervised by this dedicated group of people.

In the recent past curative services were provided by the provincial administration of the Cape Province of South Africa which subsidised the 21 mission hospitals whereas mental, tuberculosis, leprosy, prophylactic and medico-legal services were provided by the Department of Health of the Republic of South Africa through the agency of district surgeons and two state hospitals.

In 1970 all health services in Transkei were taken over by the South African Department of Health as agents for the Department of Bantu Administration and Development. This new arrangement afforded the necessary framework for the integration of services, permitting the practice of 'total care' of patient and community without an artificial division between prophylactic and therapeutic services.

A regional office of the South African Department of Health was opened in Umtata in January 1971 under the control of a regional director and deputy regional director. A supervisor of nursing services initiated the nursing section during the six months she was seconded to Umtata from East London in South Africa.

This regional office was established in order that the necessary structure could be created for a wholly independent Transkeian Department of Health. During these intermediate years a number of peripheral clinics were established and controlled by the regional office. Each was staffed by one dually trained nursing sister.

The Transkeian Department of Health was established on 1 April 1973 when the first Minister of Health was appointed and the regional director and assistant regional director became Secretary and Assistant Secretary respectively.

Problems

The topography of Transkei is such that in many areas it impedes the provision of health services. It varies from warm, humid, appropriately vegetated coastland through midland plains to rugged mountain country at an altitude in excess of 2 000 m. The generous rainfall of the coastal areas during the wet months often makes communication by road difficult.

Another limiting factor is trained manpower.

Mothers are encouraged to deliver in district clinics rather than at home, in case of complications. All infants are immunised against smallpox, tuberculosis, poliomyelitis, diphtheria, whooping cough, tetanus and measles.

There is a shortage of medical and paramedical personnel in most fields. Nevertheless, Transkei is better endowed than most Third World countries in this respect. There are 136 full-time medical practitioners for a total population of 1,8 million, and the country has at its disposal a large well-trained nursing staff of the highest calibre.

The population of Transkei is by no means homogeneous. There are at least ten major ethnic groups and in each group there are detectable differences in custom, needs and expectations which must be taken into account in the implementation of a health care system.

The distribution of the population in Transkei is such that only three per cent may be described as urban, whereas the remaining 97 per cent are rural. The complications of vast urban aggregations are not yet experienced in Transkei, but the high percentage of the rural population brings about its own problems, such as the difficulty of maintaining adequate communications and lines of supply.

Policy

In the light of the foregoing the Department of Health of the Republic of Transkei has set itself the following broad objectives:
* To provide as high a level of clinical care to as many of the population as possible.
* To provide preventive services as an integral and vital component of the health care system.
* To provide a diagnostic and therapeutic service as close to the community as possible.
* To involve, and promote as far as possible the participation of the community in health affairs.

The commitment therefore is to render total health care to individuals within their community through their community.

In order effectively to implement this policy within the confines of the various limiting factors – available funds, the difficult terrain, the shortage of trained manpower and the diversity of the population – the Transkei Department of Health has adopted the only course open to it – at least in the initial phases of development. A health service, as comprehensive as possible, is provided in breadth rather than depth. In circumstances such as those prevailing in Transkei, it is obviously in the interests of the nation as a whole to provide some services for as many people as possible, rather than to concentrate expenditure in a few areas to provide sophisticated facilities there.

Thus, it was decided early on that primary services should be proliferated at the periphery, while

sophisticated services should be centralised so as to provide for the entire Transkei.

An intermediate stage between the periphery and the central sector was also considered necessary to control, guide, and stimulate activities at the periphery and to provide services such as stores and transport. This permits lower capitalisation with regard to transport and accommodation.

In practice this means a system where the periphery is served by rural district clinics which are controlled by hospitals in the intermediate sector which in turn are served by a central referral hospital in Umtata, the capital city.

Clinics

These units provide primary health care to the community in which they are situated. There are two main functions – prevention and treatment.

Prevention is achieved by means of immunisation and, most importantly, health education, and the importance of this function cannot be overemphasised in terms of the saving of human life and the promotion of the overall well-being of the community.

Each child is protected against smallpox, tuberculosis, poliomyelitis, diphtheria, whooping cough, tetanus and measles. This sustained and compulsory programme of immunisation means that these scourges will soon become only morbid memories to entire communities.

Health education is a potent and important weapon in the fight against preventable illness. It involves perforce the staff of the clinic with the community for it is the community which they must teach. In the course of their daily ministrations the staff discuss matters of hygiene which have relevance to the community, such as the nature and means of preventing venereal disease, the necessity to bring to the clinic any child who fails to thrive, the danger of a chronic cough, the importance of balanced nutrition and the consequences of malnutrition. Each clinic is provided with a small garden to demonstrate that vegetables can be grown without expensive farm equipment.

The advantages of family spacing are discussed, as are the means of achieving planned parenthood.

This hospital at Mkambati is one of 22 mission hospitals taken over by the Transkeian Department of Health in the course of 1975 and 1976. Transkei's comprehensive health services owe much to the endeavours of the early missionaries.

It is clear that the clinic and nurses must be integral parts of the community. Therefore, the nurses are exposed as much as possible to the community which they serve. They are encouraged to join in community activities – those of the church, parent-teacher associations and cultural committees. In this way they identify themselves with their respective communities which, in turn, learn to respect and trust their nurses. And having won the respect and trust of the members of the local community, the nurses are in a far better position to persuade them to accept the new regimen of community health.

The second function of the clinic is to provide the means for easily accessible medical care. If a member of the community requires medical care, he reports to the district clinic where he is seen by a nursing sister.

The sister will ascertain whether the condition can be treated in the clinic and, if so, will provide the necessary treatment. If the condition cannot be treated, or if the patient fails to respond to treatment, or if the sister is unable to make a diagnosis, the patient is referred to the second level of the care system, namely the intermediate hospital. If necessary, the hospital will despatch an ambulance to transport the patient. In emergencies the patient may be transported by air.

Maternity services are also an important function of the clinic and mothers are encouraged to deliver in the clinic rather than at home. At the first sign of complications, the patient is immediately transferred to hospital.

At least two sisters are attached to each clinic to ensure that it can provide a comprehensive service 24 hours a day.

These sisters are trained in both general nursing and midwifery and have undergone a period of training and orientation for clinic duty. A domestic assistant is also provided to assist in cleaning the clinic.

The clinic comprises a consulting room, a maternity room and a store-room, as well as accommodation for the nursing staff. The appearance and construction of clinics vary greatly but it is generally found that six rooms meet these requirements. The basic clinic with nurses' accommodation consists of six rondavels. The clinic, as part of the community, is constructed of the same materials as other accommodation in the vicinity.

The temptation to provide larger clinics with more facilities and staff is ever present, but this is resisted in terms of the policy of providing "some to all" and not "all to some".

Previously, these clinics were controlled directly from the head office of the Department of Health in Umtata but this system of control was found to be inadequate owing to the remoteness of the controller from the controlled.

Today district clinics are under control of the hospitals and their staff are on the establishments of these hospitals, which are relatively closely situated and therefore better able to exercise control and supply transport, medicines and stores. Since the clinic staff are on the establishment of the hospital they are easily withdrawn to the hospital when it is necessary for them to be given refresher courses.

Special orientation courses are provided by some hospitals for sisters entering the clinic services. These are also made available to the staff of all hospitals.

There are also a number of non-departmental clinics in Transkei. These are either run by the tribal authority or by various missions not attached to hospitals. In these cases the Transkeian Department of Health subsidises the salaries of the staff by more than 87 per cent.

Although there are already 131 clinics in Transkei, the objective is to provide at least 400 such clinics, strategically located throughout the entire country.

Each clinic has a committee consisting of representatives of the local tribal authority, the medical superintendent and other dignitaries. This committee provides liaison between clinic and community and advises the staff and medical superintendent of the needs of the community. It is also a useful means of bringing information from the hospital or the Department of Health to the notice of the tribal authority and the community.

Intermediate hospitals

These hospitals have vital roots in the community through their district clinics, and are responsible for all the functions of these clinics.

For reasons of control, Transkei has been divided into a number of health areas, each under the control of an area hospital, the medical superintendent of which is the area health superintendent who is responsible for total health care in his area. If necessary, assistance is given by the head office in the execution of certain functions, for instance the provision of health inspectors.

Each health area has an advisory board which includes the magistrate of the district concerned and representatives of tribal authorities, as well as senior hospital staff.

Like the clinic committee, this board provides liaison between the community and the officials serving that community.

Apart from their district health activities, the hospitals provide a high level of therapeutic services. The average medical practitioner in these hospitals is called upon to perform a variety of complex tasks which would astound many of his colleagues in more technologically advanced countries. The experience of these practitioners is rapidly gained owing to the pressures of the society in which they work and live.

Many hospitals play an important role in training nurses: many have training schools attached to them. This is of particular importance, as nurses are trained within the professional environment in which they will be working.

Of the 31 hospitals in Transkei, 22 were previously mission hospitals and much is owed to the dedication of the founders and their successors.

Central referral hospital

Umtata Hospital is the referral hospital of Transkei. Patients admitted to this hospital are largely those referred from peripheral hospitals for further investigation and management.

The hospital is registered with the South African Medical and Dental and Nursing Councils for the training of interns and general nurses respectively. It is anticipated that it will shortly be approved for the training of specialists under the wing of the University of Cape Town Medical School.

The admission figures for recent years were 71 227 in 1972, 64 143 in 1973, 100 147 in 1974 and 146 795 in 1975.

Many cases admitted to the maternity department are referred from peripheral hospitals and clinics for management of obstetrical complications.

A family planning clinic is available to give advice and assistance to those who require its services.

The orthopaedic department utilises beds, apart from those in the hospital, at the Bedford Orthopaedic Centre approximately five km distant. This centre is supervised by Sisters of the Dominican Order.

Owing to the accelerating growth of the population of Transkei and the high standard of medicine practised in this hospital, the demand for beds far exceeds the supply.

In order to meet these growing needs, a new hospital is presently being planned. It will be most modern in design and provide accommodation for 1 100 patients. The total estimated cost is $27,5 million which will be spent over eight years. Facilities will include advanced equipment in the fields of radiology, medical technology and clinical diagnostics.

The hospital has also been designed to provide training for nurses in post-basic courses such as public health, ward administration, nursing administration, nursing education and theatre technique. Interns and specialists will also be trained.

Laboratory services

Nearing completion in Umtata is a large medical laboratory which will provide a sophisticated pathological service for the entire Transkei. In addition to diagnostic facilities, the laboratory will provide forensic services for the whole country.

Each hospital in Transkei has its own laboratory capable of handling its daily needs. Technically, these laboratories are controlled by the central laboratory in Umtata and administratively by the hospital at which they are situated. Laboratory facilities vary greatly from hospital to hospital, depending on the requirements of the practitioners operating in that area.

The new central laboratory will provide an important back-up service which will put at the disposal of the entire Transkei the highly sophisticated facilities available in Umtata.

Nutritional rehabilitation

The relatively high incidence of deficiency diseases, particularly kwashiorkor, is one of the major problems faced by the official health services of Transkei. There is ample evidence to suggest that this is to a large extent due to ignorance of the need for dietary balance and protein intake in particular, rather than to poverty. Kwashiorkor is frequently found in moderately wealthy families with

The backbone of Transkei's health services is the district clinic. There are 131 such clinics dotted all over the country, as well as 32 mobile teams in the field, which dispense medicine and administer inoculations on the spot as and when required.

appreciable numbers of cattle and, therefore, supposedly an adequate supply of milk.

In fact, dietary deficiencies are the root cause of many disease conditions in Transkei. Various expert investigations have shown that in good years the diet is generally adequate in calories and protein, even if it is low in animal protein, fat and some mineral salts. It is also high in carbohydrates and crude mineral fibre. This particular diet would appear to protect Transkeians against a number of diseases to which Whites are prone, such as appendicitis, gall-stones, peptic ulcer, atherosclerosis and coronary artery diseases and certain types of cancer. On the other hand, they not only appear to have little resistance to acute infections, particularly of the respiratory system, but deficiency diseases are common. In addition, certain forms of cancer – notably of the oesophagus, liver and cervix – are common.

The staple diet is maize – in various forms. A recent survey revealed that virtually all Transkeians eat maize regularly every day. This is in varying degrees supplemented by sorghum and dry beans. Vegetables are grown and consumed in varying quantities. The most popular are pumpkin and cabbage. More exotic varieties, such as spinach, peas, cauliflower and tomatoes are grown and eaten to a much lesser extent.

To the outsider one of the most surprising facts of the Transkeian diet is the small quantity of meat consumed. There are nearly two million large stock units (cattle, sheep, pigs and goats) in Transkei, but these are hardly ever slaughtered and consumed to feed the family. Virtually the only animals killed for domestic consumption are those which have grown too old to be of any value. The animals, cattle in particular, are kept for their prestige value and as tokens of wealth. A Transkeian citizen's bank statement is the number of cattle penned every night. On the whole, animals are killed only for feasts and to appease the ancestral spirits. Most families run their own little flock of chickens and some, particularly those in the mountains, hunt small wild animals and birds. Overall, however, very few Transkeians, particularly in the rural areas, claim to eat meat more than once a month. In fact, in a recent investigation the majority claimed to eat meat only once in three to six months.

Milk is part of the staple diet but fresh milk is rarely used, except to supplement the diet of very young babies. Most of the available milk is soured in calabashes to serve as a drink for the whole family.

In addition, there are various traditional taboos to complicate matters. For example, many rural

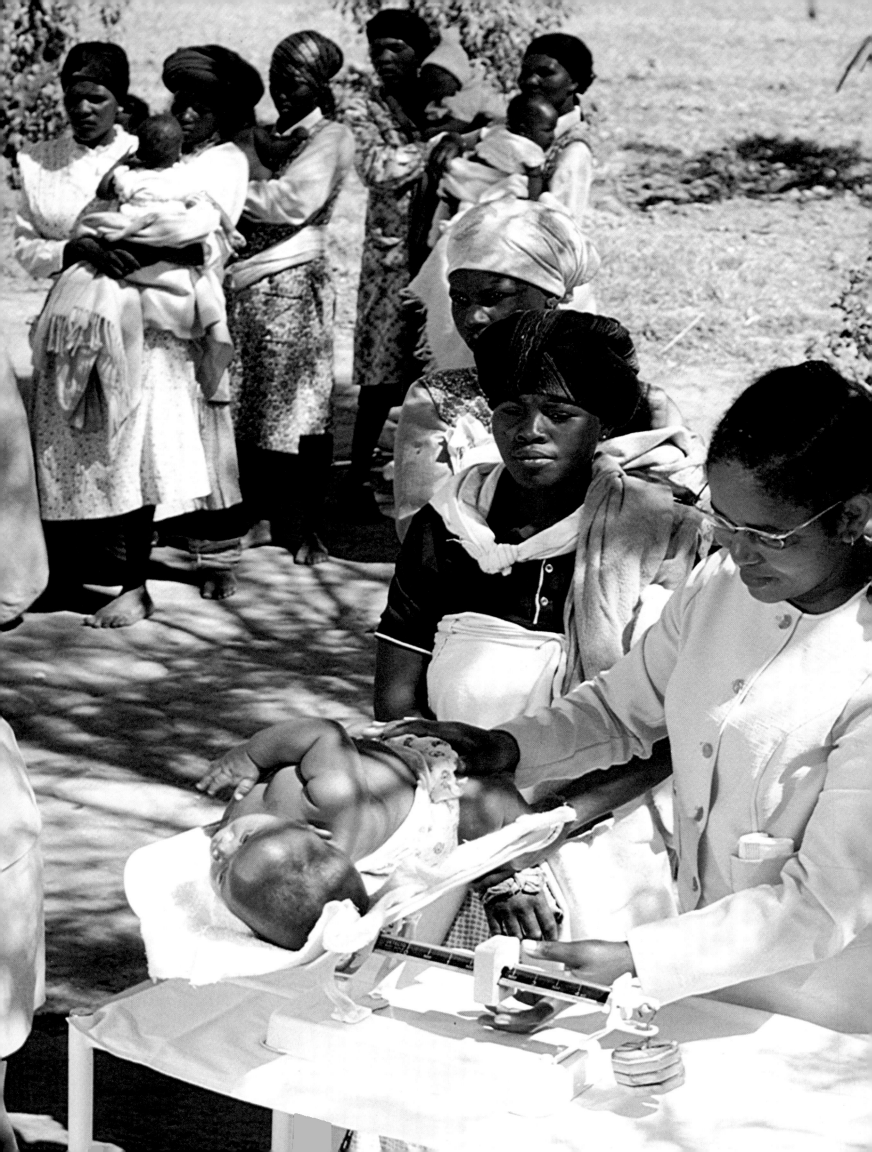

women are still not allowed to eat eggs and young girls are not supposed to drink milk while they menstruate.

The initiative in combating kwashiorkor was taken by mission hospitals which introduced nutritional rehabilitation units to their hospitals. These were known as 'kwashikraals'.

The purpose of these units is to educate in as practical a manner as possible as many of the population as can be reached. An obvious audience are the mothers of children afflicted with this condition. Whilst the child is receiving treatment in the hospital, the mother receives tuition in the kwashikraal. Frequently children with kwashiorkor also manifest other conditions, such as chest infections, gastro-enteritis or tuberculosis as this deficiency disease lowers resistance to infection.

The physical structure of the kwashikraal is hardly prepossessing in Western terms as it comprises no more than two or three grass-topped rondavels with an external open hearth for cooking – a virtual replica of the home situation, in other words. The mothers are taught how to prepare nutritious balanced meals from the means at their disposal in the home situation.

A garden is attached to each kwashikraal and mothers are not only instructed how to grow vegetables but are also taught which vegetable to choose to grow. This function is also shared by the district clinics, each of which has a demonstration garden.

Nutritional rehabilitation is clearly an area where close co-operation between the Departments of Agriculture, Education and Health will be of great advantage to Transkei, as each can assist in the elimination of this preventable condition and its complications.

School nursing

The school rooms of today hold the adult generation of tomorrow. The Department of Health of Transkei tries to exploit this fact to the full. A comprehensive programme is in operation to detect any disease, overt or covert, to immunise and to teach the children proper standards in hygiene and nutrition in particular, and health in general. A number of school nurses are employed

Visiting day for mothers at a rural clinic. These clinics provide primary health care to the community, and general health education is one of their most potent weapons in the fight against disease among Transkeians.

whose function it is to examine every child at school, to detect any undesirable condition and to treat where possible or, where necessary, refer to the hospital in the area. All children are inoculated against smallpox, measles, diphtheria, whooping cough, tetanus, poliomyelitis and tuberculosis.

Teachers play a vital role in the successful implementation of the school nursing programme. They provide the necessary continuity between visits by the school nurse and underscore what has been said in health education talks. They also supervise the administration of tablets to those children who are on continuation therapy against tuberculosis.

To improve the general state of health of school-children, health education teams have been sent into the field to motivate the local communities to organise school-feeding schemes. Each child pays 29 cents a month towards a fund which is used to buy high-protein soup powder or skimmed milk powder.

The same health teams are also trying to encourage schools to start their own vegetable gardens so that the produce may be used in the preparation of soup for the feeding scheme. Steady progress is also being made in this regard.

Training and recruitment

At present health care is based on the nurse because there are not yet enough medical practitioners. This policy is merely a temporary expedient dictated by circumstances and all possible steps are taken eventually to replace the present system with one based on the medical practitioner.

To this end, Transkei has made available to its citizens generous financial assistance which permits any son or daughter to study medicine or a paramedical subject at a university in South Africa. All students are awarded pupil professional status and paid a monthly salary whilst studying. Success in university examinations ensures an increment each year.

In return for this financial assistance, the student is bound to serve in the Transkeian Department of Health for a number of years equivalent to those during which he studied. This system applies to all students in the medical and paramedical fields, such as radiology, pharmacy, physiotherapy, clinical psychology and dietetics.

Training facilities for doctors are provided at the Universities of Natal and the Witwatersrand in South Africa. In addition, the Medical School for Blacks at the Garankuwa Hospital near Pretoria

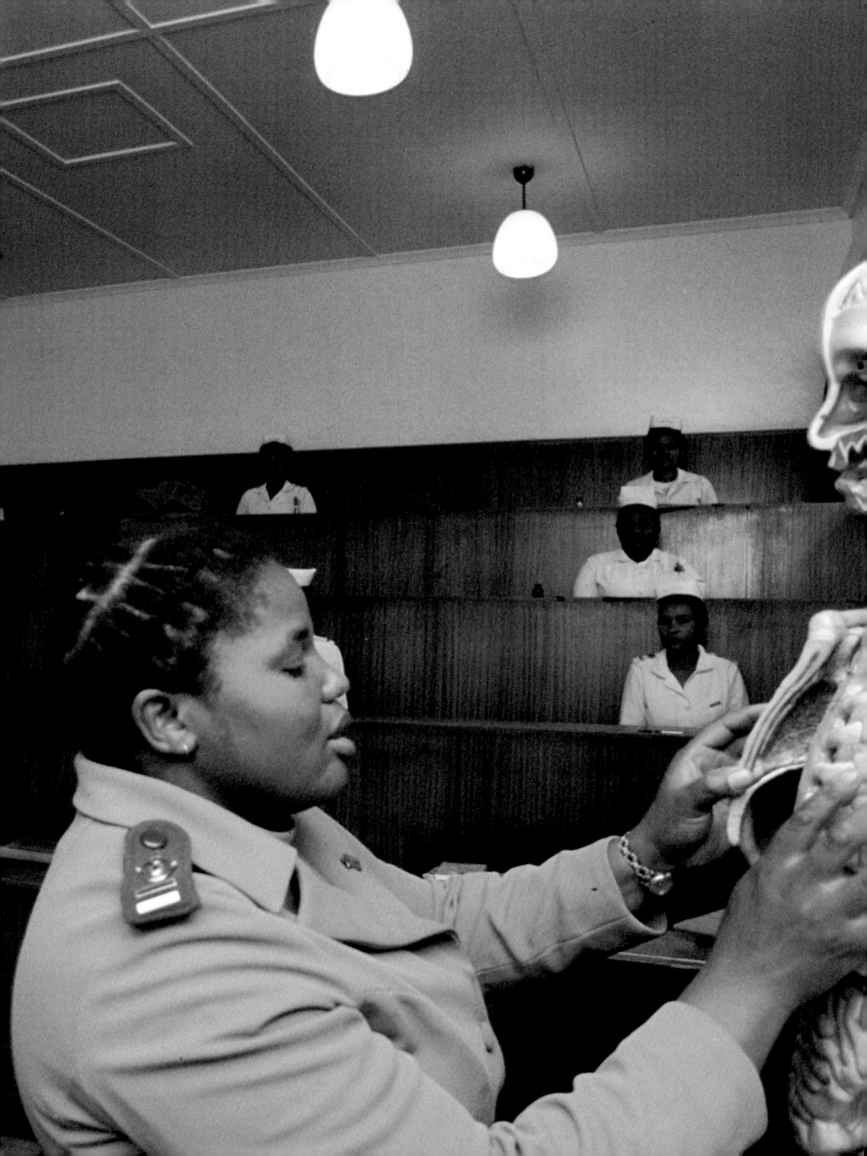

will become available for this purpose in the near future.

Prospective dieticians may pursue four-year B.Sc degree courses at the University of Natal. Pharmacists are trained at Rhodes University in Grahamstown, South Africa, and at the University of Zululand in KwaZulu, another Black homeland.

Edendale Technical College in Pietermaritzburg, South Africa, provides tuition in medical technology. Practical training is given in hospitals both in Transkei and in South Africa.

Training of nurses in Transkei is far advanced as is evidenced by the large number of trained nurses in the country. Many of them were trained in hospitals in South Africa and have brought with them a great deal of expertise and experience. This also ensures that local standards are in all respects equal to those of the Republic of South Africa. The number of nursing training posts in Transkei for the various categories are: general 391, midwifery 119, enrolled 495, and nursing assistants 764. Training for post-basic courses is not yet provided, but a course in public health nursing will be commenced in Umtata in the near future.

Professional bodies

All Transkei medical practitioners are still registered with the South African Medical Council, but it is expected that the Transkeian Medical and Dental Council will soon replace its South African counterpart. It will be composed entirely of Transkeian citizens, although legislative provision will be made for the Minister of Health to appoint non-Transkeians, should this be necessary in specific circumstances. Registration with this council will be obligatory for all medical practitioners in Transkei.

The South African Nursing Council is still the registering body for nurses in Transkei, but a Transkeian Nursing Council will be formed in the near future which will establish rolls and registers for all categories of nurses practising in Transkei, and be responsible for the control, discipline, training and examination of nurses.

Legislation has been passed providing for the establishment of a nursing association. To safeguard the interests of the profession and maintain its present high standard, membership of this

Nurses are trained at most hospitals in Transkei. The number of training posts for the various categories of nurses exceeds 1 700. Training for post-basic courses is not yet provided but a course in public health nursing is to be introduced at Umtata hospital soon.

statutory body will be compulsory for all nurses, and members will elect representatives on a regional basis. All members will be Transkeian citizens.

Therapeutic services were for many years provided in the main by mission hospitals which were fully subsidised by the State. During the course of 1975 and 1976 all these mission hospitals were taken over and became State hospitals. This means that all staff members are now either civil servants or are seconded or contracted to the Department of Health of Transkei. Thus career opportunities for the staff are open throughout the civil service and no longer only in one hospital.

A major advantage of State control of hospitals is standardisation of materials and administrative techniques. This means not only considerable material savings but also permits greater flexibility in the transfer of staff who no longer have to learn a new work situation, whenever they are relocated. Nevertheless, it is hoped that the valuable work done by mission hospitals will continue not only in the clinical and religious field, but also in the recruitment of staff.

The future

In order to meet its long-term requirements, Transkei will pay particular attention to training suitable candidates for jobs in all categories of the health service. In particular, it will seek to provide an adequate supply of paramedical personnel. Adequate provision will also be made for training assistants in dentistry, anaesthetics and other clinical fields. These assistants will work under the guidance of medical or dental practitioners and permit a far better utilisation of the limited number of professionals available in these categories.

The establishment of more district clinics is a priority, as it is the district clinic which permits decentralisation of health services to provide primary facilities at the doorstep of the patient in order to make the general health service more efficient.

Like all developing countries, Transkei is experiencing a shortage of medical practitioners, and one of the most pressing needs for the future will be as rapid as possible an increase in the number of practitioners and specialists. The government of Transkei, however, is very much aware of this need and has undertaken to do everything in its power to alleviate the shortage both by encouraging as many Transkeians as possible to train as doctors and by recruiting suitably qualified practitioners from South Africa or elsewhere to practise in Transkei.

Chapter Seven

The System of Justice

As is the case with any other country, the legal system of Transkei has two components: the law applicable in any given legal situation and the administration of such law.

At the time the British annexed to the Cape Colony the territories comprising the present Transkei, the civil law of the Cape Colony was, by and large, Roman-Dutch Law, as was the criminal law save where it had been superseded or amended by legislation. Within the annexed territories there existed an unwritten system of tradition and rules which had evolved from the way of life and needs of the people, and the general principles of which were generally known to the people. This system was and still is referred to as tribal or customary law and, as its description implies, varied from tribe to tribe and from locality to locality but such variations were in detail rather than the general overall pattern.

The government of the Cape Colony from the outset made legislative provision for the recognition and application of the prevailing system of tribal law in civil matters involving members of one or other of the tribes, and that position still obtains in Transkei, being enshrined in Section 53 of the Republic of Transkei Constitution Act.

However, where litigants were not members of a

Scene in a magistrate's court. The country is divided into 28 magisterial districts and the magistrate is to a great extent the hub of the judicial and administrative process of his district. So far, nine magistrates are Transkeians. In due course they will all be Transkeians.

tribe or where tribal law made no provision for a particular problem, Roman-Dutch Law or statutory law applied and that is still the position today. Unless or until specifically repealed by the Republic of Transkei Constitution Act, all pre-independence statutes of the Republic of South Africa remain in force in Transkei until such time as they are amended or repealed by the Transkeian legislature. A discussion of tribal law and the practical effect of its survival side by side with Roman-Dutch Law follows at the end of this chapter.

In the field of criminal law, a penal code was enacted by the Parliament of the Cape Colony in 1886 and although officially entitled the "Native Territories Penal Code," has always been and still is generally known as the Transkeian Penal Code. It amounted in fact to a codified restatement of the criminal common law, with relatively minor changes to deal with certain problems peculiar to the Transkeian Territories. With very few amendments, this penal code has stood the test of time and still embodies the criminal law applicable in Transkei. Together with various statutory crimes created as a result of legislation passed either by the Republic of South Africa or by the Transkeian Legislative Assembly prior to independence, this has been made applicable to Transkei as a whole by the Republic of Transkei Constitution Act, and all criminal law applies to all persons within the boundaries of Transkei, irrespective of creed or colour.

Chiefs' Courts

Chiefs and certain headmen are empowered to

hear and determine civil claims arising from tribal law and custom and brought before them by Black Transkeians against Blacks resident within their respective areas of jurisdiction. They also have circumscribed jurisdiction to try criminal offences arising from contraventions of the common law or of tribal law and custom. For practical purposes, the list of such offences may be regarded as limited to theft, common assault, neglect of children and offences regarding the registration of births and deaths and against public health. Offenders may not be sentenced to imprisonment or subjected to corporal punishment (unless the offender is an unmarried male under thirty years of age) nor may a fine imposed exceed 2 head of large stock or 10 head of small stock or $46.

The chief's court serves a useful purpose in that it ensures swift justice in petty matters. No records are kept of the proceedings and the appeal which, in both civil and criminal matters, lies to the court of the magistrate, takes the form of a re-hearing of the whole matter.

With the exception of the chiefs' courts, the Transkeian administration of justice is modelled upon the system prevailing in the Republic of South Africa which in turn has to a large extent, especially in regard to Supreme Court practice, adopted and adapted the British system to its own circumstances.

Magistrates' Courts

Transkei is divided into 28 magisterial districts. The magistrate of each district is to a great extent the hub of the judicial and administrative process of his district, since it is he and his staff who deal not only with the hearing of cases both civil and criminal, but also with the registration of births and deaths, welfare payments, automobile licences, and a host of other matters involving the day to day administration of the district. The magistrate is a civil servant. He usually starts his career as a clerk in the magistrate's office, receiving in-service training in the various branches of the office's activities, whilst at the same time attending courses for the civil service law examinations which qualify him for promotion to the magistrate's bench. There comes a time when he takes his seat on the Bench as an assistant magistrate, hearing both criminal and civil cases, and in due course he progresses to the stage where he becomes the magistrate of a particular district.

A magistrate's court has both civil and criminal jurisdiction but its punitive powers are strictly limited. There are two regional magistrates whose sole function is to preside over criminal trials with increased punitive jurisdiction.

In addition to the 28 district magistrates there are two regional magistrates who perform no administrative duties and have no civil jurisdiction. Their sole function it is to preside over criminal trials, Transkei being divided into two regional divisions for the purposes of the geographical jurisdiction of the regional magistrate. A regional magistrate's court has jurisdiction over all offences except treason and murder, and a case of rape where the accused demands, before plea, that his case be heard in the Supreme Court.

In practice, however, this does not mean that all other offences are necessarily tried by the court of the district magistrate whose jurisdiction in the matter of punishment is strictly limited. Considerations such as the previous criminal record of the accused or aggravating circumstances surrounding the offence often render it advisable that certain offences be tried by whichever of the two superior courts, i.e. the regional magistrate's court or Supreme Court, could in the opinion of the Attorney-General impose a sentence commensurate with the gravity of the offence. If, in such a case, the Supreme Court is regarded as the proper forum, a preparatory examination is held in a magistrate's court (unless the Attorney-General has ordered a summary trial in the Supreme Court, as he is empowered to do in cases where he deems it in the interests of justice). The purpose of the preparatory examination is to determine the strength of the State's case against the accused and if in the opinion of the presiding magistrate a *prima facie* case has been made out, the accused is committed for trial in the Supreme Court.

The record of the preparatory examination proceedings is sent to the Attorney-General. The latter is a civil servant (and a qualified advocate) appointed by the President and is the counterpart of the British Director of Public Prosecutions. Unlike his American namesake, he has no investigative powers, the investigation of crime being the sole prerogative of the Transkeian Police. He has the final word in regard to all prosecutions subject only to the authority of the Minister of Justice who in practice does not interfere with his discretionary powers.

After studying a preparatory examination record, the Attorney-General may take one of several courses. He may indict the accused in the Supreme Court on whatever offence the evidence discloses, or he may charge the accused with such offence in the regional magistrate's court, or he may remit the matter for trial to the district magistrate who conducted the preparatory examination, in which case the district magistrate's powers are increased to enable him to impose imprisonment not exceeding twelve months or a fine not exceeding $1 150, his ordinary jurisdiction being six months and $575 respectively. The regional magistrate's upper limits of jurisdiction are 3 year's imprisonment and $1 725 fine respectively. In certain cases, for example stock theft, the legislature has empowered magistrates to pass sentences in excess of their ordinary jurisdiction.

Any person charged with any offence committed within any district or regional division may be tried by the court of that district or of that regional division. This jurisdiction has been extended by statute to permit the trial, within a district or regional division, of persons who have committed offences within two miles beyond the boundary of such district or regional division.

In civil matters the jurisdiction of the district magistrate's court is limited by statute. Broadly speaking, the magistrate has no jurisdiction to hear matters where the status or mental capacity of a person is in dispute, or matters relating to succession, testamentary or otherwise, or wherein the claim exceeds $1 725, unless the defendant is being sued on a liquid document, in which case $3 450 is the maximum amount claimable in the magistrate's court. The regional magistrate's court has no civil jurisdiction.

Supreme Court

From the first annexation in 1879 up to 31 July 1973 jurisdiction at the superior court level over the geographical area which is now Transkei was exercised firstly by a division of the Supreme Court of the Cape Colony and later by a division of the Supreme Court of South Africa, the Eastern Cape Division. In practice this meant that the judges of the Eastern Cape Division rode circuit four times a year in Transkei to deal with criminal cases, and civil cases were heard at the seat of that court in Grahamstown. On 1 August 1973 the jurisdiction of the Eastern Cape Division over Transkei was transferred to the newly established Transkeian High Court. A senior judge of the Eastern Cape Division was seconded to the Transkeian High Court as its first Chief Justice and in October 1975 a second judge was similarly seconded. On 26 October 1976 the title of the court was changed to the Supreme Court of Transkei but its composition and jurisdiction remained unchanged.

Appointment of Judges

The Republic of Transkei constitution makes provision for the appointment by the President of a Chief Justice and as many other judges as the President deems necessary from time to time. Prior to his appointment, a judge must have been either a judge of the Supreme Court of South Africa or of a superior court prescribed by a resolution of Parliament, or an advocate of ten years' standing in such courts or in the Supreme Court of Transkei, and the Chief Justice, prior to his appointment, must have been a judge of any one of the aforementioned courts. No judge may be removed from office, save by the President upon an address from the National Assembly requesting such removal on the grounds of misbehaviour or incapacity.

Jurisdiction

The Supreme Court has jurisdiction over all persons residing or being in the Republic of Transkei and has power to hear and determine all civil and criminal matters, proceedings or causes arising within Transkei, save that it is not competent to enquire into or pronounce upon the validity of any legislation of the Transkeian Parliament. It also hears all appeals, criminal and civil, from magistrates' courts and has the power to review the proceedings of such courts. It automatically reviews all proceedings in the district magistrate's court where a sentence of imprisonment exceeding 3 months or a fine exceeding $58 or corporal punishment has been imposed. In all such cases, a certified transcript of the evidence is sent to the Supreme Court for perusal by a judge who certifies that the proceedings have been in accordance with justice, if he is satisfied that that was the case. If he is not satisfied, he may query any aspect of the district magistrate's decision or sentence, and thereafter either set aside or amend his findings and/or sentence to accord with justice. During 1975 some 1 400 matters were dealt with by way of automatic review. The advantages of this procedure for both the accused and the administration of justice are self-evident.

In practice, the Attorney-General only refers matters to the Supreme Court which are so serious that an appropriate penalty would be beyond the jurisdiction of the magistrates' courts. Except where minimum or maximum sentences are prescribed by law, the punitive jurisdiction of the court is unlimited and includes the death sentence. There is no jury system in Transkei and both criminal and civil trials are presided over by a single judge. In any criminal case the judge is entitled to summon to his assistance either one or two assessors who are chosen for their knowledge of the issues involved in the case to be heard. In practice they are usually magistrates; they participate in the decision of the court, on matters of fact, but the judge alone gives rulings of law and imposes the sentence, but he invariably consults his assessors on the latter. Where the judge sits with assessors, the decision of the court as to the guilt or otherwise of the accused is arrived at by a majority vote. Although not

obliged to do so, a judge always elects to sit with assessors if, from his prior reading of the preparatory examination record, he believes that there is a possibility that the death sentence may be imposed if the accused is convicted. In any application, civil trial or appeal where questions of tribal customs followed in Transkei are involved, any court, including the Supreme Court, may summon to its assistance in an advisory capacity such assessors as the court may deem necessary, and the opinions of such assessors must be recorded and form part of the record of the proceedings.

Appeals from the Supreme Court at present lie to the Appellate Division of the Supreme Court of South Africa, but the establishment of a Transkeian Appeal Court is envisaged.

Legal Practitioners

Transkei has followed the English and South African practice of a bar divided into advocates and attorneys. Both are officers of the Supreme Court, but except in special circumstances and then only with the leave of the Chief Justice, an attorney may not appear in the Supreme Court, but must engage the services of an advocate to represent his client. As a general rule, advocates on the other hand may not act for a client directly without having been engaged to do so by an attorney acting on behalf of the client. There are two exceptions to this rule. Firstly, in all cases where by law the death sentence may be imposed if the accused were to be convicted, and the accused cannot afford legal representation, the court appoints an advocate to appear for the accused and his fee – a prescribed one – is paid by the State. Such pro Deo counsel acts without the intervention or assistance of an attorney, but occasionally in complex cases attorneys are appointed on the same basis to assist the advocate in the preparation of his defence. Secondly, by tradition, an accused who has not engaged the services of an attorney is entitled to ask that any advocate present in court represent him for whatever fee – usually a very small one – the accused is able to pay in cash. This form of defence is known as a dock defence and the tradition of the bar demands that counsel act, provided the accused is able to tender a minimal or token amount. In addition, Transkei has a legal aid system for indigent litigants. It is financed by the State and its activities are confined to the magistrates' courts, since in view of the pro Deo and dock defence systems there is no real call for the opera-

At Independence the establishment of the Transkeian Police provided for 929 officers and other ranks. Twenty Black Transkeians held commissioned rank. They were assisted by several White officers seconded by South Africa.

tion of the legal aid system in the Supreme Court.

Both attorneys and advocates may appear in a magistrate's court and before any other quasi-judicial body where legal representation is permitted, but the advocate must in all cases be instructed by the attorney on behalf of the client. The advocate looks to the attorney for his fees and not to the client.

All attorneys and advocates who were entitled to practise in Transkeian courts before independence are entitled to practise in such courts after independence, but those not so entitled must be admitted to practise by the Supreme Court of Transkei. An advocate must have a Bachelor of Laws degree, obtained after not fewer than five years' study, and before being allowed to practise must undergo four months' pupillage under the supervision of one or more experienced advocates. In order to qualify for admission, an attorney must have passed the prescribed examinations (a degree course specially designed for aspirant attorneys or a Bachelor of Laws degree) and have served articles of clerkship with a qualified attorney for a prescribed period and have passed a practical examination in the practice of an attorney.

Department of Justice

From the establishment in 1963 of the form of self-government destined to culminate in independence gained on 26 October 1976, the Transkeian Department of Justice pursued a policy of training as many Black Transkeians as possible to take over posts formerly held by Whites in the department. At independence there were 40 legally qualified Black Transkeians in the department and in nine of the 28 district offices the entire staff, including the magistrate, consisted of Black Transkeians. In the other 19 districts either only the magistrate or the magistrate and one assistant magistrate were White.

Police

The establishment of the Transkeian Police at independence provided for 929 officers and other ranks. In addition several White members of the South African Police remained with the Transkeian Police on secondment until such time as their services would no longer be needed. Twenty Black Transkeians hold commissioned rank ranging from the Commissioner to lieutenants.

Prisons

The Transkeian Department of Prisons has an establishment of 520 permanent staff members. It is run on the same organisational lines as the Army

and the Police, with equivalent ranks. There are 14 commissioned officers and 8 warrant officers. Of the 22 prisons under the department's jurisdiction, 21 are situated in various towns and villages other than Umtata, the capital city. The policy is to accommodate prisoners serving sentences of less than two years in the area in which they are sentenced.

Wellington Prison at Umtata has been built to conform to the most modern standards. It is designed for prisoners with sentences of two years and more. A Prisons Board reviews all individual long-term sentences from time to time and grants parole in appropriate cases.

All persons sentenced in Transkei are housed in prisons in Transkei. The average daily prison population for the first 10 months of 1976 was 2 100, which indicated a low incidence of crime in Transkei.

Tribal Law and Custom

Without an insight into the structure of Transkeian tribal society, it is not possible to arrive at a proper understanding of the legal system which it evolved and which fulfilled its needs so well, and which is referred to generally as tribal law and custom.

All Transkei tribes allow polygamy. The basic unit of the tribe is the family, comprising the kraal head and his wife or wives and children. (In this context kraal means a group of huts, often enclosed by a hedge of aloes.) A polygamist has two main wives, and in some tribes he may have three; any further wives he may marry are subordinate wives. Generally, each wife creates a "house" and the various houses collectively constitute the kraal head's kraal, which is subject to his guardianship and control. A house is defined by statute as "the family and property, rights and status, which commence with, attach to, and arise out of, the customary union of each Bantu woman".

Except in the case of a chief a man's first wife is always known as his *great wife,* and she and her issue become the entity known as the great house, which is ranked as the principal house in the kraal. As a rule, each house occupies its own hut, with the great wife's hut usually built opposite the gate of the cattle kraal. The second wife is the right-hand wife, and her house, the right-hand house, stands to the right of the great hut. The third wife married is the *Qadi* (rafter, or support) to the great house, and her hut goes to the left of the great hut. The fourth wife is the *Qadi* to the right-hand house, and her hut is situated to the right of that of the right-hand wife. If additional wives are married, they are alternatively "rafters" of the great house or the right-hand house. The group of huts comprising a kraal is constructed in a semi-circle which, if the nature of the site permits, faces east, and the circular cattle kraal stands in the open segment of the circle. Each house represents a separate and distinct entity, having its own separate rights and identity. As a rule, a wife's rank depends upon the position in the chronological order in which the wives were married.

A kraal head could have two distinct kinds of property: his general estate, or kraal property, and house property. The latter comprises all property specifically allotted to a house by the kraal head from his kraal property; any dowries which may have accrued to the house through unions entered into by daughters of that house; fines paid for the seduction of such daughters; and the earnings of the wife and her minor children. Moreover, if the kraal head has allotted a land to a house, all the fruits accrue to that house. Kraal property may be derived from inheritance, from fruits of any land cultivated by the kraal head, from his own earnings, or from fines received as damages for adultery committed with his wife.

The customary fines payable as compensation for delicts, such as seduction and adultery, were traditionally reckoned in cattle. Dowry was also paid in cattle. When horses and small stock were introduced into the country, these were often used as well, ten sheep or goats being reckoned as equivalent to one beast. Later, with the introduction of cash, an alternate standard value was adopted for each beast. This was varied at intervals so as to bring it into line with prevailing market values. Presently it stands at $92 per beast, fines and dowries nowadays often being paid in cash, or cash and livestock, and seldom solely in the latter.

The fine for adultery varies from three to five head of cattle. Adultery, like seduction, is common and it is customary for the husband to condone it. Indeed, adultery *per se* does not generally constitute an adequate cause for dissolving a customary union, unless there is accompanying conduct on the part of the wife which amounts to a repudiation by her of the union. The tribal world is very much a man's world, and not only does the husband's adultery fail to furnish his wife with grounds for divorce, but she is not entitled to claim compensation from the other woman.

The Transkeian Department of Prisons has an establishment of 520 permanent staff members, including 14 commissioned officers and eight warrant officers, administering 22 prisons. The photograph shows a senior official enjoying a game of tennis.

The property of a kraal is held in communal ownership by the family as a unit, but under the administration and control of the kraal head. Hence the rule which makes the kraal head jointly and severally liable, together with the wrongdoer, to compensate the victims of all delicts committed by unemancipated inmates of his kraal.

The tribal law of succession is based on primogeniture. This principle is, however, modified in a polygamous household in that the senior or general heir is the eldest son of the great wife, even if he is not the first-born son of the kraal head, whilst the eldest son of each house (whether he be a major or a minor) succeeds to the property of that house. Provision is made for succession to houses lacking a son. No female may inherit property. The heir steps into the shoes of the deceased kraal head, succeeding to all his rights and obligations. One of the latter is the duty to support the widow and minor children of the house.

The majority of Transkei's residents to some extent still order their lives in accordance with this traditional legal system.

They are free to marry by Christian or civil rites. Many who do so, nevertheless enter into an ancillary dowry agreement. The dowry is paid by the intending husband to his intended wife's father or guardian. Charges that tribal law treats women as chattels are, however, unfounded and are based on a misconception of the function fulfilled by the dowry which has, indeed, been described as "the rock on which the customary union is founded". So much so, that many Transkei Blacks who intend marrying by Christian or civil rites do not feel properly married unless they have paid a dowry for their wives. The dowry is somewhat analogous to a deposit paid by the groom as a token of his honourable intentions. Should the husband ill-treat his wife, she may return to her guardian and, under certain circumstances, he will find that the union has been dissolved and that he has forfeited his dowry. Conversely, should the wife's conduct indicate an intention to repudiate the union, her husband may dissolve the union and claim restoration of the dowry. All these considerations tend to have a stabilising effect on customary unions and, where a civil or Christian marriage is backed by a dowry contract, this factor serves to reinforce the bonds of matrimony.

Customary unions remain common to this day,

An official in a magistrate's court. As in Britain, the bar is divided into advocates and attorneys. Usually, an attorney may not appear in the Supreme Court, but must engage an advocate to represent his client there. Transkei has a legal aid system for indigent litigants.

although the practice of polygamy is disappearing as men increasingly tend to confine themselves to a single wife.

Tribal Law and Custom and Roman-Dutch Law

The co-existence of Roman-Dutch law and tribal law creates a more flexible legal system which is better adapted to the requirements of a society in transition and in which some citizens adhere to the traditional way of life while others are either partially or wholly detribalised.

The Transkeian Constitution Act provides that in all proceedings involving questions of tribal customs, it shall be in the discretion of the court to decide such questions in accordance with the tribal law applying to such customs. In the absence of agreement to the contrary, the customary law to be applied is that observed at the place where the defendant resides. If there is more than one custom in operation at that place, the custom observed by the defendant's tribe is applied. In this way, a conflict of laws has been avoided.

Transkeian tribal law, like most less developed legal systems, did not distinguish between crimes and delicts (civil wrongs), and assault did not found a cause of action for compensation. However, the Black assault victim is not without a remedy: he may found his claim for compensation on Roman-Dutch Law.

In a sense, therefore, Black Transkeian litigants may "have the best of both legal worlds", whilst their White counterparts are confined to the Roman-Dutch Law.

A further example of the flexibility of the Transkeian legal system is to be found in the law of succession. The tribal law of inheritance is equitable for as long as it operates amongst families following the traditional way of life for which it was formulated. It may lead to unjust consequences, however, where the family is detribalised. Suppose a deceased *paterfamilias* were survived by three children, all daughters, whom he had educated for the teaching and nursing professions and who, when they began earning, regularly remitted a substantial portion of their salaries to their father, thereby increasing his estate. Upon his death without a will, his entire estate would devolve upon a male relative, such as a brother or nephew. This result can be obviated if the *paterfamilias* bequeaths his estate by will to his wife or daughters. When two spouses contract a marriage, they thereby assume a nuptial status under Roman-Dutch law which subsequently governs all matters of status arising out of the marriage.

Chapter Eight

Agriculture

The agricultural potential of Transkei is beyond dispute. Annual rainfall varies from 1 200 mm along the coast to 660 mm in the south and 880 mm in the north, which is much higher than the average for Southern Africa. In fact, the six principal rivers and their tributaries – all perennial – account for about 23 per cent of the total run-off of the Republic of South Africa and Transkei together. Irrigation potential, therefore, is considerable. (See chapter on The Country).

The total area of Transkei is 4,4 million ha, of which 4,2 million ha is available for farming. Of this area, 383 000 ha is suitable for crop production. The soils vary in quality: some are very fertile, but all are at least able to support average crops. Climatic conditions, together with rainfall and soils, are such that Transkei can grow a remarkably wide variety of crops and produce enough cattle for sale to earn at least $34,5 million a year, to say nothing of sheep and wool.

Wherever modern and proficient methods of husbandry are applied, this potential has been fully realised. Flourishing tea and fibre plantations have been established. Yields much above average have been attained on irrigated land of which there will soon be 9 500 ha, and on rain-fed experimental plots at the Tsolo College of Agriculture 30 bags of maize per hectare are harvested every year.

The agricultural potential of Transkei is considerable and wherever modern methods of cultivation have been applied, this potential has been fully realised. Thirty bags of maize per hectare have been harvested on experimental plots.

On the whole, however, this potential lies largely unexploited. Like many other African countries, Transkei does not produce enough food to feed its Black population of 2,2 million. In fact, about half the maize consumed every year is imported from the Republic of South Africa. The average maize yield is a little more than two bags per hectare and in 1974/75 only $1 840 000 was realised from 11 000 cattle sold at 162 auction sales. This, despite a comprehensive extension service run for the benefit of farmers throughout the country by the Department of Agriculture and Forestry.

There are various interrelated reasons for this modest performance, all rooted in a life-style and set of customs fashioned over many centuries. The fact of the matter is that the Cape Nguni have never been farmers in the accepted sense of the term. The men were warriors, hunters and nomadic stock-owners.

From time immemorial the main components of the daily diet were meat and wild fruits and vegetables gathered in the veld. Later crops – mostly maize, millet and sorghum – were grown to supplement this diet, but the responsibility for these crops was exclusively that of the women and children. It was their function to till the soil as best they could, plant whatever seeds were available and harvest whatever they could gather.

Until the middle of the eighteenth century, when they first met the vanguard of the White pioneers in the south-eastern corner of South Africa, the Cape Nguni were continually on the move, in search of better pastures for their cattle. This meant that there was no permanency to their agriculture.

They practised what has been described as 'shifting agriculture': whenever a piece of cultivated land was exhausted, eroded or, when it was on a steep incline, even completely washed away by floods, the family or tribe simply moved on to make a fresh start elsewhere.

In those early years, therefore, farming, i.e. both animal husbandry and agronomy, was in the first place a way of life – not a commercial enterprise undertaken to produce surpluses which could be sold or bartered for other commodities. Both livestock and crops were tended merely to meet the modest daily subsistence needs of the family or tribe. The notion of production for sale on a market was entirely foreign to them.

Once their southerly migration was halted by the White pioneers who had taken possession of the uninhabited virgin lands south-west of the Great Fish River, the Cape Nguni had to make do with the land they had occupied – some of the best watered and most fertile in Southern Africa. But all they knew was the subsistence agriculture their womenfolk had practised for centuries.

After a series of nine so-called Kaffir Wars between the Nguni and the Whites of the Cape Colony, the former were subjected to British rule and by a process of annexation, started in 1879 and completed in 1894, the area now known as Transkei was joined to the Cape Colony. There were no further wars to be fought.

Given their traditional lack of interest in agriculture, it was to be expected that whenever they needed cash for some purpose or other, the able-bodied menfolk would leave their land in Transkei to sell their labour on White farms and – later – mining and industry. This was done on a temporary basis: the men would return to their tribal lands at the end of summer to resume their traditional existence, for after the harvests had been gathered there would be enough to eat and drink.

Generally, this pattern, together with the traditional system of land tenure, persists to this day and represents one of the major obstacles to sound agricultural development in Transkei. There is no individual ownership of land in Western terms: the land belongs to the tribe as a whole. The chief of the tribe allots a certain area of land to the head of each family and each family has the right to claim a piece of land for cultivation and to depas-

Two young farmers demonstrate what can be done when modern cultivation methods are applied. The irrigation potential of the country is considerable and the Transkei Development Corporation has done much to promote vegetable production under irrigation.

ture an unlimited number of stock on the commonage. These animals are not bred and reared to be marketed, however, but merely so that their numbers may serve as a token of the owner's wealth and status in the tribe.

Thus even today there is the anomalous situation – in Western terms – that in a total population of 2 200 000 Blacks there are no fewer than 383 800 'farmers' in Transkei. Each of these has on average 6,4 large stock units (one large stock unit = 1 beast = 6 sheep) and the usufruct to about 12,5 ha of land of which 2,5 ha is arable. Even in the most favourable circumstances, this type of holding would be highly uneconomical. Certainly, it does not lend itself to the practice of market-orientated agriculture.

In these circumstances, because there was no agricultural tradition and since 'everybody's property is nobody's responsibility', the agricultural methods applied were destructive in the extreme. When owing to poor practices a piece of land was rendered unproductive, the family concerned would merely approach the chief for compensatory land.

The first noteworthy effort to improve the situation was made in 1935 when a system of planned land utilisation was introduced to reclaim and conserve the soil. The results were poor, however, owing to a lack of scientific know-how among the planners and a natural resistance on the part of the Blacks to control measures which they did not understand.

Ten years later the South African government published a White Paper which proclaimed a 'new era of reclamation' for the Black areas of the country, including Transkei. While steps were immediately taken to achieve the goals set out in the White Paper, it soon became clear that the pace of destruction was still far outstripping that of reclamation. In the early 'fifties, the South African government decided that the time had come to tackle this problem with all the expertise at its disposal and appointed the Commission of Enquiry into the Socio-Economic Development of the Black Areas within the Union of South Africa (better known as the Tomlinson Commission, after the chairman). The report of the commission was published in 1954, and ever since has served as the blueprint for development in all Black areas, including Transkei.

Incidentally, the commission had found that by 1954 no less than 30 per cent of Transkei was badly eroded, 44 per cent moderately so, while only 26 per cent of the land was intact.

Planning

In implementing the recommendations of the commission, each land unit under the control of a headman or chief was designated an administrative area which would serve as basis for the entire planning and conservation programme. There are no fewer than 943 such administrative areas in the 28 districts of Transkei. The total land surface area involved is nearly four million ha and includes land not in tribal possession but acquired by the South African Bantu Trust for development as farm land.

The basic objective of these planning programmes is the reclamation and conservation of natural resources – soil, water and vegetation. Cultivation is limited to consolidated blocks of soil suitably protected against erosion. This is essential since about 75 per cent of Transkei's land surface is mountainous or hilly, while only eleven per cent may be classified as gently rolling or flat. Eroded and infertile lands on a steep incline are excised and, wherever possible, replaced by fertile and virgin soils. The lands are then properly fenced to keep livestock out. Protection against erosion is provided by grass strips and more particularly by training banks constructed by the engineering division of the Department of Agriculture and Forestry. Training banks are erected along every third grass strip and have more than proved their worth in conserving the soil of Transkei.

Pasture is fenced into camps and provided with stock-watering points. The whole system is designed to permit rotational grazing so that the natural pasture may be restored and conserved. All fencing is done by private local contractors, but the materials, tools and equipment are supplied by the Department of Agriculture and Forestry. Livestock numbers are limited to the carrying capacity of the pasture. Various factors are taken into account in determining the carrying capacity of any land unit or ward within a unit – soil, water, veld type and the condition of the natural cover.

At the same time a comprehensive effort is made to separate farmers from non-farmers and move the latter off farm lands. Cultivation and grazing rights are given only to those family heads who had these rights prior to the introduction of the planning programme. Those who do not have these rights are moved into residential sites which are selected and surveyed in advance. These families are generously compensated for all improvements

Most Transkeian farmers still use oxen to plough their fields. In recent years much has been done to rationalise land utilisation. Wherever possible, eroded or infertile lands on steep inclines are withdrawn and replaced by virgin lands.

on their old sites and are allowed to transfer all salvageable materials to the site on which their new house is to be built. The number and size of these residential plots depend on the population and area of the land unit concerned.

In this way various families living scattered all over the countryside are brought together in properly planned residential areas which in some instances are beginning to assume the aspect of viable and self-supporting villages, with their own schools, shops, churches and other community centres. Each residential area or developing village is provided with its own water supply, either by means of boreholes, protected fountains or weirs across rivers or streams. The water is piped to points in the centre of the residential area where all residents have easy access to it.

Apart from food and water, the average Transkeian family's greatest need is wood – firewood for cooking and heating and timber (poles and laths) as hut-building material. Thus, the planning programme envisages the establishment of adequate woodlots on all those land units which have no supplies of their own. Progress in establishing these woodlots has been slow – mainly owing to the severe droughts of recent years and the slow growth rate of the trees used.

During the past 20 years remarkable progress has been made with this planning programme. To date, no less than 61,4 per cent of the available farm land of Transkei has been planned as outlined above. All planning is done in close co-operation with the appropriate tribal and regional authorities. When the headman and residents of a particular administrative area or land unit indicate that they wish their land to be planned, the Department of Agriculture and Forestry or its agents consult the local tribal authority. If there are no objections, detailed plans for the area are drawn up in consultation with the headman or chief and his local committee. Afterwards the plans are explained to the people at a meeting convened by the magistrate of the district, and later also to the tribal authority. The people may accept or reject the plan in toto or they may suggest amendments which are duly considered. The plans in their final form are then submitted to the Minister of Agriculture and Forestry for his approval. Once the plans are gazetted in terms of the Transkeian Development Act (no. 10 of 1966), they acquire force of law and legal sanctions may be applied to ensure their implementation.

Animal production

Traditionally, the Transkeian farmer has always been a stock-owner. Animal husbandry has never

been a commercial undertaking, however. Animals are not bred and reared to be sold. Instead, the number of cattle, horses, donkeys, sheep and goats a man possesses is a measure of his wealth and status in the community. Animals serve as a form of currency to be converted into cash only when needed. They are still the main component of lobola – the token that the young bridegroom gives to his prospective father-in-law to show that his intentions are honourable.

Social customs and traditions are not the only factors militating against a prosperous cattle industry in Transkei. Land tenure – described earlier – is another limiting circumstance. Traditionally, grazing has always been communal and no effort was made to prevent selective grazing by animals. As soon as the stock had exhausted a particular grazing area, they were simply moved to the next. This type of casual husbandry is certainly not conducive to the production of stock of high quality.

In addition, the carrying capacity of the natural grazing of Transkei is not very high – on average only one large stock unit (i.e. one head of cattle or six sheep) per hectare. Ideally, the country should carry no more than 1,8 million head of cattle or large stock units. This number is perhaps not very large, but it is nevertheless a potential source of great wealth for the people of Transkei, for if a turnover of about 15 per cent – reasonable by world standards – could be achieved and maintained, it would mean an annual income at current prices of at least $34,5 million.

At present the animal population is more than 2 044 000 large stock units, made up of 1 300 000 head of cattle, 2 500 000 sheep, 1 400 000 goats and 120 000 equines. This gives some idea of the extent of overgrazing practised in Transkei today. As indicated in Table 1, however, the position has improved slightly during the past few years – owing largely to the efforts of the Transkeian Department of Agriculture and Forestry. The severe drought of 1968/69 had reduced the number of large stock units from 2 049 000 the year before to 1 780 000. The following year the number increased alarmingly by more than 140 000, but has been maintained fairly constantly at that level ever since.

The Transkeian Department of Agriculture and Forestry is doing much to improve the situation in an effort fully to exploit the potential of animal

The rains have come and two teams of oxen are inspanned to plough the fields as quickly as possible. In terms of current development programmes, cultivation is limited to consolidated blocks suitably protected against erosion.

husbandry in the country. No fewer than 2 628 000 hectares – 62 per cent of the total farming area – have been planned, as outlined earlier. This means inter alia that the scattered homesteads of old have been concentrated into surveyed residential sites and that each area has been allotted sufficient grazing for the number of livestock to be grazed. In addition, a system of veld management and grazing control has been introduced. This is based on the rotational use of two or more camps. More recent planning envisages one herd on four camps, one of which is rested for a whole season while the other three are grazed in rotation. As a first step in implementing this policy, the various veld types were determined by aspect and soil type and thereafter properly fenced. The rested camps are so designed that animals do not have to traverse them when they are brought to the others to be grazed. The number of animals to be carried is carefully determined by the capacity of the natural grazing of the area.

Sheep and wool

It is not certain how or when the first sheep were introduced into Transkei but it is generally believed that they were originally brought in from neighbouring White farms by labourers who had been paid in sheep in lieu of cash.

At present there are some 2 500 000 sheep in Transkei and the annual clip is in the vicinity of 27 000 bales. Each sheep yields about 1,7 kg of wool. These production figures are not nearly as high as they might have been but here, too, progress has been slow in persuading farmers to adopt progressive breeding and management practices. Extension work among sheep farmers has been going on for more than 20 years and during the past ten years this has been backed up by a scheme whereby the Department of Agriculture subsidises the purchase by farmers of improved rams for breeding purposes. During this period Transkeian sheep farmers have acquired about 600 rams of good quality a year.

In 1967 the Department of Agriculture and Forestry initiated a system of collective shearing sheds for Transkeian sheep farmers. At present there are 63 of these sheds in which 247 000 sheep were shorn in the 1974-75 season. These collective shearing operations have made a valuable contribution to the improvement of the wool industry of Transkei. In the first instance they have ensured better prices for the local farmer by selling the clip directly to the agents of the South African Wool Board, the sole buyer of Transkeian wool, thereby eliminating speculative profits by private agents and buyers in Transkei. Secondly, they have considerably enhanced the quality of the Transkeian product by ensuring that the clip is properly classed and sorted.

Each shearing shed is controlled by a committee of local farmers who perform their duties under the guidance of officials of the Department of Agriculture and Forestry which also finances the construction of the sheds. Agricultural co-operative companies have a major share in the proper functioning of many of these sheds. In all those districts where such companies are operative, they order the wool sacks and all other requirements of the sheds, organise and supervise the consignment of the baled product and see that every farmer receives his due for his clip. In the absence of an agricultural co-operative company, these functions are performed by the shearing shed committees with the assistance of officials of the department. It is the intention of the department that all these sheds should eventually be run by co-operative companies.

Veterinary services

Certainly, disease is no longer a serious limiting factor in Transkeian animal husbandry. In fact, few African countries can boast more disease-free herds or flocks. The four main cattle scourges – contagious bovine pleuropneumonia, rinderpest, East Coast fever and anthrax – have been wiped out. This has been achieved either by massive inoculation programmes in the early days or by stringent precautionary measures, such as compulsory dipping and strict control over all movements of cattle in the country, which are at present applied mainly to prevent tick infestation and tick-borne diseases which are fairly prevalent in Transkei. The most important of these are probably gall-sickness and redwater fever.

The dipping programme is enforced by a large staff of stock inspectors in the employ of the veterinary branch of the Department of Agriculture and Forestry. They not only supervise the actual dipping operations, but also inspect livestock for signs of disease, keep stock registers up to date, control cattle movements and advise on such matters as improved management, immunisation and the control of internal parasites which are a continual threat to the health of Transkei's cattle population.

Each year the stock inspectors also immunise all cattle against anthrax and quarter-evil, all sheep against quarter-evil and all heifer calves against brucellosis. This service is performed nation-wide free of charge. In addition, they assist farmers in dosing against internal parasites and in castrating bulls and rams at the owners' request.

The veterinary branch maintains a fully equipped laboratory at Umtata which handles a wide range of clinical diagnostic tests. The routine work of the laboratory includes the annual examination of some 120 000 spleen smears from cattle dying or slaughtered in Transkei. This investigation serves as a monitor for the occurrence of tick-borne and other diseases.

The veterinary branch is also engaged in several long-term research projects. Perhaps the most important at present is a survey of trace elements in the natural grazing of Transkei in order to determine deficiencies or excesses. Some 2 000

Table 1   Average crop yields, 1963 – 72 and 1974 – 75

Crop		Total yield (tonnes)	Area planted (ha)	yield (kg) per ha
Maize	1963 – 72	130 535,2	545 931	239,0
	1974 – 75	90 340,5	409 764	220,5
Sorghum	1963 – 72	6 098,7	32 709	186,3
	1974 – 75	4 382,2	39 662	110,5
Legumes	1963 – 72	1 524,2	22 377	68,4
	1974 – 75	4 845,6	30 892	156,8

Note: Figures for the districts of Herschel and Cacadu (Glen Grey), which were added to Transkei in December 1975, are not included.

livers have already been analysed by means of atomic absorption spectrophotometry. Once the results have been analysed, the scientists of the veterinary branch will be able to advise on the formulation of supplementary stock 'licks' for Transkeian cattle.

Surveys to be initiated shortly include one of the occurrence of internal parasites in sheep and cattle, and one to determine to what extent ticks have become resistant to dipping chemicals used at present.

Whenever assistance is needed, it is always readily given by Onderstepoort, the world famous veterinary research institute north of Pretoria in South Africa. In fact, the senior staff of the Transkeian veterinary branch were all trained at Onderstepoort and all vaccines used in the immunisation programmes are imported from Onderstepoort.

Apart from its wide-ranging extension service among Transkeian farmers, the veterinary branch also undertakes the training of both its own personnel and students of agriculture. All formal lectures in animal health given to students at the Tsolo College of Agriculture are conducted by the branch.

But the major task in education remains the extension service designed to persuade the Transkeian farmer to improve the quality and health of his stock and to adopt a more commercially minded approach to his farming operations. The veterinary branch conducts a regular series of formal lectures, informal discussions and practical demonstrations for the benefit of farmers all over the country.

Table 2 Land utilisation Planning and Conservation works Completed, 1966 – 1975

Year	Conservation schemes prepared	Area prepared ha	Fencing done km	Grass strips done km	Lands demarcated	Residential sites demarcated	Woodlots established
Up to 1965	337	1 307 631	12 662	200 405	62 897	138 341	1 413
1965 – 66	20	101 702	3 449	4 069	11 191	10 257	832
1966 – 67	40	93 383	4 483	3 938	10 791	28 041	398
1967 – 68	20	71 631	3 725	2 990	6 343	17 129	463
1968 – 69	9	36 181	2 208	3 080	7 141	18 192	248
1969 – 70	46	109 353	3 138	4 432	7 310	15 342	280
1970 – 71	35	130 139	2 218	2 833	4 666	13 558	602
1971 – 72	39	175 840	4 188	2 376	4 746	16 290	119
1972 – 73	18	80 958	4 168	2 953	8 114	35 637	53
1973 – 74	19	95 217	1 519	2 158	13 151	12 905	51
1974 – 75	17	77 117	1 289	2 015	10 848	24 598	58
Total 1965 – 75	263	971 521	30 385	30 844	84 301	191 949	3 104
Grand Total	600	2 279 152	43 047	231 249	147 198	330 290	4 517

Note: Figures for the districts of Herschel and Cacadu (Glen Grey), which were added to Transkei in December 1975, are not included.

Table 3   Livestock in Transkei, 1959 – 1960 to 1974 – 1975

Year	Cattle	Sheep	Goats	Equines	L S U
1959/60	1 392 041	2 209 063	1 022 409	93 796	2 134 132
1961/62	1 354 416	2 309 605	1 003 076	97 017	2 003 546
1963/64	1 419 226	1 929 774	995 920	117 845	2 024 686
1965/66	1 331 486	1 940 397	1 022 267	111 531	1 936 781
1967/68	1 313 317	2 483 566	1 229 606	117 156	2 049 337
1968/69	1 083 310	2 311 824	1 219 663	108 305	1 780 197
1969/70	1 116 901	2 824 692	1 339 967	111 681	1 922 700
1971/72	1 184 989	2 604 480	1 314 229	114 264	1 950 920
1973/74	1 194 181	2 347 830	1 330 312	119 760	1 926 964
1974/75	1 214 078	2 238 942	1 218 596	115 409	1 905 743

Note: One LSU (Large Stock Unit) = 1 head of cattle or 6 sheep or goats

Note: Figures for the districts of Herschel and Cacadu (Glen Grey), which were added to Transkei in December 1975, are not included.

Table 4   Composition of cattle herds, 1969 – 1975

Year	Heifers	Cows	Oxen	Bulls
	Percentage of Total			
1969	24,6	30,1	35,7	9,6
1970	24,1	31,8	34,5	9,6
1971	22,4	32,0	35,0	10,6
1972	23,3	32,2	33,6	10,9
1973	23,8	31,9	32,8	11,5
1974	23,4	32,1	32,5	12,0
1975	23,7	33,0	32,0	11,9

Note: Figures for the districts of Herschel and Cacadu (Glen Grey), which were added to Transkei in December 1975, are not included.

Table 5 Growth of Co-operative Companies, 1967 – 1975

Year	Number of Companies	Total Membership	Total sales to members $	Outstanding advances to members $	Secured loans (outstanding) $
1967	1	1 339	42 125	42 757	44 550
1968	4	3 002	77 577	84 742	79 465
1969	6	6 210	139 240	199 315	177 140
1970	6	10 009	173 113	310 730	244 322
1971	6	12 803	221 982	375 769	320 272
1972	6	15 290	213 716	439 337	484 346
1973	6	16 877	256 577	508 293	523 052
1974	6	16 356	223 011	486 601	454 831
1975	10	19 640	375 353	498 407	521 526

The exchange rate of the Rand as at 1976/08/31 was R1,00 = $1,15.

Note: Figures for the districts of Herschel and Cacadu (Glen Grey), which were added to Transkei in December 1975, are not included.

Table 6   Growth of Collective Shearing Sheds, 1969 – 1975

Year	Number of sheds	Number of sheep shorn	Mass of wool (kg)	Average yield per sheep (kg)	Value of wool sold $
1969	21	23 500	32 830	1,4	14 817
1970	29	56 343	95 888	1,7	30 857
1971	31	93 705	146 343	1,6	39 820
1972	33	141 405	222 000	1,6	82 347
1973	39	132 317	211 707	1,6	182 511
1974	43	129 171	186 547	1,6	94 264
1975	63	182 834	246 872	1,4	178 561

The exchange rate of the Rand as at 1976/08/31 was R1,00 = $1,15.

133

In addition, the Animal Slaughter, Animal Products and Hygiene Act of 1967 confers on the veterinary branch the duty to maintain standards of excellence at all public abattoirs and other places where meat is handled for public consumption, including the meat processing plant at Umtata. There are 17 abattoirs in urban areas and nearly 200 in country districts.

This facet of the branch's work is certain to increase in importance in future as it will have to play a vital role in eradicating the so-called zoonoses, i.e. those animal diseases which may affect man.

Crop production

Most crops in Transkei are grown on dry lands; irrigation is only a very recent innovation. The most important crops are maize (the staple food), grain sorghum and legumes.

On the assumption that a soil depth of at least 60 cm and an incline of no more than 15 per cent is required for effective tilling, the total arable area of Transkei is 383 000 hectares, or 8,7 per cent of the total land area. Some 600 000 hectares are at present planted to dry-land crops. This indicates the extent to which marginal soils are worked.

The accompanying table shows that over the years there has been a marked fluctuation both in the area planted to the three main crops and in total and average yields. The most alarming fact revealed by the table is that in 1974-75 the average yield per hectare of both maize and sorghum decreased markedly, compared with the average for the ten years 1963-72. On the other hand, that of legumes more than doubled during the same period.

The average yield per hectare of all crops is very modest – far below the actual potential of the land. There are various reasons for this. The first and most important lies in the traditional system of land tenure and the average Black man's attitude to agriculture, described earlier. This attitude prevails to an overwhelming extent to this day: tilling the soil and tending crops are left to the women and children of the family. Broadly speaking, agriculture in general and crop production in particular, is not yet looked upon as a possible source of income. Rather, it is a way of life and the final resource on which a man falls back if his efforts

Extension officers and stock inspectors are trained at Tsolo, Transkei's college of agriculture about 55 km from Umtata. The college's sheep flock of 350 comprises mostly Dohne Merinos. Wool production has considerable potential.

elsewhere fail. When cash is needed for whatever reason, the man will rather sell his labour in a factory either in Transkei or in South Africa.

This pervading lack of interest in agriculture as a commercial venture is one of the major obstacles faced by the Department of Agriculture and Forestry and by other development agencies, such as the Transkei Development Corporation. Coupled with this, and flowing from it, is the traditional system of land tenure which militates against the establishment of economic units. Another factor contributing to the low yield is lack of training. The Tsolo College of Agriculture does not train prospective farmers, only stock inspectors and extension officers to be employed by government. The official extension services are broadly based and extremely active but customs and traditions of centuries simply cannot be altered overnight.

Those farmers who have broken with tradition and would like to apply modern methods, find that they are up against another hampering circumstance – lack of capital. Apart from the co-operative credit societies (discussed elsewhere) and the Transkei Development Corporation, there are hardly any sources of capital for the Transkeian farmer, and unless he succeeds in acquiring the necessary capital, he is unable to buy proper tillage and planting equipment, sufficient quantities of fertiliser and certified high-yield seed.

In these circumstances Transkei does not produce enough crops to meet the requirements of its own population. In fact, about half the maize consumed each year is imported from South Africa. In 1974-75 more than 188 000 tons of maize and maize meal were bought from South Africa. Similarly, large quantities of other grains, mainly grain sorghum, vegetables and other crops have to be imported each year.

Transkei Development Corporation

What to do about this situation, which repeats itself in most Black African countries? Apart from the broad plans aimed at a rationalisation and modernisation of the agriculture industry in general, described earlier, agricultural experts in Transkei believe that the approach most likely to bring immediate and measurable improvement is project farming which envisages production on non-tribal land of industrial crops which may be either exported to be processed elsewhere or, preferably, serve as the basis of local processing industries which, in turn, will provide job opportunities for the people of Transkei.

It is in this field that the Transkei Development Corporation (TDC) will play a major role in future. The agricultural division of the TDC was established in 1973 to assist the Transkeian Department of Agriculture and Forestry in exploiting the full potential of the soil and water resources of the country. Capital expenditure by the division on agricultural development increased from $490 680 in 1973-74 – the first year of operation – to $6,1 million in the 1975-76 financial year.

To date the activities of the agricultural division of the TDC have been largely experimental in nature and mostly associated with beef cattle, dairy products and irrigation farming. For the immediate future the Corporation has set its sights on the intensive production of a variety of cash, vegetable, grain and fodder crops as well as red meat and fresh milk, for which there is a growing demand, both in Transkei and South Africa. A wide range of experiments are in progress in order to determine possible yields and production problems and costs. Only the most promising crops will be incorporated in future large-scale production programmes.

This type of project has three immediate advantages. Firstly, because capital is available and the most modern production methods are used, the yield per hectare is increased both dramatically and immediately. Transkeian farmers receive intensive practical training on these projects and, above all, they are shown by example that the land can be a source of wealth. Thirdly, substantial numbers of job opportunities are created on the land. So far, more than 1 000 Transkeians have been employed on projects launched by the agricultural division of the TDC. Such projects also promote infrastructural development in that houses for employees, barns and access roads have to be built.

Project farming enterprises will to a great extent rely on irrigation and consequently the area under irrigation will be substantially increased during the next few years. The TDC in particular is keen to produce under irrigation fruit and vegetables, which will be canned or frozen for export. Large parts of Transkei are ideally suited to the production of a large variety of such crops.

Irrigation

As stated earlier, irrigation is a recent develop-

The Magwa tea estates in the district of Lusikisiki cover an area of 830 ha, on 490 ha of which the tea is mature and in full production. This undertaking is an excellent example of the type of project farming which holds much promise for the future of Transkei.

ment in Transkei. The potential is vast: the country is blessed with abundant rainfall, and several perennial rivers account for nearly 25 per cent of the run-off of the entire Republic of South Africa and Transkei together. The soils, particularly those in the river valleys, are deep and fertile. It has been calculated that some 20 000 ha of land can be irrigated. Irrigation farming, however, is a specialised and expensive undertaking and it needed a powerful agency, such as the Transkeian government, to give the necessary impetus to development in this field. When Transkei was granted self-government in 1963, only a modest area of 268 hectares was under irrigation. Most of the schemes were very small – ranging in size from 2,5 ha to 12 ha – and were initiated for experimental purposes. Most ended in failure, owing mainly to lack of expertise and capital on the part of the farmers and, in some instances, the inadequate size of the individual plots.

Progress in recent years has been substantial, however. The Malenge scheme (240 ha), largest of those in existence before 1963, is doing well. The major problem experienced there – aluminium toxicity – has been solved by the application of lime and since 1969 crop production has been improved almost beyond recognition. Good yields of potatoes, maize, dry beans, wheat, cabbage, Japanese radish and Italian rye have been maintained. The last two crops are grown to supplement the winter fodder of the large dairy herd run in conjunction with the scheme.

Large quantities of vegetables are also grown on the Orange Grove scheme near Umtata, which was recently enlarged from 5 ha to 7,75 ha. Most of the produce is sold in Umtata where, in 1975, the city council constructed a new market building for that purpose.

The largest development projects since 1963 are the Qamata and Ncora irrigation schemes. Qamata is situated at St Marks, 17 km below the Lubisi Dam on the Indwe River. The dam has a capacity of 157 million m³ and, on completion, the irrigation scheme itself will be 3 566 ha in extent. The dam has a double-curvature concrete arch wall and a water depth of 35,7 metres. Water released from the dam into the river is diverted by the Lante weir into the scheme's main canal which is 29 km long and has a capacity of 2,5 cumecs. The dam was completed on 23 April 1968 and in the same year the first 90 plots of 1,28 ha each were allotted to farmers. To date, 1 240 plots have been issued to individual farmers, in addition to a portion of 127 ha which was allocated to the agricultural division of the TDC. Altogether an area of some 2 300 ha is under flood irrigation and the remaining 1 200 ha will be developed for sprinkler irrigation. The main crops grown are wheat, maize, lucerne, dry beans and vegetables.

The latest and by far the largest irrigation scheme is Ncora which is some 5 600 ha in extent and mainly under gravity-fed sprinkler irrigation. Only about 700 ha will be flood-irrigated. Water is obtained from the Ncora Dam on the Tsomo River which has a capacity of 181,25 million m³ and a water depth of 33,5 metres. Water is taken to the scheme through a series of pipelines and canals, a tunnel and a major syphon pipe. This system can discharge water at a rate of five cumecs but the actual rate is automatically adjusted by means of a series of float valves to suit any fluctuations in demand. No crops have been produced yet – the dam was only completed in 1973 – but it is expected that the first 400 ha will be brought into production by the end of 1976. The estimated total cost of the scheme is $22 million.

When the Ncora scheme is complete and fully developed, some 9 500 ha in all will be under irrigation in Transkei.

The engineering services branch of the Department of Agriculture and Forestry not only constructs soil conservation works and dams for irrigation schemes, but also builds and maintains water supply schemes for several towns and rural settlements. The most important of these are the following:

The water supply scheme for Butterworth, the most important industrial town in Transkei, consists of two dams, of which the main one, an earth embankment 23 metres high, with a capacity of 21 million m³, is on the Xilinxa River. This dam discharges water into the river system when it is needed and a 13-metre concrete gravity section weir with a capacity of 1,8 million m³ on the Gcuwa River collects the water and, in turn, discharges it at the municipal filtration works.

Umtata, the capital city, is supplied by a dam with a capacity of 260 million m³ on the Umtata River. The dam consists of an earth embankment some 35 metres high and water is taken by pipeline to the municipal filtration works.

The town of Cofimvaba in the west is supplied from an earth-fill dam with a capacity of 13,24 million m³. The water is taken to the town through a pipeline some 23 km long.

State projects

Project farming is, however, not confined to irrigation schemes, nor is it undertaken only by the agricultural division of the TDC. The Transkeian Department of Agriculture and Forestry has played a leading role in establishing such intensive farming enterprises. So far it has sought mainly to establish industrial crops of which the most important are tea, coffee and Phormium tenax (New Zealand hemp).

The first experimental plantings of tea were made at Umgazi forest station in the district of Umzimvubu (formerly Port St Johns) in 1958. These were not successful, however, and in 1960 new experimental plots were laid out at the Ntsubane station in the Lambasi area in the district of Lusikisiki. Results were much more encouraging here and subsequently a feasibility study was carried out which indicated that conditions in this area were favourable for large-scale tea production. Consequently the Department of Agriculture and Forestry decided to develop a tea estate in this area, to be called Magwa, after the Magwa Falls nearby. A nursery was established with seed imported from Mozambique and in 1965 the first 50 ha was planted to seedlings from this nursery.

Today the Magwa tea estate comprises an area of 830 ha, on 490 ha of which the tea is mature and in full production. In 1969 a tea factory with a capacity of 16 000 kg of green leaf a day was built on the estate by the engineering services branch of the Department of Agriculture and Forestry. The capacity of the processing plant is now being increased to 20 000 kg a day.

All tea produced on the Magwa tea estate is sold in South Africa by a prominent firm of tea brokers in Johannesburg. So far the firm has sold 880 tonnes of tea at a total value of $776 250. In the 1974/75 season alone 365 tonnes realised $514 050, while employment was provided for nearly 2 000 workers.

Much encouraged by this success, the department in 1969 began to develop a second tea estate – in the Majola area of the Umzimvubu district. In 1970 about 35 ha was planted to seedlings. The estate now covers an area of 280 ha and on at least 80 ha the tea has already reached maturity. Some 500 men and women are employed and a processing plant will be built on the estate in the near future.

Some progress has also been made in the establishment of coffee plantations. Seedlings of the Arabica type were imported from Natal in 1965 and planted at Lambasi, not far from the Magwa tea estate. Additional seedlings were raised in a new nursery in the district of Umzimvubu. In 1968, about 30 ha was planted to coffee seedlings at Glengazi but unfavourable conditions soon put an end to this experiment. Thereafter it was

decided to extend the area under coffee at Lambasi where conditions turned out to be better suited. At present, 150 ha is under coffee at Lambasi and a processing plant, commenced by the engineering services branch in 1974, will be commissioned in the near future. Meanwhile, another small area in the Umgazana Valley near Port St Johns has been experimentally planted to coffee.

Transkei may very well become an important producer of Phormium tenax (New Zealand hemp) which is used in the manufacture of grain bags, a commodity for which there is always a keen demand in Southern Africa, more particularly the Republic of South Africa which produces 100 million bags of maize and 16 million bags of wheat in a good year.

In the 1950s various fibre crops were experimentally planted and Phormium tenax proved to be the most successful. In 1955 experimental plantings were established on a large farm of the South African Bantu Trust in the Butterworth district in the south. The first plants were imported from Natal but later a local nursery was successfully established.

Soon afterwards plantations were established on four Bantu Trust farms in the Gcuwa (formerly Butterworth) district which today comprise an area of 1 053 ha which annually yields some 8 200 tonnes of green leaf.

Success in this region persuaded the department to look elsewhere for suitable areas for Phormium tenax plantations. The choice fell on the Lusikisiki district where tea was doing so well. Some 725 ha has been planted to this fibre crop in the Lambasi area. The annual yield of green leaf at 12 000 tonnes is much higher than that in Gcuwa because precipitation at Lambasi is much higher.

Developments in the Phormium tenax industry are an excellent example of the type of operation envisaged in project farming. Not only has the crop been established successfully, but a large bag factory has been commissioned in Butterworth for the manufacture of five million grain bags a year from fibre grown in Transkei or imported from Black homelands in South Africa.

Green Phormium tenax leaf produced on the Lambasi and Butterworth estates is sold to the

The Lubisi Dam on the Indwe River from which water is drawn for the 3 566-ha irrigation scheme of Qamata. The dam has a double-curvature concrete arch wall, a capacity of 157 million m³ and a water depth of 35,7 metres.

Transkei Development Corporation at $3,68 per tonne. This means that about $58 650 a year is realised from these estates. The TDC itself decorticates the leaf and sells the fibre to the bag factory at Butterworth.

Agriculturalists are agreed that other industrial crops can also be cultivated successfully on project farms in Transkei – apart from tea, coffee, Phormium tenax, fruit and vegetables. Two in particular have been suggested – sugar and cotton.

Extension services

The Department of Agriculture and Forestry operates comprehensive extension services for farmers throughout Transkei. The 280 extension officers in the field have at their disposal a full array of the most modern equipment, including two mobile film units and a host of other audio-visual aids. In a recent year more than 450 film shows were given and were attended by more than 80 000 adults and children.

Since 1970 the radio and local press have been involved on a substantial scale in bringing the value and benefits of proper agricultural methods to the populace. In that year alone a panel of extension officers made 52 broadcasts. In the following year a special programme for farmers, Engolimo, was introduced on the Xhosa service of the South African Broadcasting Corporation and no fewer than 104 half-hour programmes were broadcast. In some of these programmes farmers discussed their problems in the field and afterwards these problems were dealt with by a panel of extension officers.

In 1972 the number of programmes was increased to 156 and the audience to at least 1,7 million. Meanwhile the number of listeners' letters – always a sound barometer of the impact of a programme – had increased to more than 12 000. At present three programmes a week are broadcast to Transkeian farmers and the number of letters received from listeners has grown to more than 20 000. The programmes are still compiled around practical problems encountered by farmers in their everyday farming activities. This approach has proved to be the most effective of all.

In 1970 the department also started publication of its own quarterly agricultural extension magazine, Ulimo Nemfuyo. In addition, in recent years the department has distributed many thousands of handbills, posters, charts and pamphlets on various aspects of crop production and animal husbandry.

Meanwhile, the extension officers devote much of

their time to lectures in the field and, above all, to discussing their problems with individual farmers on a man-to-man basis.

The success or not of these efforts is not easy to gauge. Certainly, there has been no significant improvement in crop and animal production. On the other hand, the quality of livestock has been immeasurably improved during the past ten years and much has been achieved in soil conservation, proper utilisation and conservation of grazing and the orderly resettlement of rural families. Without the painstaking and tireless efforts of the extension officers, these improvements would not have been accomplished.

Training

Extension officers, stock inspectors and other officials in the employ of the Department of Agriculture and Forestry and other agencies are trained at the only agricultural college in Transkei, Tsolo, about 55 km from Umtata. In recent years enrolment at the college has been in the region of 100 and in 1976 the teaching staff was increased from 11 to 13. Fees are only $37 a year and cover tuition, all text-books, sports equipment and dues, and accommodation. Students who are unable to pay even these modest fees, may apply to the Transkeian government for a scholarship. In fact, in any one year scholarships are awarded to about one-third of the students.

The entry qualification is Junior Certificate (ten years of schooling), but in recent years students with higher scholastic qualifications have been attracted to Tsolo. For instance, of the 42 new students admitted in 1975, fourteen had completed Form IV or Form V. This means not only an improvement in the general quality of the students but also that the standard of tuition offered can be raised. In 1975 the two main courses offered were completely revised. Both the stock inspectors course and the general course last 30 months and after successful completion of either, the student is awarded the appropriate diploma which entitles him to seek employment with the government. So far it has been possible to place all diplomaed students in employment. In the past ten years alone there were 290 such students. The courses are wide-ranging and maintain a sound balance between practice and theory.

The training of extension officers does not end

Students being instructed in poultry husbandry at the Tsolo College of Agriculture. In recent years enrolment at the college has been about 100. The courses comprise both theory and practice. The grounds of the college are 1 370 ha in extent.

with the acquisition of a diploma. Each year in-service training courses for these officials are conducted throughout Transkei. The particular subjects covered vary from year to year, depending on what aspect of agriculture requires particular emphasis in any given year.

The grounds of the college comprise 1 370 ha, granted to the United Transkeian Territories General Council by the government of the Cape Colony in 1904, for the purpose of establishing an agricultural school. Today this area is utilised as follows: irrigated lands (10 ha), arable dry lands (80 ha), gardens (2 ha), orchard (one ha), cultivated pastures (30 ha), paddocks (5 ha), forest (50 ha), project farms (150 ha), buildings (10 ha), fish dams and breeding ponds (7 ha), veld fenced into grazing camps (1 024 ha). In addition, one hectare has been set aside for use by Jongilizwe College, a special training school for the sons of chiefs and headmen.

The project farms represent an interesting and highly successful facet of the training programme of the college. In their final year – i.e. after they have successfully completed 18 months of theoretical and practical training – all students are required to operate on a communal basis, four small farmsteads where they are expected to apply in practice the knowledge acquired in the classrooms. They put on several demonstrations a year and run field trials to illustrate proper fertilisation, planting times and cultivation. In addition, they are taught to draw up a balance sheet to reflect their operations. In 1974-75, for instance, the projects showed a combined net income of $2 300.

The college runs its own large herd of various breeds of cattle, largely for demonstration purposes. Of the total of 330 in 1974-75, 199 were Brown Swiss, 36 Frisians and 29 Pondo/Nguni. In the same year the herd also produced 140 000 kg of milk.

The college's sheep flock numbered 347 in 1974-75 of which the vast majority were Dohne Merino, but a flock of Dorpers was introduced recently. Wool production has considerable potential in Transkei and these sheep are used to train students in all aspects of sheep husbandry and wool production. In 1974-75 the college's flock produced 2,72 kg of wool per adult animal – which is considerably more than the average yield of Transkeian flocks.

Pigs, poultry and horses are also kept for teaching and demonstration purposes.

Similarly, much attention is devoted to instruction in field husbandry on the main farm which is

highly mechanised. About 28 ha of dry lands are put to maize every year and the average annual yield is 30 bags per hectare – which shows that the maize harvest of Transkei – about two bags per hectare – can be vastly increased by implementing proper production methods such as those applied at Tsolo. There are also two hectares of lucerne under irrigation and, for the rest, the farm produces mostly silage and hay for the livestock. National maize and sorghum trials are also held annually.

Farmers organisations

There are two main types of farmers organisations in Transkei – co-operative credit societies and co-operative agricultural companies.

The first credit society was formed in 1927 and by 1930 there were 28 such societies receiving deposits from and granting loans to members. These societies reached the peak of their activities in 1959 when there were 30 with total assets of some $57 500 and 5 500 members. Subsequent years saw a steady decline in the importance of these societies and by the end of 1975 there were only 12 left. Throughout their existence most of these credit institutions had been beset by serious problems arising from lack of proper control. Financial control has been tightened up considerably in the remaining societies and they are likely to continue to play a role of some importance in providing credit facilities to the small farmer.

Of more significance are the co-operative agricultural companies, the first of which was established in 1966. They are modelled on the agricultural co-operative societies of South Africa which have played an indispensable role in the development of South Africa's agriculture industry. Indeed, they are controlled in terms of the South African Co-operative Societies Act (no. 29 of 1939). This Act was in 1966 amended by the Transkei Legislative Assembly to provide for the appointment by the Transkeian Department of Agriculture and Forestry of a director for each co-operative company, a registrar of co-operative societies and inspectors to assist in controlling the activities of the co-operatives.

Today there are ten such co-operative companies. Not only are they financed by government loans, but the initiative for their establishment was taken by the Department of Agriculture and Forestry.

Tea pickers on the Magwa tea estates in the district of Lusikisiki. All tea produced here is sold in South Africa. In the 1974/75 season the estates employed nearly 2 000 Transkeians and produced 365 tonnes of tea. A second tea estate has been launched near Port St Johns.

They provide a wide range of services to their members. They make available at reasonable prices approved seed, fertilisers, insecticides, stock remedies and other farming requisites. They also grant credit to their members and assist in the marketing of their produce.

Not unlike the credit societies, the co-operative companies have also experienced some difficulties owing to lack of control over credit facilities. In fact, in 1973-74 these problems led to the liquidation of one of these companies. Thus, the Department of Agriculture and Forestry encourages these co-operatives as far as possible to conduct all sales to their members on a cash basis until such time as their reserve funds are strong enough to withstand losses suffered as a result of bad debts.

In the ten years of its existence the co-operative movement has made rapid strides. As the accompanying table shows, membership has grown from just over 1 300 to nearly 20 000 and sales to members increased from $41 400 to $374 900.

The future

What of the future? As stated at the outset, the potential of Transkei's agriculture industry is considerable by Southern African standards. Recently a survey was conducted on a tract of land situated in the relatively low rainfall region and comprising about eight per cent of the total surface area of the country. It showed that with proper land utilisation and modern husbandry methods this land could produce 225 000 tonnes of maize (the entire present production of all Transkei's farmers), as well as 5 000 tonnes of grain sorghum, 7 400 tonnes of beans, 17 500 tonnes of potatoes and 42 300 tonnes of hay. In addition, the land would be able to support 53 000 large stock units in terms of dairy cattle, 11 000 in terms of beef cattle and 33 000 in terms of sheep and goats!

In the high rainfall and frost-free region along the coast the climate is mild to subtropical. Here large quantities of vegetables, citrus and subtropical fruit can be produced to serve as basis for a processing and canning industry of considerable proportions.

How can this potential be realised? There seems to be one major requirement above all else – that the subsistence agriculture of today be in large measure replaced by commercial farming by both development agencies and individual farmers. This presupposes that many of those thousands who currently look upon the land merely as part of their daily existence and heritage will somehow have to be persuaded to vacate it so that it may be judiciously exploited on a large scale.

Chapter Nine

Forestry

An area of at least 295 000 hectares – or 6,7 per cent of the total surface area – is suitable for afforestation. So far, 192 844 hectares have been set aside as forest reserve. Of this area, some 70 000 ha are under indigenous forest and 61 000 ha have been put under plantations – mostly pine, eucalyptus and wattle.

In the financial year 1974/75, the 61 000 ha of plantations produced 382 000 m³ of timber in the form of logs, poles, laths, droppers and firewood. Total revenue accruing to the State was $1 950 095. This figure can be increased many times over when the full forestry potential of Transkei is exploited.

Like the promotion of general agriculture, the preservation of indigenous forests and afforestation in Transkei have always been beset by peculiar problems. Progress has been slow, mostly because the Xhosa lacked a conservationist tradition and a realisation of the full economic potential of afforestation. In fact, the early history of Transkeian forests is one marked by unchecked despoliation and complete neglect of regeneration and replenishment. As the Nguni tribes centuries ago moved south-east into what is today Transkei, they denuded the indigenous forests, stripping them of wood and timber suitable for firewood and for building kraals (cattle pens) and huts. The chiefs

Hundreds of thousands of saplings being prepared for transplantation in Transkei's forests. Most plantations belong to the State and are managed by the Department of Agriculture and Forestry. In 1974/75 they produced 380 000 m³ of timber.

exercised little or no control over this injudicious exploitation.

Even when the Transkeian Territories were taken over by the government of the Cape Colony after the war of 1877/78, no special arrangements or laws were made for the protection of forests and most accessible forests continued to be despoiled by woodcutters. Gradually, however, some of the magistrates began to take a personal interest in the preservation of natural forests and told the people not to cut wood in certain forests. This prohibition proved ineffective, however, and for a long time there was virtually nothing to stop the rapid destruction of forests.

In 1889 the jurisdiction of the Department of Forestry of the Cape Colony was extended to cover the three territories of Transkei, Tembuland and East Griqualand and, in 1902, Pondoland. The Cape Colony's Forest Act (no. 28 of 1888) was considered too stringent and a special set of regulations was drawn up and proclaimed. In terms of these the people could still get their wattle and firewood free of charge on a written permit issued by the magistrate of the district, on condition that cutting took place under the supervision of forest officers and that no seedlings or saplings on the reserve list were cut. This provision soon became a dead letter, however, owing to the enormous number of permits issued and the insufficiency of staff to control the cutting activities.

Because it had to restrain the destruction that had been carried on unchecked for years, the Department of Forestry was at first far from popular and when in 1895 the Prime Minister of the Cape Col-

ony, Cecil John Rhodes, visited the Transkeian Territories, he informed the people in Umtata that he had decided that the small and inferior forests should be used by the people under the supervision of the magistrates, and the remainder preserved.

In his annual report for 1895 the Conservator of Forests said: 'These instructions have now been carried out in almost all districts of the three territories and the Forestry Department loses a little over half the area of forests, and also vast areas covered with sugar-bush, besides other large areas covered with thorn bush'.

In subsequent years the demarcation of forests to be preserved proceeded apace, but so, unfortunately, did the denudation of the forests which had been handed over.

In 1898 it was reported that the process of destruction had to a certain extent been checked in the demarcated forests. Meanwhile, however, the rapidly increasing population meant an ever greater demand for hut-building materials and it was proposed that special plantations should be established to grow wattles and poles.

This proposal was adopted and plantations were established in many parts of the territories. By 1901, 55 550 ha had been set aside as forest reserve. Of this area, 33 489 ha were indigenous forests and 400 ha plantations.

In 1910 the undemarcated forests were returned to government control and eventually taken over by the Department of Forestry of the Union of South Africa and administered in terms of the Forest Act of 1913. Previously – in 1912 – a policy was adopted whereby no more free removals were allowed from a forest as soon as it was demarcated.

In 1914 forests not recommended for demarcation were handed over to the headmen in all districts (except, provisionally, Eastern Mpondoland) and the Department of Forestry ceased to issue free permits. Those who required free forest produce approached their respective headmen.

When Transkei was granted self-government in 1963, it immediately established its own Department of Agriculture and Forestry which took control of all forests. Transkei's own Forest Act was promulgated in 1969.

Some 61 000 hectares have been put under plantations in Transkei – mostly pine, eucalyptus and wattle. An area of at least 295 000 ha, or 6,7 per cent of the total surface area, is suitable for afforestation and therefore a potential source of wealth.

Progress has been such that today the area of forest reserves is 192 844 ha of which some 70 000 ha are indigenous forest and 61 000 plantations.

Indigenous forests

Natural forests occur in two fairly well-defined areas – the cool southern and eastern slopes of the inland mountains and along the coast.

High forests are found in scattered small to comparatively large patches both inland and near the coast. They are similar in composition to those of the eastern Cape Province of South Africa, but also contain species more common to the north, such as Natal mahogany (*Trichilia emetica*), Umzimbeet (*Millettia grandis*) and flat-crown (*Albizia adianthifolia*). The most important species are yellowwoods (*Podocarpus latifolius, Podocarpus falcatus* and *Podocarpus Henkelii*), stinkwood (*Ocotea bullata*), lemon-wood (*Xymalos monospora*), black ironwood (*Olea capensis var. macrocarpa*), Camdeboo stinkwood (*Celtis africana*), etc.

Despite various control measures, most accessible high forests were heavily exploited over the years and by 1938 it was found that the average volume cut each year actually exceeded the increment. Experiments in planting indigenous trees in worked forests met with very little success. Regular working was abandoned and exploitation restricted to removal of windfalls and dead trees. Exotic trees were also experimentally planted in openings to keep down weeds and act as nurses for the regeneration of indigenous species. Camphor, Californian redwood, Australian blackwood and cypress have grown well and increased the commercial value of those forests in which they were planted, but regeneration under them is rarely successful.

In 1975 provision was made for staff to investigate conditions in the forests, classify them and plan operations in general – with a view to more intensive management.

In many parts the coast is vulnerable to wind erosion. Where this type of erosion is at its worst, sand dunes and drifts are formed. Reclaiming these drifts is one of the important functions of Transkei's Department of Agriculture and Forestry. The most vulnerable stretches of coastline have been declared demarcated areas and the coastal forests are carefully protected against destruction by both man and sand drifts.

Mangroves are found in the estuaries of many rivers, notably the Umngazana, Bashee and Ntafufu. Detailed investigations of these tree communities are now being made.

150

A few remnants of the once extensive thornveld are still to be found, for example in the Nduli Game Reserve near Umtata.

The rare Pondoland palm *Jubaeopsis caffra* is found only on the left banks of the Mtentu and Msikaba Rivers in the district of Lusikisiki, and only within the tidal reach. Another palm, *Phoenix reclinata,* occurs in large numbers in the coastal areas.

The main commercial species of the coastal forests are Cape box *(Buxus macowanii)* and sneezewood *(Ptaeroxylon utile).* Regeneration is very slow and it will be many years before the forests can be reopened for exploitation of these species.

Plantations

From the earliest days of management, plantations of fast-growing hardwoods, such as acacia and eucalyptus, were established to meet the people's need for fuel, laths and poles and other building material. There can be no doubt that these plantations were a vital factor in preventing the total destruction of indigenous forests.

Over the years, management of these plantations was adapted to the changing timber needs of the populace. Rising standards of living inevitably dictated an improvement in the structure of homes. The old-style huts were replaced by rondavels with walls of sods or wattle and daub. In consequence, the people needed more pole-sized building material and less laths. Recently, the emphasis shifted again: there is a substantially increased demand for sawn building timber.

It was only after the establishment in 1936 of the South African Bantu Trust – a national developmental body for all Black areas in South Africa – that large areas of mountain land in Transkei could be reserved for afforestation. The Second World War intervened, and actual afforestation on a large scale could only be commenced in the 'fifties. In 1957 the central Department of Forestry in Pretoria handed over to the South African Bantu Trust all its forests and plantations in Transkei but continued to manage these on behalf of the Trust.

By 1951, some 17 000 ha had been put under plantations, and by March 1965 there were 108 plantations with a total area of 41 000 ha. About 25 per cent of this area was planted to eucalyptus and wattle for the production of firewood and hut-building material, while the remainder comprised coniferous plantations for the production of saw timber.

In March 1975, the 61 255 ha of plantations were made up as follows: 46 051 ha of soft-woods, 10 660 ha of eucalyptus, 2 648 ha of wattle and 1 896 ha of other species. These plantations belong to the State and are managed by the Department of Agriculture and Forestry. In addition, 1 587 ha of wattles are owned by village management boards.

In 1974/75 these plantations produced 381 694 m^3 of logs, poles, laths, droppers and firewood. Of this, 42 397 m^3 was sold to state sawmills and preservative plants, 146 112 m^3 to long-term private contractors and 193 186 m^3 to other purchasers. This volume of timber was processed and sold as follows: 105 706 m^3 saw timber, 103 580 m^3 pulp-wood, 59 953 m^3 poles, 5 425 m^3 laths and droppers, 95 474 m^3 firewood and 11 556 m^3 kraal-wood. In the same year state sawmills produced 3 246 m^3 furniture and box timber, 9 164 m^3 structural timber, 839 m^3 dressed timber, 372 m^3 hardwood and 7 412 m^3 treated poles and droppers.

In 1974/75 the forest industry as a whole provided employment for 7 500 people. When finally the full forestry potential of Transkei is realised, this industry will be able to support many times that number. This is of great significance to the future economic development of Transkei as the country will need every job opportunity that can be created within its borders with a view to reducing the large number of migrant workers who have to sell their labour outside Transkei.

A substantial proportion of the timber produced is exported to the Republic of South Africa, but in proportion as living standards rise and the local demand for timber increases, the volume of timber available for export will decrease. In fact, it has been estimated that by the year 1990 the entire production of the area under plantations today will be needed to meet all local requirements and that thereafter timber will have to be imported unless the plantations are increased substantially. Such a situation – where timber will have to be imported – is, however, unlikely to occur. Not only has Transkei the physical resources – land, soil and climate – for the development of a comparatively large forest and timber industry, but the government is very much aware of the economic benefits to the country of full but judicious exploitation of the potential. So much so that there is a distinct possibility that private initiative will sooner or later be involved on a large scale. Already 28 sawmills are in the hands of private entrepreneurs, including a large one in the Umzimkulu district which was commissioned in March 1976. It was established in co-operation with the Transkei Development Corporation and represents a capital investment of some $3,5 million.

Chapter Ten

Social Security

The concept of official social services is relatively new to Transkei; yet in the financial year 1976/77 the Transkei government budgeted $ 23 304 750 for social benefits – the largest single item of expenditure in the national accounts.

Since time immemorial the social system of the Cape Nguni, of whom the Xhosa people are a segment, has been such that the needy and destitute are cared for by the family or clan as a whole. In the early days, before contact was made with the White man and his systems, there was no government or authority which expended monies on allowances, pensions or grants. It was the duty of the young to care for the aged, and the privilege of the healthy and strong to see to the needs of the handicapped – all within the context of the family, clan or tribe.

To a considerable extent this is still the position today, particularly in the more remote parts of the country. In proportion as industrialisation and, consequently, urbanisation of the population has increased, the people of Transkei have been subjected to the same kind of pressures which in other developing or developed countries have tended to disrupt family and community life and detrimentally affect the social security inherent in the fabric of traditional society and social systems.

A nursing sister on her way to hospital. In many areas of social security there is close liaison between the Transkeian Departments of Health and the Interior, particularly in the field of disability grants. This year $23-million will be spent on social services.

First in the field of organised social services were the various Christian denominations, notably the Methodist, Anglican, Roman Catholic and Dutch Reformed Churches, all of whom have done valuable work in Transkei and to this day play an indispensable part in the overall national programme for caring for the needy, destitute and handicapped. Several of their institutions, notably the Efata School for the Blind and Deaf of the Dutch Reformed Church and the Holy Cross Children's Home of the Roman Catholic Church, are models of their kind and much beloved and respected by all the people of Transkei.

Transkei has always followed the same system in providing social and welfare services as that applicable in the Republic of South Africa: the State and various private organisations have entered into an unwritten but highly effective partnership. The State has assumed responsibility for pensions and various disability grants, while it subsidises the work of private organisations in virtually all spheres of social work.

At some time or another, many private welfare organisations of South Africa entered the field in Transkei. Notable among the earliest efforts were those of the Cripple Care Society of East London and Border, backed by the National Council for Cripple Care of South Africa. First in the field with a number of trained welfare workers was the South African Bantu Trust (SABT), a general developmental agency for all Black homelands called into being by the Bantu Land and Trust Act of 1936. The social workers were all women and were trained at the agricultural college at Tsolo near Umtata. The training course was later discon-

tinued and these workers ceased to operate, but while they were active, they blazed the trail for all other welfare workers who came after them.

The situation was materially altered in 1963 when Transkei became the first Black homeland to be granted self-government in terms of the central government's policy of separate development for the various peoples of South Africa. Among the State departments established by the government of Transkei in 1963 was that of the Interior and on 1 August 1964 a Black social science graduate of the University College (now University) of Fort Hare was appointed welfare officer in this department. In the financial year 1966/67 four more officers were appointed – one each for the regional authority areas of Maluti, Qaukeni, Gcalekaland and Emigrant Thembuland. In 1969 their ranks were increased by two more officers. Today the welfare section of Transkei's Department of the Interior is staffed by 16 welfare officers. The officer in control is styled Chief Welfare Officer and is stationed at head office in Umtata. The others are located at various points throughout the country. They are all highly qualified: many are in possession of a BA degree in social sciences and the remainder are diplomaed students in social welfare work.

The major function of these officers is co-ordinating existing welfare services and assisting in the development of community social services. They also administer national relief schemes as and when required. The major operation so far in this field was executed in 1969 when droughts over several seasons had culminated in severe hardship among several sections of the population. Over a period of six months some 9 500 people were provided with emergency employment in thirteen stricken areas and no fewer than 300 000 children of pre-school and primary school age were given a daily ration of protein-enriched food. These emergency relief services were carried over into 1970 when 7 350 adults were employed and 360 000 toddlers were fed emergency rations.

In addition, the welfare section of the Department of the Interior administers the payment of pensions and grants payable to the aged, and to chronically ill and indigent persons. They are also closely involved in the provision of public health services, particularly the administration of clinics in rural areas.

A new housing estate for factory workers at Butterworth. In rural areas Transkeians build their own homes, but at the growth points housing is provided by various agencies, notably the Transkei Development Corporation, in conjunction with the entrepreneur.

As stated earlier, provision of social services in Transkei, as in the Republic of South Africa, is the joint responsibility of both the State and private organisations. Before a private organisation is allowed to operate in Transkei, it has to be registered with the Transkeian Department of the Interior in terms of the provisions of the Welfare Organisations Act, 1947 (No. 40 of 1947). Current policy is that only those organisations are registered whose management committees comprise only Transkeian citizens, but all foreign assistance is welcomed, particularly in those fields where there are not yet sufficient qualified Transkeian personnel to launch or run the welfare organisation. What usually happens in these instances is that South African Whites advise and assist Transkeian committees until such time as they are capable of administering the operation themselves.

External organisations, usually under White management, may not initiate independent operations in Transkei. Instead, the law requires that they co-operate with existing Transkeian organisations on a basis mutually agreed upon. The law also allows Transkeian welfare organisations to affiliate with national institutions in the Republic of South Africa.

This is of material advantage to Transkei as local bodies benefit from the experience and expertise of long established organisations operating in the same fields. The only requirement is that a copy of the draft document of affiliation be submitted for approval by the Transkei Department of the Interior a month before the affiliation is due to take effect.

The Holy Cross Children's Home at Cala was established in August 1967 and provides accommodation for one hundred children in need of care. The home is subsidised by means of grants-in-aid on the same level as those applicable in the Republic of South Africa.

Until quite recently adoption by law of orphans or abandoned children was unkown in Transkei. As stated earlier, such children have traditionally been cared for by the family or clan. As elsewhere, however, the process of industrialisation and urbanisation has led to an increase in the number of abandoned children who cannot be cared for in the traditional family context. Such children are usually admitted to the Holy Cross Home until suitable adoptive parents can be found. The numbers involved are not large by international standards but – as elsewhere – the number of adopted children is exceeded by those awaiting adoption.

Transkei's physically handicapped are catered for by the Efata Welfare Organisation of the Dutch

Reformed Church, the Ikwezi Lokusa Rehabilitation and Sheltered Employment Scheme and the Ilinge Handicraft Centre, a State institution.

The Efata Welfare Organisation has developed out of the Efata School for the Blind and Deaf and today trains handicapped Blacks in spinning (mohair) and weaving, masonry, carpentry and needlework. It also trains blind persons as telephone switchboard operators. Most of the trainees have school certificates from the Efata School for the Blind and Deaf.

Similarly, pupils who complete their schooling at the Glen Avent Special School for Cerebral-Palsied mostly proceed to the Ikwezi Lokusa Rehabilitation and Sheltered Employment Scheme where they are provided with sheltered employment. As in the case of Efata, the handicapped workers are housed in hostels while a modest amount is deducted from their weekly wages for board and lodging.

These two institutions accept handicapped people not only from their own schools – Efata and Glen Avent – but also any others for whom accommodation can be found. As a matter of policy, a certain number of physically fit workers are also admitted as it has been established that handicapped people are far more likely to adapt successfully to the exigencies of everyday life if they associate with normal people as much as possible.

Pensions and Grants

The accompanying table shows that in the financial year 1974/75 the Transkei government paid out $12 774 515 in pensions and grants to 97 319 recipients of all descriptions – old-age pensioners and people handicapped in one way or another.

Social pensions are paid and administered in terms of the Transkei Pensions Act, 1965 (No. 10 of 1965). Old-age pensions are paid to all males who have reached the age of 65 and to all females 60 years and older.

Disability grants are paid to those certified more than 50 per cent unfit for remunerative work in the open labour market and are awarded on either a permanent or temporary basis, depending on the chief disabling factor and the degree of disability. For instance, if the chief disabling factor is tuberculosis and the district surgeon decides that the

patient may be cured of the disease, the grant is payable for a specified period of not less than one year. On the other hand, those who have lost an arm or leg are considered completely unfit and awarded a disability grant on a permanent basis. The minimum age for the payment of such grants is 19 years in the case of blind persons and 16 years in all other cases, unless the person concerned is still a scholar at some educational institution.

Social benefits are paid every second month – in January, March, May, July, September and November. On each of these six pay days every recipient is paid a basic pension of $2,30 plus an allowance of $32,20. These amounts compare favourably with those paid in most other Black African countries.

Special benefits are paid to workers injured while on duty. In terms of the Workmen's Compensation Act, 1941 (No. 30 of 1941) of the Republic of South Africa (still applicable in Transkei) an Accident Fund was established to compensate those workers disabled in the line of duty, or who contract a scheduled industrial disease. All employers contribute to this fund. When the disablement exceeds 30 per cent, Black workers are usually paid a lump sum. These monies are invested on behalf of the workers concerned and the interest is paid into trust accounts which are administered by the welfare section of the Transkei Department of the Interior. Payments are usually made every second month but from time to time the beneficiary may apply for an advance.

Table 1. Pensions and grants awarded in 1974/75

	Number of beneficiaries	Amount paid out $
Old-age pensioners	67 717	8 866 878
Blind persons	1 614	216 416
Disability grantees	27 532	3 631 542
Needy ex-soldiers	16	2 398
Discharged lepers	440	57 279
	97 319	12 774 515

The exchange rate of the Rand as at 1976/08/31 was R1,00 = $1,15.

A typical Transkeian family group in the rural areas. One of the major functions of the official welfare services is to involve such families throughout Transkei in social services for the benefit of the local community. Some $13-million a year is spent on grants and pensions.

Chapter Eleven

The National Economy and Demography

Over the past decade and more, a sound basis for economic development has been laid in Transkei. In the three years prior to independence, various development agencies, including the Transkei government, expended $350 million to promote inter alia economic growth in Transkei.

Progress in industrialisation has been particularly notable in recent years. By March 1975, 24 new industries had been established in Transkei by South African and other foreign entrepreneurs. This represented a capital investment of nearly $33 million.

Much is being done to improve the infrastructure necessary for further economic expansion. Expenditure in this regard has increased by more than 100 per cent since 1972/73. The country has a network of 8 800 km of roads and more than 200 km of railways. A new international airport and a large automatic telephone exchange are due to be commissioned soon.

In addition, Transkei has established a tradition of political stability coupled with sound government administration. The country was granted self-government in 1963 and from that year in particular Transkeians gradually took over from South African officials the responsibility for the administration of their own country.

The construction industry of Transkei is hard pressed to keep up with the demand for new buildings, particularly in the capital Umtata. One of the new projects nearing completion in Umtata is a sports stadium which will also be used for other purposes.

Perhaps the country's greatest economic asset is the size and quality of its labour force. During the past few years some 24 000 workers have entered the labour market each year. These men and women have shown a remarkable degree of adaptability to an industrialised system of production. And behind this labour force is one of the most successful educational systems in all of Black Africa.

Transkei has another major advantage over most other developing African countries: on its doorstep is a vast and ready market, comprising not only the Republic of South Africa with its large purchasing power, but also several other developing countries, such as Lesotho, Botswana, Swaziland and Rhodesia.

Like that of most developing countries in Africa, Transkei's economy is dualistic in nature. This means that most people are still engaged in subsistence activities, particularly in the agricultural sector, while a relatively small but thriving industrial and commercial sector has been established which has an assured potential for growth. A Black entrepreneurial class is emerging, largely due to the efforts of the Transkei Development Corporation, a statutory body which, in one form or another, has been active in Transkei since the early 'sixties. Today it has a share capital of some $87 million.

As in most developing African countries, the greatest challenge for the future lies in agriculture, which has not yet been commercialised to any marked extent. It is largely still tied to the so-called 'cattle-complex' and the belief that every tribesman is entitled to occupy land for farming (see the

chapter on Agriculture). A prerequisite for development in agriculture is land reform, and land reform presupposes a radical modification of traditions and attitudes acquired over many centuries. Even in this difficult area there has been some notable progress in recent years.

National accounts

As in the case of most developing countries, it has as yet not been practicable to compile a complete set of national accounts for Transkei. Estimates have, however, been made of the gross domestic product (GDP), gross national income (GNI) and fixed investment of the public sector.

The GDP has been estimated since 1959/60. Owing to recently improved accounting methods, as well as the more reliable information that has become available since 1969/70, the estimates for the period before 1969/70 are not directly comparable with those made for the period after 1969/70. In the discussion that follows, the accounts are those of Transkei before the transfer of the districts of Herschel and Glen Grey from Ciskei to Transkei in December 1975.

The increase in the GDP of Transkei from $50,1 million in 1959/60 to $71,6 million in 1968/69 represents an average annual growth rate of 4,3 per cent (see Table 1). The fluctuations in the GDP (notably in 1960/61, 1966/67 and 1967/68) are largely due to the variability in agricultural production which comprises the biggest component of the GDP. Owing to the prevalence of traditional farming methods, agricultural production in any given year is closely related to the rainfall of that year.

From 1969/70 to 1973/74 the GDP increased from $97,2 million to $150,9 million – an average annual increase of 11,9 per cent, varying from 3,3 per cent in 1970/71 to 20,9 per cent in 1971/72. This growth rate is significantly higher than that of the period 1959/60 to 1968/69.

While agriculture, hunting, forestry and fishing made the largest contribution to the GDP (an average of 34,8 per cent over the period 1959/60 to 1973/74) manufacturing, electricity, gas and water and construction showed the most rapid growth. Their contribution increased from 13,6 per cent in 1969/70 to 15,2 per cent in 1973/74. This increase is in large measure attributable to the successful

The Transkei Development Corporation has played a major role in development. By March 1975 it had invested $38,18 million in its own enterprises, including two plants to decorticate sisal for the manufacture of grain bags in Butterworth.

efforts which have been made to promote industrial development at Umtata and Butterworth. This trend is likely to continue as further industrial activity in these and other centres of Transkei is stimulated.

Even now, the economy of Transkei is showing signs of becoming more market orientated. Table 1 shows that non-market production increased at an average annual rate of 9,8 per cent after 1969/70, compared with an average annual increase of 13,5 per cent in market production during the same period. At the same time there was a decline – from 46,2 per cent in 1969/70 to 42,2 per cent in 1973/74 – in the share of non-market production.

Animal and plant production have been the main contributors to total agricultural production (with 61,7 and 34,8 per cent respectively in 1973/74). The major single contributions to the GDP in 1973/74 were made by maize (33,1 per cent) and cattle (19,4 per cent).

Prior to 1968/69 there was virtually no mining and quarrying at all. Production increased from $14 950 in 1969/70 to $88 550 (0,1 per cent of the GDP) in 1970/71, however, and then declined to $11 500 in 1973/74.

The value added to production by manufacturing, electricity, gas and water and construction showed an average annual increase of 14,3 per cent after 1969/70, while the relative contribution of this sector to the GDP also increased, particularly in the latter period. The contribution of the market production in this sector increased from 28,9 per cent in 1959/60 to 43,0 per cent in 1973/74.

The contribution by trade, catering and accommodation to production showed an average annual increase of 4,5 per cent before 1969/70 and 8,7 per cent after 1969/70. The contribution of this sector to the GDP also increased from 11,6 per cent in 1959/60 to 13,4 per cent in 1973/74.

As far as transport, storage and communication are concerned, the value added to production increased by 10,7 per cent a year prior to 1969/70 and by 7,1 per cent after that year. Except in the last three years of the period under review, there was a sustained increase in the relative contribution of this sector to the GDP.

The value added by the sector finance, insurance, real estate and business services rose at an average annual rate of 5,3 per cent before 1969/70 and by 11,2 per cent a year afterwards. The relative contribution of this sector to the GDP remained fairly constant.

Table 1. GDP of Transkei according to type of economic activity and market and non-market production, 1959/60 – 1973/74

Economic activity	$'000											
	1959/60		1960/61		1961/62		1962/63		1963/64		1964/65	
	Amount	%	Amount	%	Amount	%	Amount	%	Amount	%	Amount	%
Agriculture, hunting, forestry and fishing	21 538	43,0	26 029	45,5	23 466	41,8	25 293	42,2	26 651	41,7	21 274	34,6
Market	4 448		4 158		4 049		4 686		4 793		3 375	
Non-market	17 090		21 871		19 417		20 607		21 858		17 899	
Mining and quarrying (Market)	—	—	—	—	—	—	—	—	—	—	—	—
Manufacturing, electricity, gas and water, and construction	2 942	5,9	3 811	6,7	3 404	6,1	3 557	5,9	4 004	6,3	4 003	6,5
Market	850		918		1 045		1 120		1 326		1 490	
Non-market	2 092		2 893		2 359		2 437		2 678		2 513	
Manufacturing	1)											
Market												
Non-market												
Electricity, gas and water												
Market												
Non-market												
Construction												
Market												
Non-market												
Wholesale and retail trade, catering and accommodation (Market)	5 805	11,6	6 596	11,6	7 393	13,1	8 186	13,6	8 979	14,0	9 776	15,9
Transport, storage and communications (Market)	1 107	2,2	1 187	2,1	1 395	2,5	1 643	2,7	1 837	2,9	2 025	3,3
Finance, real estate and business services	1 676	3,3	1 789	3,1	1 905	3,4	2 006	3,4	2 112	3,3	2 217	3,6
Market	1 178		1 283		1 390		1 482		1 578		1 673	
Non-market	498		506		515		524		534		544	
Community, social and personal services	17 065	34,0	17 744	31,0	18 593	33,1	19 329	32,2	20 372	31,8	22 221	36,1
Market	9 528		10 071		10 785		11 373		12 276		13 978	
Non-market	7 537		7 673		7 808		7 956		8 096		8 243	
Public administration (Market)	3 459	6,9	3 820	6,7	4 167	7,4	4 475	7,5	4 947	7,7	6 119	9,9
Education services (Market)	3 964	7,9	4 026	7,0	4 096	7,3	4 166	6,9	4 377	6,8	4 737	7,7
Health services (Market)	1 270	2,5	1 314	2,3	1 520	2,7	1 659	2,8	1 802	2,8	1 858	3,0
Other marketed services (Market)	835	1,7	911	1,6	1 002	1,8	1 073	1,8	1 150	1,8	1 264	2,1
Subsistence services (Non-market)	7 537	15,0	7 673	13,4	7 808	13,9	7 956	13,2	8 096	12,7	8 243	13,4
Grand Total	50 133	100,0	57 156	100,0	56 156	100,0	60 014	100,0	63 955	100,0	61 516	100,0
Market	22 916	45,7	24 213	42,4	26 057	46,4	28 490	47,5	30 789	48,1	32 317	52,5
Non-market	27 217	54,3	32 943	57,6	30 099	53,6	31 524	52,5	33 166	51,9	29 199	47,5

1) Not available.

	1965/66		1966/67		1967/68		1968/69		1969/70		1970/71		1971/72		1972/73		1973/74	
$'000	Amount	%	Amount	%	Amount	%	Amount	%	Amount	%	Amount	%	Amount	%	Amount	%	Amount	%
	26 443	38,1	34 078	42,7	22 786	31,7	19 694	27,5	36 394	37,4	31 775	31,7	43 922	36,2	43 085	33,6	53 157	35,2
	4 497		4 809		4 620		5 118		2 957		2 639		3 200		4 967		5 833	
	21 946		29 269		18 166		14 576		33 437		29 136		40 722		38 118		47 324	
	—	—	—	—	—	—	1	—	15		89	0,1	43	—	29	—	12	
	3 795	5,4	4 584	5,7	4 902	6,8	4 840	6,8	13 230	13,6	15 174	15,1	17 326	14,3	19,256	15,0	22 957	15,2
	1 664		1 909		2 171		2 599		4 097		5 383		6 644		7 533		9 875	
	2 131		2 675		2 731		2 241		9 133		9 791		10 682		11 723		13 082	
									10 185	10,5	11 011	10,9	12 116	10,0	13 600	10,6	15 196	10,1
									2 759		3 059		3 409		3 977		4 340	
									7 426		7 952		8 707		9 623		10 856	
									147	0,1	167	0,2	170	0,2	231	0,2	245	0,1
									147		167		170		231		245	
									—		—		—		—		—	
									2 898	3,0	3 996	4,0	5 040	4,1	5 425	4,2	7 516	5,0
									1 191		2 157		3 065		3 325		5 290	
									1 707		1 839		1 975		2 100		2 226	
	10 568	15,2	11 364	14,2	12 170	17,0	12 956	18,1	14 359	14,8	15 852	15,8	16 816	13,9	18 439	14,4	20 222	13,4
	2 240	3,2	2 308	2,9	2 414	3,4	2 849	4,0	5 126	5,3	5 850	5,8	6 481	5,3	6 484	5,1	6 867	4,6
	2 326	3,6	2 459	3,1	2 575	3,5	2 652	3,6	5 268	5,4	6 249	6,2	6 710	5,5	7 278	5,7	8 314	5,5
	1 773		1 895		2 001		2 068		2 946		3 589		3 863		4 239		5 077	
	553		564		574		584		2 322		2 660		2 847		3 039		3 237	
	23 983	34,5	25 078	31,4	26 988	37,6	28 619	40,0	22 815	23,5	25 461	25,3	30 168	24,8	33 625	26,2	39 400	26,1
	15 594		16 538		18 291		19 764		22 815		25 461		30 168		33 625		39 400	
	8 389		8 540		8 697		8 855		—		—		—		—			
	7 301	10,5	7 594	9,5	7 637	10,6	8 243	11,5	10 015	10,3	11 074	11,0	13 291	10,9	14 194	11,1	16 208	10,7
	4 942	7,1	5 281	6,6	6 785	9,5	7 291	10,2	7 365	7,6	8 270	8,2	9 832	8,1	11 661	9,0	13 659	9,0
	1 996	2,9	2 225	2,8	2 374	3,3	2 644	3,7	2 772	2,9	3 244	3,2	3 962	3,3	4 457	3,5	5 968	4,0
	1 355	1,9	1 438	1,8	1 495	2,1	1 586	2,2	2 663	2,7	2 873	2,9	3 083	2,5	3 313	2,6	3 565	2,4
	8 389	12,1	8 540	10,7	8 697	12,1	8 855	12,4	—		—		—		—			
	69 355	100,0	79 871	100,0	71 835	100,0	71 611	100,0	97 207	100,0	100 450	100,0	121 466	100,0	128 196	100,0	150 929	100,0
	36 336	52,4	38 823	48,6	41 667	58,0	45 355	63,3	52 315	53,8	58 863	58,6	67 215	55,3	75 316	58,8	87 286	57,8
	33 019	47,6	41 048	51,4	30 168	42,0	26 256	36,7	44 892	46,2	41 587	41,4	54 251	44,7	52 880	41,2	63 643	42,2

The exchange rate of the Rand as at 1976/08/31 was R1,00 = $1,15.

The sector community, social and personal services added 6,1 per cent a year before 1969/70 and 14,7 per cent a year thereafter.

The public sector has played an important role in the growth and development of the Transkeian economy. In the latter years of the period under review, its contribution to the GDP was in the region of 30 per cent. Throughout the entire period there was a steady annual increase in the value added to production by this sector.

Although the contribution by Black Transkeians to the GDP declined somewhat in relative terms – from 80,0 to 72,7 per cent – prior to 1969/70, their contribution in absolute terms to production increased significantly. After 1969/70 their relative contribution to the GDP remained fairly constant, fluctuating between 78,0 and 80,6 per cent.

Whether the growth rate or the structural change in the GDP is taken as criterion, it is clear that appreciable development has already occurred in the economy of Transkei.

The gross national income (GNI) of Transkei increased from $106 million in 1960 to $468 million in 1973 (see Table 2). The GNI represents the income derived by permanent inhabitants of Transkei (including those temporarily absent) from participation in production both inside and outside Transkei.

The GNI per capita increased by 201,7 per cent – from $67 in 1960 to $201 in 1973. Significant, too, is the fact that the relative contribution of Black Transkeians to the GNI increased from 92,0 per cent in 1960/61 to 96,3 per cent in 1973/74.

Table 2 shows that the largest proportion of income is earned by migrants working outside Transkei. Migrant income has had an increasingly important effect on the Transkeian economy. This is evident from the increase of its relative contribution to the GNI from 48,3 per cent in 1960/61 to 69,6 per cent in 1973/74.

The gross fixed investment by the public sector in Transkei is given in Table 3. There was a sustained increase in capital investment between 1959/60 and 1973/74, except for 1972/73 when the South African government temporarily curtailed funds.

Table 2. The GNI and income per capita, 1960/61, 1970/71 and 1973/74

National accounts estimates	1960/61		1970/71		1973/74	
	Amount	%	Amount	%	Amount	%
Gross national income ($ million)	105,8	100,0	300,5	100,0	468,4	100,0
Blacks	97,3	92,0	286,2	95,3	450,9	96,3
GDP	46,2	43,7	78,2	26,1	121,7	26,0
Commuters	—	—	2,0	0,7	3,2	0,7
Migrants	51,1	48,3	206,0	68,5	326,0	69,6
Non-Blacks	8,5	8,0	14,3	4,7	17,5	3,7
Income per capita ($)						
GDP (Blacks)	33,4		46,0		63,3	
GDP + commuters (Blacks)	33,4		47,2		64,4	
GNI (Blacks)[1]	62,1		138,0		192,1	
GNI (Blacks + Non-Blacks)[2]	66,7		143,8		201,3	

1) GNI (Blacks) = GDP (Blacks) + commuters + migrants

2) GNI = GDP (Blacks) + commuters + migrants + income of permanent non-Black inhabitants.

The exchange rate of the Rand as at 1976/08/31 was R1,00 = $1,15.

The South African Bantu Trust, a general developmental agency for all Black homelands, was the major investor until 1970/71, after which the Transkei government, with $8,6 million (31,1 per cent) in 1971/72 and $13,9 million (49,1 per cent) in 1973/74, played an increasingly important role as it progressively took over the functions of the SABT in Transkei.

In 1973/74 the SABT's investment was largely accounted for by the establishment of towns and the purchase of land.

Significant contributions to investment in Transkei have been made by the Transkei Development Corporation, formerly the Xhosa Development Corporation, the Cape Provincial Administration, local government and the central government departments of South Africa.

Agriculture and forestry
This is fully discussed in separate chapters elsewhere in this book.

Mining
Deposits of minerals such as travertine, zircon, rutile and ilmenite, suitable for mining, have been found, while platinum group metals, sulphides of copper and nickel and coal deposits are known to occur in Transkei.

Geological surveys also indicate the presence of large deposits of dolerite. The presence of kaolinitic clays and soils, suitable for the manufacture of bricks and ceramics, is also postulated in view of the prevailing climatic conditions. The geological formations of Transkei are such as to make it seem worthwhile to pursue further exploration into the occurrence of uranium.

Exploration by diamond-drills has confirmed the presence of approximately one million cubic metres of travertine on the banks of the Umzimvubu river and 100 000 m³ at the Insinuka Spring. The Bantu Mining Corporation, which was founded in 1969 to promote mining development in all the traditional Black homelands, is planning to exploit both deposits. The travertine may be used either for agricultural lime or bricks.

Activity in the mining sector is expected to gain momentum in proportion as the results of new research and prospecting ventures become available.

Industry
To obviate the need for any further migration of workers from the country, it has been estimated that, between 1975 and 1980, 27 960 new jobs would have to be created in Transkei every year.

As yet, there is little potential in the mining sector and restructuring the country's agricultural sector on market orientated lines will release rather than absorb more labour. It thus seems clear that Transkei, like most developing countries, will have to rely mainly on industrial development as the primary field of employment. The need for industrial development is further underlined by the fact that the country is geographically isolated from major industrial concentrations in South Africa. There is therefore not much opportunity for Transkei residents to obtain employment in South Africa on a commuter basis. Consequently, a large number leave the country as migrant labourers. In 1975 there were some 7 000 commuters and 360 000 migrant labourers.

Unlike many developing countries, which face barriers to the export of manufactured products to developed countries, Transkei has free access to the Southern African market. In addition, the purchasing power of Transkei's Black population amounted to $170 million in 1974/75, providing some scope for the local production of certain consumer goods.

The concessions granted by the South African government to industrialists establishing factories at Transkeian growth points, such as Butterworth and Umtata, as well as the relatively low wage structure at these growth points, will help Transkei to pursue an export-orientated strategy of industrialisation.

Industries in Transkei have so far been established in three ways – by White industrialists in terms of the so-called agency system, by way of enterprises established and managed by the Transkei Development Corporation (TDC) and by the independent activity of Black businessmen. The feasibility of establishing industries on a tripartite basis, involving each of these three groups as shareholders in a single undertaking, is at present being investigated.

In 1968 the South African government announced that its policy of encouraging the decentralisation of industries from the major metropolitan areas would be extended to include the establishment of industries on an agency basis in the traditional Black homelands. This implied that while the industrialist would receive certain concessions and would be assisted by government-sponsored economic and social infrastructural

Table 3. Gross fixed investment by the public sector, 1959/60 to 1973/74

Year	$'000				
	S.A. Government				
	General government departments		SABT		Sub-total
	Amount	% of total	Amount	% of total	
1959/60	558	44,9	—	—	558
1960/61	627	32,2	—	—	627
1961/62	991	39,9	—	—	991
1962/63	1 567	46,8	—	—	1 567
1963/64	2 377	64,1	—	—	2 377
1964/65	468	9,5	—	—	468
1965/66	1 565	19,4	—	—	1 565
1966/67	3 677	37,4	—	—	3 677
1967/68	4 353	41,1	—	—	4 353
1968/69	838	7,1	4 728	40,0	5 566
1969/70	1 080	6,1	7 156	40,2	8 236
1970/71	452	2,5	6 890	38,2	7 342
1971/72	859	3,1	8 574	30,9	9 433
1972/73	1 189	6,2	4 657	24,4	5 846
1973/74	1 436	5,1	5 286	18,6	6 722

$'000							
Public enterprises and corporations		Cape Provincial Administration and local White authorities		Transkei government and other Black authorities		Total	
Amount	% of total	Amount	% of total	Amount	% of total	Amount	% increase on previous year
—	—	540	43,6	143	11,5	1 241	—
736	37,8	486	25,0	97	5,0	1 946	56,8
835	33,5	561	22,6	99	4,0	2 486	27,8
948	28,2	545	16,3	292	8,7	3 352	34,8
111	3,0	848	22,8	375	10,1	3 711	10,7
362	7,3	1 531	30,9	2 589	52,3	4 950	33,4
491	6,0	1 379	17,1	4 643	57,5	8 078	63,2
539	5,5	1 533	15,6	4 080	41,5	9 829	21,7
889	8,3	828	7,8	4 533	42,8	10 603	7,9
1 604	13,6	328	2,8	4 316	36,5	11 814	11,4
4 806	27,0	398	2,2	4 365	24,5	17 805	50,7
3 344	18,6	562	3,1	6 790	37,6	18 038	1,3
8 524	30,7	1 012	3,7	8 747	31,6	27 716	53,7
1 310	6,8	1 755	9,2	10 212	53,4	19 123	− 31,0
5 178	18,2	2 400	8,4	14 131	49,7	28 431	48,7

The exchange rate of the Rand as at 1976/08/31 was R1,00 = $1,15.

development, he would not be able to obtain ownership rights on any land or building in the homeland. In addition, the industrialist signs a contract agreeing that after a specified period (usually 25 years) the enterprise will be sold to Black citizens of the homeland.

The concessions, subject to change, granted to industrialists establishing plants at the growth points Butterworth and Umtata are very favourable by international standards.

The interest rate on loans to finance all assets, excluding land and factory buildings, is the base rate (the long-term domestic stock rate plus 0,5 per cent) less 7,5 per cent. Loans are granted on 80 per cent of the value of land and buildings and 45 per cent of other assets. Land and buildings are regarded as sufficient security for the loans. The subsidised interest applies for a minimum of 10 years. The interest rate on loans to finance factory buildings is the base rate less 3,5 per cent. The South African government also assists with the provision of housing for White personnel which is leased at 2,5 per cent of the cost of the house.

In addition, income tax is reduced by an amount equal to 50 per cent of all wages paid to Blacks employed for the first seven financial years of the plant's operation, and by 30 per cent of the book value (for income tax purposes) of manufacturing plant at the end of the first financial year after establishment. This may be utilised in equal amounts over a period of three years.

These concessions may be converted into non-taxable cash grants if tax is not payable and the concessions cannot be utilised.

All approved costs incurred in moving a factory from the congested Pretoria-Witwatersrand-Vereeniging and Durban-Pinetown areas of South Africa are also reimbursed. In addition, certain transportation rebates are granted, as well as certain percentual preferences on tenders for the supply of manufactured goods to the South African government.

In Transkei, industrial growth through this agency system has taken place mainly at Butterworth. By 31 March 1975, 24 industries had been established under this system – 15 at Butterworth, three at Umtata and six, mainly sawmills, in the rest of Transkei. Another industrial area, Ibeka, is

Building cranes have virtually become a permanent component of the Umtata skyline. Building and construction by the Transkei government, in particular, increased appreciably during the period immediately before independence.

now being developed at Butterworth by the TDC with a view to establishing more agency industries. By March 1975, $1,7 million had been invested in infrastructure there.

Total investment in industries operating under the agency system increased rapidly since 1971 – from less than $5 million to $32,9 million by 31 March 1975 (see Table 4). By 31 March 1975, $6,9 million had been spent by the TDC on housing for agency industrialists and on infrastructure.

By 31 March 1975, 3 531 Transkeians were employed in these industries. Of this labour force, 48 per cent was employed in wood and related product concerns and 40 per cent in textile, clothing and leather industries. By 31 March 1976 the number of Transkeians employed in agency industries had increased to 4 824.

The TDC establishes industries not only on the agency system, but has also established several financed by its own funds. These industries – weaving, furniture and sack factories, three bakeries, two decortication plants and a brewery – employed 1 283 Transkeians in March 1975.

At present the Transkeian entrepreneur is mainly involved in activities in the tertiary sector. Less than two per cent of the business loans granted by the TDC to Transkeian entrepreneurs has been used in secondary sector activity.

Those Transkeians who have ventured into the industrial sector have directed their efforts mainly towards meeting the needs of the local market.

By helping Blacks to establish themselves as industrialists, the proposed tripartite arrangement could have an important bearing on future industrial development in Transkei.

Building and construction

The rate of building and construction work in any developing country is closely related to the pace of economic development. The sustained expansion of the national product of Transkei in the past few years has made increasing demands on the building and construction sector. In addition, the infrastructure created by this sector tends to promote further development in the agricultural and industrial sectors.

Activity in this sector includes the design, production and maintenance of buildings, houses, roads and bridges.

Building and construction by the Transkei government has increased appreciably in the past few

years, particularly at Butterworth and Umtata.

The Transkei government and the SABT budgeted $11,7 million for building and construction in 1974/75, with dams and reservoirs being allocated 11 per cent of the total, boreholes 11 per cent, roads 10 per cent and primary schools 12 per cent.

The TDC has also made important contributions in this sector. It has established infrastructure, erected housing units in Umtata and Butterworth and built factories and commercial buildings.

Black contractors are at present involved in the construction of houses, schools, clinics and extensions to hospitals, and new ways are constantly being found to involve an increasing number of Black entrepreneurs, managers and skilled workers in this strategic sector.

Table 4. Cumulative investment and employment in agency industries in Transkei, 1974 and 1975

Item	Year	
	31 March 1974	31 March 1975
Investment ($'000):		
Total	13 490	32 923
TDC[1]	7 465	20 189
Industrialists	6 025	12 734
Number of establishments	17	24
Black employment	2 287	3 531

1) Building, loans and share capital

The exchange rate of the Rand as at 1976/08/31 was R1,00 = $1,15.

An old (foreground) and new (background) bridge on the road to Port St Johns. The debris in the foreground is a reminder of a recent summer's deluge when the bridge was inundated. The Transkeian government spends $1,2 million a year on roads and bridges.

Commerce and services

There has been sound progress in the commercial and service sector. Until comparatively recently, non-Blacks dominated the commercial sector in Transkei, but of late a vigorous Black entrepreneurial class has started to emerge. By 1974 there were 2 592 Black commerce and service enterprises, more than double the number in 1961 (see Table 5). This is in large measure due to the financial assistance and training in managerial skills given by the TDC. Business loans granted by the TDC to Black businessmen increased from 402 ($3,9 million) on 31 March 1972 to 732 ($7,9 million) on 31 October 1975.

The so-called Transkei Adjustment Committee is also making a major contribution to the establishment of a Black entrepreneurial class. This committee, active since 1964, buys up the businesses or enterprises of those Whites who wish to leave the country. These are initially managed by the TDC until such time as a suitably equipped Transkeian can be found to take over.

Indicative of the progress made by Blacks in the development of Transkei's tourist potential is the fact that by 1975, 29 hotels, including the Transkei Hotel in Umtata, were managed by Blacks.

The purchasing power of Blacks in Transkei doubled in the space of five years, from $85 million in 1970/71 to $170 million in 1974/75, and to stimulate activity in the commercial sector, a formula for the establishment of enterprises is being developed similar to that applicable in the industrial sector, whereby White skill is involved through the agency system. This will make it possible for White and Black entrepreneurs to launch a 'tripartite company', together with the TDC to the advantage of both consumers and Black traders. This means that an increasing number of chain stores, supermarkets and hypermarkets will in time be established in Transkei if the authorities find it possible to make 'tripartite companies' acceptable to the people. Such expansion of activities in the commerce and services sector of the economy will offer increased opportunity for the growth of an entrepreneurial class, which will be particularly significant for future development.

Infrastructure

The annual expenditure on infrastructure which since 1972/73 has more than doubled (from $6,8 to $13,9 million) has been an important stimulus for economic development in Transkei.

The country has 8 800 km of roads and 209 km of railways. The Transkeian government spends $1,2 million a year on the construction of roads and

Table 5. Type and number of commerce and services enterprises in Transkei[1] owned by Blacks, 1974

Type of enterprise	Magisterial district									
	Bizana	Gcuwa	Cala	Cofimvaba	Xhora	Engcobo	Siphaqeni	Idutywa	Centane	Libode
RETAIL TRADE AND ALLIED SERVICES	73	79	50	65	20	101	86	64	70	52
General dealer	55	69	44	46	16	75	60	54	58	41
Butcher	1	2	3	1	1	4	12	2	4	–
Fresh produce	–	–	1	1	–	–	1	–	–	1
Speculator	14	1	–	3	2	4	6	5	5	–
Filling station	–	–	1	–	–	–	–	–	–	1
Bottle-store	1	1	–	1	–	–	–	–	–	–
Hawker	1	5	1	8	1	2	5	3	–	1
Shoemaker	–	–	–	–	–	3	–	–	–	–
Combined shop	1	1	–	2	–	–	1	–	3	8
Other	–	–	–	3	–	13	1	–	–	–
CATERING AND ACCOMMODATION SERVICES	8	6	7	7	22	11	9	18	5	10
Restaurant and cafe	7	6	6	6	21	8	8	17	2	10
Fish and chips shop	–	–	–	–	–	–	–	–	–	–
Hotel and motel	1	–	1	1	1	3	1	1	3	–
TRANSPORT	–	–	–	–	1	2	–	2	–	–
Bus service	–	–	–	–	–	2	–	2	–	–
Other	–	–	–	–	1	–	–	–	–	–
PERSONAL SERVICES	–	–	–	–	–	4	–	–	–	–
Dry-cleaner	–	–	–	–	–	1	–	–	–	–
Hairdresser	–	–	–	–	–	1	–	–	–	–
Undertaker	–	–	–	–	–	1	–	–	–	–
Other	–	–	–	–	–	1	–	–	–	–
Total	81	85	57	72	43	118	95	84	75	62

1) TDC enterprises excluded.

Lusikisiki	Matatiele	Maxesibeni	Mt. Fletcher	Kwabhaca	Mqanduli	Nqamakwe	Ngqeleni	Umzimvubu	Qumbu	Tabankulu	Tsolo	Tsomo	Umtata	Umzimkulu	Gatyana	Total
118	156	54	84	180	84	110	53	15	101	48	73	76	179	181	104	2 276
91	132	29	78	121	59	93	36	14	85	43	62	59	137	71	70	1 698
8	10	6	4	11	1	4	3	1	5	4	1	3	4	16	1	112
–	–	2	–	–	1	–	1	–	–	–	5	4	4	3	2	26
5	3	3	1	20	17	4	3	–	10	–	1	–	8	23	26	164
4	–	1	–	1	1	1	–	–	–	–	–	2	3	–	–	15
1	–	1	–	–	–	–	–	–	–	–	–	–	–	3	–	8
7	6	10	1	27	5	8	9	–	1	1	4	8	1	60	3	178
–	–	–	–	–	–	–	–	–	–	–	–	–	–	–	–	3
1	5	1	–	–	–	–	1	–	–	–	–	–	2	5	–	31
1	–	1	–	–	–	–	–	–	–	–	–	–	20	–	2	41
21	22	8	14	15	7	8	4	4	10	15	14	6	23	12	20	306
21	22	7	14	15	7	8	4	4	10	15	13	4	21	11	19	286
–	–	–	–	–	–	–	–	–	–	–	–	–	–	1	–	1
–	–	1	–	–	–	–	–	–	–	–	1	2	1	1	1	19
–	–	–	–	–	–	–	–	–	–	–	–	–	–	–	–	5
–	–	–	–	–	–	–	–	–	–	–	–	–	–	–	–	4
–	–	–	–	–	–	–	–	–	–	–	–	–	–	–	–	1
–	–	–	–	–	–	–	–	–	–	–	–	–	–	1	–	5
–	–	–	–	–	–	–	–	–	–	–	–	–	–	–	–	1
–	–	–	–	–	–	–	–	–	–	–	–	–	–	–	–	1
–	–	–	–	–	–	–	–	–	–	–	–	–	–	1	–	2
–	–	–	–	–	–	–	–	–	–	–	–	–	–	–	–	1
139	178	62	98	195	91	118	57	19	111	63	87	82	203	193	124	2 592

bridges. All railways in the country were built by the South African Railways and after independence will continue to be run by that organisation for as long as required.

Until independence the only direct air links between Transkei and South Africa were by means of light aircraft flying between Umtata, on the one hand, and the cities of Durban and East London, on the other. Nearing completion at Umtata is a new international airport which will be able to handle all jet aircraft currently in use and will link Umtata directly with Johannesburg and, from there, with the rest of South Africa and the world.

Transkei also has a comprehensive postal and telecommunication service. By independence, most of the 38 post offices were staffed by Transkeians. A large new automatic telephone exchange is to be commissioned in Umtata which will link the capital with the nation-wide South African automatic system and, through that, with the rest of the world.

Electricity is now mostly supplied through the national grid of South Africa's Electricity Supply Commission (ESCOM), although some smaller centres still generate their own power, mostly by way of diesel motors driving generators of varying capacities (see the chapter on Umtata).

Water is no problem in Transkei. As pointed out elsewhere, precipitation is comparatively high and there are several large perennial rivers, notably the Umzimkulu, Umthamvuna, Umtentu, Umzimvubu, Umtata, Bashee and the Great Kei. Several dams have been built on these and other rivers to store the abundant supply of water for agricultural, urban and industrial use and more will be constructed in due course.

Two of the largest dams are Xonxa and Lubisi. The Xonxa is on the White Kei River, in the newly acquired Cacadu (Glen Grey) district. The Lubisi Dam with a capacity of 156 million m³ on the Indwe river, supplies water mainly for the Qamata irrigation scheme. Other dams in Transkei include the Ncora, Toleni, Majola, Gcuwa, Belfort, Magwa, Qwili-Qwili, Mtanga, Mbulu, Ndabakazi, as well as the Xilinxa, the main source of water for Butterworth.

The possibility is being investigated of linking the Umtata Dam, at present under construction, to two waterfalls in the area with a view to generating

By March 1975 the Transkei Development Corporation had granted 692 loans to Transkeians to launch their own enterprises, mostly in the retail trade, and these have benefited greatly from the wholesale outlets established by the Corporation.

hydro-electric power for Umtata. The estimated cost of this project is $12,6 million. In fact, a number of Transkei's rivers may be harnessed for generating hydro-electric power and in future it may well become economically feasible to exploit this potential further.

Demography and labour

The resident population of Transkei at independence was estimated at 2,5 million, and if the relatively high rate of increase is maintained, the total population is expected to reach 7,7 million by the year 2020.

The last official census was that of 1970. The total *de facto* population of Transkei in that year was 1 751 142, of whom all but 17 211 were Black. As pointed out earlier, on 1 December 1975 the districts of Herschel and Cacadu (at that time called Glen Grey) which previously were part of Ciskei, the other Xhosa homeland in South Africa, were added to Transkei. If the population enumerated in these two districts in 1970 is added (as has been done in Table 6), the total population of Transkei in 1970 was 1 933 010 (1 914 190 Blacks, 10 134 Whites, 8 676 Coloureds and 10 Asians). Of this total some 95 per cent (1 817 514) were Xhosa, four per cent South Sotho and one per cent Zulu. Members of other Black ethnic groups represented a negligible percentage.

The table also shows that the vast majority of Black Transkeians – about 98 per cent – were settled in rural areas. The Coloureds were fairly evenly divided between rural and urban areas and more than three-quarters of the Whites were living in urban areas, with the largest concentration in Umtata, the capital city.

The Zulu and South Sotho segments of the population are found mostly in the districts of Transkei which border on the traditional homelands of these peoples. Thus, 91 per cent of Transkeian Zulu live in the Umzimkulu area which borders on the South African province of Natal in which KwaZulu, homeland of the Zulu nation, is situated. The South Sotho of Transkei are mostly concentrated in three districts bordering on the independent Kingdom of Lesotho. These are Mount Fletcher (41,5 per cent of all Transkeian South Sotho), Matatiele (35,5 per cent) and Herschel (17,8 percent).

The population density of Transkei in 1975 was approximately 50 persons per km². This figure takes into account the total area of Transkei after the inclusion of the districts of Herschel and Cacadu, as well as the relatively small areas still to be added after independence.

Table 6. De facto population of Transkei enumerated in 1970

District	Urban Areas				Rural Areas				Grand Total
	Xhosa	Other Blacks	Whites	Coloureds	Xhosa	Other Blacks	Whites	Coloureds	
Bizana	756	40	133	128	96 966	517	92	143	98 775
Cacadu (Glen Grey)	889	8	159	162	102 478	63	189	205	104 153
Centane	239	3	80	3	59 499	8	324	11	60 167
Cofimvaba (St Marks)	799	15	130	254	66 668	2	83	–	67951
Engcobo	1 510	–	298	11	96 586	32	103	261	98 801
Gatyana (Willowvale)	413	–	118	19	76 868	12	120	–	77 550
Gcuwa (Butterworth)	1 738	14	872	125	37 208	129	99	17	40 202
Herschel (Sterkspruit)	131	56	122	–	63 191	13 443	108	664	77 715
Idutywa	1 718	–	680	291	49 443	–	54	4	52 190
Kwabhaca (Mt Frere)	1 938	38	264	191	71 820	49	30	434	74 764
Libode	327	2	64	213	59 462	–	19	40	60 127
Lusikisiki	847	25	144	141	124 642	96	97	703	126 695
Matatiele	103	265	–	–	55 039	27 300	25	86	82 818
Maxesibeni (Mt Ayliff)	1 076	31	82	177	38 396	409	27	10	40 208
Mt Fletcher	561	319	88	37	35 906	30 876	11	164	67 962
Mqanduli	294	3	51	21	65 694	11	148	23	66 245
Ngqeleni	571	–	58	48	76 967	11	82	287	78 024
Nqamakwe	306	–	54	21	54 899	6	54	21	55 361
Qumbu	435	2	77	181	62 879	965	31	145	64 715
Siphaqeni (Flagstaff)	500	9	52	181	64 691	14	16	87	65 550
Tabankulu	571	–	51	112	66 876	1 021	22	30	68 683
Tsolo	1 424	5	111	207	61 623	41	87	52	63 550
Tsomo	307	2	14	54	41 207	10	29	–	41 623
Umtata	20 024	205	3 542	1 067	74 598	116	241	181	99 974
Umzimkulu	2 375	391	220	556	64 116	20 058	183	304	88 203
Umzimvubu (Port St. Johns)	–	9	86	78	32 475	–	–	–	32 648
Xalanga	4.423	22	140	308	30 627	22	23	212	35 777
Xhora (Elliotdale)	404	–	32	–	42 011	1	115	6	42 569
	44 679	1 464	7 722	4 586	1 772 835	95 212	2 412	4 090	1 933 000
								Asians	10
									1 933 010

The most salient feature of the *de facto* population of Transkei is its youthfulness: about 47 per cent of all Transkeians are under 14 years of age. Another notable feature is that at certain times of the year (when migrant workers are selling their labour outside Transkei), there are twice as many women as men in the age group 15 to 64 years. In 1970 the economically non-productive segment of the population – those under 14 and those over 65 years of age – was 51,2 per cent. This fact gives some idea of the dependency burden carried by male Transkeians in the prime of their years.

The total of 1 914 190 enumerated in 1970 re-presented about 58 per cent of the *de jure* population of Transkei. Over a period of many years, large numbers of Transkeians have for varying periods of time migrated to the more developed areas of South Africa. Many of these are migrant labourers (8 per cent of the *de jure* Transkei population in 1970) who sell their labour in South Africa for a specified period, usually less than a year, and return to Transkei after the conclusion of the contract. Others are absent for extended periods. In 1970 there were more than one million Transkeians in White South Africa.

In this regard Transkei is in an average position, compared with the remaining Black homelands in South Africa. The fact of the matter is that despite the development programmes in agriculture and industry during the past few decades, and particularly during the past ten years, there are as yet not sufficient job opportunities to meet the needs of all those who enter the labour market every year. This situation is similar in nature, if not in degree, to that pertaining in Europe where comparatively large numbers of workers from the less developed countries find employment on a continuous basis in the highly industrialised countries, such as West Germany and France.

Economic development in Transkei has in many respects been hampered because such a large number of able-bodied men work in urban centres in South Africa owing to lack of employment opportunities in Transkei. Many of these migrants return for only a short period every year. Since a large proportion of the migrant's income is sent back to his family, labour is regarded as one of Transkei's chief 'export products'.

There is a real need to provide employment for people entering the labour market in Transkei. Hence the efforts, described earlier, to encourage industrialists to establish factories on an agency basis in Transkei, mainly at Butterworth and Umtata.

Estimates of the increase in the number of potentially economically active Transkeians (15-64 years), are given in Table 7. These estimates are based on ratios between male and female found to be applicable in Black populations throughout South Africa.

The table shows that over the 30-year period from

Table 7. Estimates of potentially economically active Transkeians (15-64 years), 1970-2000

Year	Male I	Female II	Female (45,8%) III	Total (I + III)	5-yearly increase	Average annual increase
1970	535 320	601 160	275 330	810 650	–	–
1975	614 280	689 830	315 940	930 220	119 570	23 910
1980	706 600	793 510	363 430	1 070 030	139 810	27 960
1985	811 920	911 890	417 650	1 229 570	159 540	31 900
1990	928 960	1 043 340	477 850	1 406 810	177 240	35 450
1995	1 059 770	1 190 260	545 140	1 604 910	198 100	39 620
2000	1 205 480	1 353 920	620 100	1 825 580	220 670	44 130

1) Herschel and Cacadu (Glen Grey) are included

1970 to 2000, the potential labour supply will increase by 125,2 per cent – from 810 650 to 1 825 580 and that the average annual increase will rise from 23 910 for the period 1970-75 to 44 130 for the period 1995-2000. This projected growth rate gives some idea of the tempo at which employment opportunities in Transkei will have to be created if the percentage of migrant workers from Transkei is not to increase. The average annual increase in the Black labour force between 1973 and 1975 was estimated at 25 430 (Table 8). Of this number, 15,2 per cent were provided with employment in Transkei, chiefly in the tertiary sector as government employees. Few additional employment opportunities could be created in the border industrial areas adjacent to Transkei and the majority of the new workers may thus be viewed as potential migrants (21 500 or 84,5 per cent).

In 1975, 845 489, or 34 per cent of the total Black population were economically active (see Table 9). The potential labour supply, on the other hand, was 930 220 (see Table 7). It would therefore appear that many people were either voluntary or involuntary unemployed in 1975. This was, in fact, not so. Included in the estimates of the potential

labour supply were persons between the age of 15 and 64 years who were still at some training institution. It should also be noted that, for various reasons, in the developing economy of Transkei, the potential of economically active females in the age group 15 to 64 years is considerably lower than in the rest of South Africa. Thus the potential labour supply is actually much less than 930 220.

Table 9 shows that in 1975, 478 489 were economically active in Transkei, while 360 000 were active as migrant labourers and 7 000 were working on a commuting basis outside Transkei.

In the same year there were 417 500 households (Table 10) in Transkei. This means that, on average, 1,1 person per household had found a job in Transkei itself. If the total number in employment, 845 489 (Table 9), is taken as base of the calculations, it means that two persons in every household were in employment, either in Transkei itself or outside.

It should be noted, however, that 80 per cent, or 383 800, of those active in Transkei were engaged in the agricultural sector on a non-wage earning

Table 8. Average annual increase in demand and supply of Black labour in Transkei, and demand in border areas, 1973-75[1]

Supply and demand	Average annual increase	Percentage
I. Supply of Black labour	25 430	
II. Demand for Black labour in Transkei	3 870	100,0
Primary sector	80	2,1
Secondary sector	900	23,2
Tertiary sector	2 890	74,7
III. Supply of Black labour employed in Transkei (II as percentage of I)		15,2
IV. Demand for commuters	60	
V. Total demand in Transkei and border areas (II plus IV)	3 930	
VI. Supply of Black labour employed in Transkei and border areas (V as percentage of I)		15,5
Potential supply of migrants (I minus V)	21 500	

1) Herschel and Cacadu (Glen Grey) excluded

basis. In view of the modest output of this sector, it is evident that many of these 383 800 may be termed disguised unemployed, since they make little or no contribution to the output of this sector.

This surplus labour, as well as the projected increase in the potential labour supply of Transkei, will therefore have to be absorbed mainly by the secondary and tertiary sectors.

Domestic income and expenditure

This discussion on the income and expenditure of Transkeian households is based on a study carried out in three homogeneous areas in the country – urban, semi-urban (village) and rural. The findings of this pilot study may reasonably be applied to the country as a whole and are summarised in Table 10.

It was found that 96,7 per cent of the population lived in rural areas and that the average size of households throughout Transkei was 5,5 persons (5,6 in rural areas, 4,3 in urban areas and 4,0 in villages).

The salient feature of the findings is that households in the semi-urban and urban areas have a much higher income than those in rural areas.

A large proportion of the income is received in the form of goods and services (33 per cent), and the remainder ($232 million) as cash. Income from non-household members outside Transkei amounted to $72 million.

The average annual income of households in the various regions is given in Table 11. The fact that income of households in semi-urban areas ($2 746) is considerably higher than in urban

Table 9. Estimates of migrant labourers, commuters and Blacks economically active in Transkei, 1975

Type of employment	Number	Percentage
Wage earners in the economic sectors	94 689	11,2
Primary sector	1 084	0,1
Agriculture	941	0,1
Mining	143	0,0
Secondary sector	11 977	1,4
Manufacturing	6 273	0,7
Private construction	5 704	0,7
Tertiary sector	81 628	9,7
Trade and services	21 723	2,6
Transport	1 078	0,1
Government	43 874	5,2
Other	14 953	1,8
Non-wage earners in the agricultural sector	383 800	45,4
Migrant labourers	360 000	42,6
Commuters	7 000	0,8
Total	845 489	100,0

($1 793) and rural areas ($767) is largely due to the many government employees in the villages.

Salaries and wages constituted the major component of income (between 86 and 88 per cent) in the semi-urban and urban areas. In rural areas, net profits from farming accounted for 32 per cent, salaries and wages for 21 per cent and contributions from non-household members for 30 per cent of household income. More than 75 per cent of this came from outside Transkei, mainly from migrant labourers in South Africa.

A similar study conducted in 1971 in the districts of Tabankulu and Gatyana found that the average annual income for Black households was $287, and that this was fairly representative of Black households throughout the rural areas of Transkei at that time. This means that from 1971 to 1975 the income of rural Black households increased by 27 per cent a year on average. Over the same period, growth rates for income derived from farming, wages and salaries and contributions from non-household members, were, 43, 42 and 18 per cent a year respectively.

Total cash expenditure by Black households on goods and services amounted to $270,7 million in 1975 (Table 12). Expenditure on food accounted for 44,6 per cent of the total. Households in rural areas spent more on food (47,6 per cent) than those in urban areas (33,3 per cent) and semi-urban areas (21,5 per cent). This is largely attributable to the difference in income levels between the three areas.

Other important expenditure items include trans-port (10,5 per cent), furniture and household appliances (8,7 per cent) and clothing (5,2 per cent).

Total expenditure in kind by Black households accounted for $104,1 million. This included such items as clothing received from, and housing subsidised by, employers and agricultural products used for subsistence purposes.

While 90,2 per cent of expenditure occurred inside Transkei, less than 33 per cent of all goods and services purchased was produced locally. The potential for local production of consumer goods and services is therefore considerable.

The role of government

In a developing country such as Transkei, government tends to play a more active role in the development process than is the case in developed Western economies. Often in such a developing country, there is a marked lack of physical and social infrastructure which discourages the private sector from involvement in the economy. In these circumstances, government has to step in and provide the required social and physical infrastructure and generally create an atmosphere more attractive to private sector activity.

In the case of Transkei, the meaning of 'government' has varied considerably, depending on the period of development. Prior to 1963, when Transkei was granted self-government, all official development agencies were those of the central government of South Africa. These were mostly departments of state, notably the Departments of

Table 10. Population and total income of Black households in rural, semi-urban and urban areas, 1975

Area	Income		Households		Population	
	$'000	Percentage	Number	Percentage	Number	Percentage
Rural	306 194	88,3	399 460	95,7	2 225 000	96,7
Semi-urban	24 871	7,2	9 250	2,2	37 000	1,6
Urban	15 760	4,5	8 790	2,1	38 000	1,7
Total	346 825	100,0	417 500	100,0	2 300 000	100,0

The exchange rate of the Rand as at 1976/08/31 was R1,00 = $1,15.

Table 11. Average annual income of households according to type of income, 1975

Type of income	Rural		Semi-urban		Urban		Total	
	$	Percentage	$	Percentage	$	Percentage	$	Percentage
WAGES AND SALARIES								
Cash wages	149,40	19,49	2 215,73	82,40	1 526,35	85,13	219,81	26,98
Cash bonus	4,01	0,52	99,79	3,71	48,35	2,69	6,84	0,84
Free clothing	0,10	0,01	5,47	0,20	4,25	0,24	0,32	0,04
Free food	0,82	0,11	4,74	0,18	11,59	0,65	1,14	0,14
Free transport	0,55	0,07	–	–	3,05	0,17	0,58	0,07
Free housing	–	–	–	–	0,67	0,04	0,16	0,02
PROFIT FROM OWN ENTERPRISES								
Agriculture: Cash	6,76	0,88	0,01	0,01	–	–	6,36	0,78
Agriculture: Other	237,18	30,94	76,73	2,84	16,52	0,92	224,53	27,56
Private activities	16,65	2,17	23,11	0,86	24,54	1,37	16,62	2,04
Other	27,26	3,56	50,96	1,90	28,67	1,60	27,29	3,35
INCOME FROM PROPERTY AND INVESTMENT	0,86	0,11	7,27	0,27	5,73	0,32	1,06	0,13
PENSIONS	49,04	6,45	18,73	0,70	22,21	1,24	46,92	5,76
CONTRIBUTIONS								
Cash – Transkei	49,29	6,43	69,57	2,59	12,12	0,68	47,99	5,89
Cash – Elsewhere	167,16	21,81	84,08	3,13	23,44	1,31	159,12	19,53
In Natura – Transkei	2,85	0,32	4,93	0,18	3,00	0,08	2,77	0,34
In Natura – Elsewhere	11,41	1,49	3,69	0,14	1,51	0,17	10,83	1,33
PAYMENT FROM BOARDERS	9,66	1,26	4,46	0,17	56,37	3,14	10,34	1,27
PART-TIME WORK	5,95	0,78	12,05	0,45	–	–	5,87	0,72
FREE HOUSING	27,32	3,57	5,52	0,20	4,51	0,25	25,91	3,18
OTHER	0,24	0,03	1,97	0,07	–	–	0,24	0,03
Total	766,51	100,00	2 688,81	100,00	1 792,88	100,00	814,70	100,00

The exchange rate of the Rand as at 1976/08/31 was R1,00 = $1,15.

Table 12. Total cash expenditure by Black households inside and outside Transkei, 1975

| Item | $'000 Area | | | | | | | | |
| | Rural Transkei | | Semi-urban Transkei | | Urban Transkei | | Total Transkei | | |
	Inside	Outside	Inside	Outside	Inside	Outside	Inside	Outside	Total
Food	99 988	10 831	4 860	219	4 737	–	109 585	11 050	120 635
Clothing	8 742	2 918	1 030	234	1 066	60	10 838	3 212	14 050
Housing	5 658	–	2 964	–	1 622	–	10 244	–	10 244
Fuel and light	8 425	1 833	714	30	396	–	9 535	1 863	11 398
Transport	21 628	–	3 902	699	2 141	–	27 671	699	28 370
Medical services	2 324	588	62	15	111	–	2 497	603	3 100
Education	9 726	992	725	–	230	–	10 681	992	11 673
Insurance and funds	993	–	1 206	–	547	–	2 746	–	2 746
Recreation	657	97	437	1	53	–	1 147	98	1 245
Furniture and household appliances	16 793	3 836	1 539	444	789	200	19 121	4 480	23 601
Alcoholic drinks	6 743	1 264	473	11	505	–	7 721	1 275	8 996
Cigarettes and tobacco	2 324	60	93	2	91	–	2 508	62	2 570
Washing materials	6 128	606	306	10	269	–	6 703	616	7 319
Personal care	5 081	587	535	6	366	–	5 982	593	6 575
Communication	1 016	161	165	37	33	3	1 214	201	1 415
Reading and writing material	583	106	121	4	103	–	807	110	917
Vacation	–	–	6	–	7	–	13	–	13
Dry-cleaning and laundry	230	331	64	28	102	–	396	359	755
Miscellaneous	8 512	276	635	66	249	–	9 396	342	9 738
Taxes	1 750	–	575	–	329	–	2 654	–	2 654
Support of family	1 020	–	1 451	–	235	–	2 706	–	2 706
Total	208 321	24 486	21 863	1 806	13 981	263	244 165	26 555	270 720

The exchange rate of the Rand as at 1976/08/31 was R1,00 = $1,15.

Table 13. Expenditure by certain South African public institutions and enterprises in Transkei, 1969/70 – 1973/74

Institution	$'000				
	1960/70	1970/71	1971/72	1972/73	1973/74
A SA GOVERNMENT DEPARTMENTS	5 492	8 975	11 169	12 138	5 235
Health	2 392	6 325	7 604	7 627	–
Prisons	665	608	790	774	920
Information	–	37	41	46	49
Justice	17	–	–	–	13
Controller and Auditor-General	46	52	66	72	92
National Education	7	7	7	8	7
Public Works	141	77	159	141	123
Police	1 176	1 406	1 610	2 284	2 644
Transport	1 048	463	892	1 186	1 387
B Cape Provincial Administration	3 210	897	611	1 102	1 171
C Local authorities	1 692	2 114	2 877	3 808	4 802
D Total government sector (A to C)	10 394	11 986	14 657	17 048	11 208
E Public enterprises	4 020	4 687	4 883	5 510	6 505
South African Railways and Harbours	3 309	3 722	3 788	4 048	4 118
Posts and Telecommunications	683	949	1 068	1 156	1 311
Electricity Supply Commission	28	1	12	288	1 053
South African Broadcasting Corporation	–	15	15	18	23
Grand total (D plus E)	14 414	16 673	19 540	22 558	17 713

The exchange rate of the Rand as at 1976/08/31 was R1,00 = $1,15.

Table 14. Expenditure on a programme basis by 'government' institutions, 1973/74 – 1975/76[1]

Programme and year		Transkei Government	Department of BA & D	SABT	TDC	BMC	Total
		\$'000					
Land planning and conservation	1973/74	1 117	–	10	–	–	1 127
	1974/75	1 960	–	53	–	–	2 013
	1975/76	1 723	–	–	–	–	1 723
Population settlement	1973/74	250	–	5 267	–	–	5 517
	1974/75	282	–	6 683	265	–	7 230
	1975/76	200	–	12 341	345	–	12 886
Employment and income	1973/74	14 243	–	–	8 658	49	22 950
generation	1974/75	13 493	–	–	16 221	12	29 726
	1975/76	15 783	–	–	25 409	270	41 462
Development of human potential	1973/74	16 352	–	46	–	–	16 398
	1974/75	26 727	–	–	–	–	26 727
	1975/76	27 464	–	–	–	–	27 464
Social services	1973/74	19 545	–	3	–	–	19 548
	1974/75	25 666	–	17	–	–	25 683
	1975/76	31 972	–	–	–	–	31 972
Government planning and adminis-	1973/74	4 994	–	–	–	–	4 994
tration	1974/75	9 331	–	383	–	–	9 714
	1975/76	13 237	–	23	–	–	13 260
Physical infrastructure	1973/74	7 876	–	264	1 617	–	9 757
	1974/75	9 539	–	739	3 581	–	13 859
	1975/76	10 593	–	1 289	4 132	–	16 014
Other	1973/74	–	2 942	–	–	–	2 942
	1974/75	–	3 007	–	–	–	3 007
	1975/76	–	3 877	–	–	–	3 877
Total	1973/74	64 377	2 942	5 590	10 275	49	83 233
	1974/75	86 998	3 007	7 875	20 067	12	117 959
	1975/76	100 972	3 877	13 653	29 886	270	148 658

1) The budgeted expenditure of the Transkei government for 1976/77 is \$158 million, an increase of 56,5 per cent on the previous year

The exchange rate of the Rand as at 1976/08/31 was R1,00 = \$1,15.

Table 15. Expenditure by the TDC in Transkei, 1973/74 – 1975/76

	1973/74		1974/75		1975/76[1])	
Activity	$'000	%	$'000	%	$'000	%
Agriculture	−220[2])	−2,2	338	1,7	3 000	10,0
Manufacturing	4 583	45,7	12 628	62,9	17 678	59,2
Construction	1 865	18,6	4 183	20,9	5 082	17,0
Commerce and services	2 675	26,7	1 934	9,6	1 519	5,1
Transport	122	1,2	130	0,6	1 694	5,7
Financial institutions	560	5,6	60	0,3	62	0,2
Community and personal services	−16[2])	−0,1	161	0,8	302	1,0
Administration	454	4,5	632	3,2	549	1,8
Total	10 023	100,0	20 066	100,0	29 886	100,0

1) Revised budgeted expenditure drawn up in July, 1975
2) Net disinvestment.

The exchange rate of the Rand as at 1976/08/31 was R1,00 = $1,15.

Table 16. Functional expenditure by the TDC in Transkei, 1973/74 – 1975/76

	$'000			
Financial year Programme	1973/74	1974/75	1975/76[1])	Total
Population settlement	–	264	345	609
Employment creation and income generation	8 407	16 222	25 409	500 38
Creation of physical infrastructure	1 617	3 580	4 132	9 329
Total	10 024	20 066	29 886	59 976

1) Revised budgeted expenditure drawn up in July 1975

The exchange rate of the Rand as at 1976/08/31 was R1,00 = $1,15.

Bantu Administration and Development, Bantu Education, Transport, Health, Justice and Public Works. Another was the South African Bantu Trust (SABT), an overall development agency created in 1936 to promote general development in all Black areas in South Africa. In 1959 the Bantu Investment Corporation (BIC) was founded to mobilise capital among Blacks in South Africa and to use this for the development of the various Black homelands. Various specialist development corporations followed in the late 'sixties and early 'seventies. Notable among these was the Xhosa Development Corporation (XDC), founded in 1965 to promote development in the two homelands of the Xhosa, Transkei and Ciskei. On 1 April 1976 this corporation was divided into two independent corporations, the Xhosa Development Corporation which is now concerned only with development in Ciskei, and the Transkei Development Corporation (TDC). Another important agency is the Bantu Mining Corporation (BMC) founded in 1969 to exploit the mining potential, however small, of all the Black homelands of South Africa.

By independence the Transkei government had taken over responsibility for expenditure by all central South African government departments as well as the South African Bantu Trust. In future public expenditure will be for the accounts of only the Transkei government and the TDC and BMC, and even in the case of the TDC an increasing number of functions will be directly controlled by the Transkei government.

Total developmental expenditure by the Transkei government and these agencies is given in Tables 13 and 14.

The increase in the expenditure of the TDC by 190,0 per cent in the period under review (Table 14) is particularly significant since it is all directly aimed at stimulating economic development.

Expenditure by the SABT is also important, since it is largely aimed at township development. In fact, in 1975/76, 91 per cent of all expenditure by the SABT concerned the settlement of population. Salaries, subsistence and transport allowances for White employees seconded to the Transkei government, fully account for the expenditure by the Department of Bantu Administration and Development shown in Table 14.

Transkeians are natural weavers and with proper instruction the country can build up a weaving industry of considerable proportions. Transkeian weaving products have been exported to South Africa for many years.

The tables show that the highest priority was given to employment creation and income generation, followed by social services and development of human potential. These three programmes accounted for 67,9 per cent of total expenditure in 1975/76.

The Transkei Development Corporation (TDC)

Like its forerunner, the Xhosa Development Corporation (XDC), the TDC seeks to promote the economic development of Transkei by initiating, financing and establishing industrial, mining, financial and other business projects. The Corporation supplies capital, technical and other assistance, specialised advice and information and promotes savings. It also assists in the take-over by Transkeians of enterprises formerly owned and run by Whites, and in the establishment of other development organisations in Transkei.

The Transkei government nominates five of the ten directors of the TDC and is accepting increasing responsibility for the finance and management of the Corporation's activities.

The expenditure of the TDC by type of activity is given in Table 15. The major share has gone to manufacturing and this increased from 45,7 per cent in 1973/74 to 59,2 per cent in 1975/76. Over the same period, expenditure on trade and service activities declined, from 26,7 per cent to 5,1 per cent. Percentage expenditure on other activities, with the exception of agriculture, has remained fairly constant. The net disinvestment of $219 650 in agriculture in 1973/74 is accounted for by the closure of a ploughing unit in Transkei.

Table 16 shows that TDC activities have been largely aimed at the creation of employment opportunities and generation of income in Transkei. Over the past three years 83 per cent of total expenditure was devoted to this programme.

Of the remaining expenditure, 16 per cent went to the creation of physical infrastructure and one per cent to population settlement.

Since the establishment of its first factory in 1968, a brewery at Zitulele, the TDC has made sound progress with its industrialisation programme, which received considerable impetus when the South African government in the same year announced a series of incentives (described earlier) for White industrialists who established factories in Transkei on an agency basis.

Following the announcement of these concessions,

the TDC embarked on a three-year development plan. In the first two years, while negotiating agency contracts with industrialists, the TDC also set about expanding the infrastructure in Transkei, particularly at the two industrial growth points, Butterworth and Umtata. As a result, by 31 March 1975, 24 industries had been established on an agency basis (see Table 4). The major share of total investment in these industries came from the TDC – 61 per cent. By 31 March 1976, agency industries employed 4 824 Blacks.

The TDC also provides a wide range of services by way of enterprises either taken over from Whites or launched on its own account. By March 1976 6 325 Blacks were employed in these concerns.

All the Corporation's projects are destined for ownership by Transkeian citizens. All Black employees thus have the prospect of eventually becoming either sole or part owners of the business undertakings in which they are employed at present.

So far, mainly commercial enterprises have been transferred to Transkeians. By 31 March 1975, the TDC had transferred to Transkeians 18 of the 31 garages it had taken over from Whites. Furthermore, Blacks held many of the senior positions in the remaining garages still owned by the TDC.

In 1970 the TDC opened the Transkei Hotel at Umtata which has proved invaluable as a training centre for Black hoteliers. Hence the fact that by 1975, 29 hotels and six bottlestores in Transkei were under Black management.

At present Blacks are also being trained to take over the more sophisticated concerns operated by the Corporation's industrial division.

By March 1975, the TDC had invested $38,2 million in its own enterprises, $7,2 million (or 19 per cent) in manufacturing concerns, including two decorticating plants at Butterworth and Lusikisiki which produce Phormium tenax fibre for the bag factory in Butterworth, and a weaving plant and furniture factory, both at Umtata.

The TDC also makes an important contribution to economic development by granting loans to Black businessmen. By 31 March 1975, 692 loans had been granted of which 78 per cent were used to

Transkei has a network of 8 800 km of roads, more than many other Black African countries of comparable size. The vast majority of these roads are not macadamised and many, especially those in the mountainous areas, require regular maintenance.

launch general dealer businesses. Assistance was also given to entrepreneurs to run hotels, bottlestores, garages and bus and transport companies. By 31 October 1975, 732 loans ($7,9 million) had been granted to Transkeians.

Black traders benefit greatly from the wholesale outlets which the Corporation has established in the major towns of Transkei. The total annual turnover of these concerns increased from $4,0 million in 1971, when they were launched, to $16,1 million for the year ending 31 March 1975.

A special division to finance Black bus operators was created in August 1974 in the Xhosa Development Corporation. In Transkei this division is now managed by the TDC whose managers and transport officers assist Transkeian bus operators, most of whom are loan holders of the Corporation, in administrative and operational matters relating to their enterprise. By 31 March 1975, $1,6 million in loans had been made available to 57 bus operators in Transkei.

The Corporation also makes available stand-by buses which operators may use when their own are temporarily out of commission owing to breakdowns or routine maintenance.

Plans are on the drawing board for a major workshop complex at Umtata and for depots at Butterworth and Queenstown.

In 1973 a separate agricultural division was created in the XDC and by 1974 a number of irrigation and dairy schemes had been launched (see the chapter on Agriculture).

At the commencement of its activities as an independent Corporation on 1 April 1976 the TDC had an estimated share capital of $87 million. Employment opportunities in projects launched by the TDC increased from fewer than 1 000 in 1968 to more than 12 000 in 1975. It has been estimated that TDC enterprise indirectly created at least another 10 000 employment opportunities for Blacks in Transkei.

Economic planning

In view of the importance of overall planning in a developing economy, such as that of Transkei, the Transkei government in 1970 adopted the planning programme budgeting (PPB) system, instead of the traditional budget vote system. The new system permits the government to establish a developmental framework within which the various national activities may be grouped according to the objectives to be realised. Thus planners are better able to determine priorities.

The main objective of the Transkei government is to settle as many Transkeian citizens as possible within the country on a basis of productive employment. Certain programmes have been formulated to achieve this objective. These are land planning and conservation, settlement of population, employment creation and income generation, development of human potential, social services, government planning and administration and infrastructure.

In addition, the Transkei Planning Committee was established in March 1972. Its members are drawn from various government departments of Transkei and from the TDC and the Bureau for Economic Research re Bantu Development (BENBO).

The committee identifies and examines problems hampering economic development in Transkei; seeks better co-ordination between government departments, the Transkei Townships Board, the TDC and the BMC and advises the Transkei government on general strategy for development.

The Transkei Planning Committee appointed planning consultants to prepare a report on the potential of certain growth points in Transkei. The towns of Umtata, Butterworth and Idutywa were investigated to determine their suitability for industrial development. These investigations have played a decisive role in the industrialisation of these towns.

Meanwhile planners in the Department of Bantu Administration and Development of the South African government have compiled an overall physical development plan for Transkei. Various government and semi-government bodies as well as private consultants were appointed to investigate aspects such as mineral potential, water resources, agricultural and tourist potential. Such a development plan, the first instalment of which was due towards the end of 1976, will enable the Transkei Planning Committee as well as various Transkei government institutions to engage in more effective physical and regional planning in Transkei.

Transkei has considerable potential for growth, particularly in the agricultural sector. With co-ordinated planning and appropriate motivation of rural communities, significant increases in production and income are bound to occur and these will be a strong base for development in the other sectors of the economy.

The vast labour potential, which has already attracted a significant number of foreign industrialists to Transkei, is still to be fully utilised. Between 1975 and 1980, 28 000 job-seekers will enter the labour market every year and the potential total labour force is anticipated to increase by 125 per cent from 1970 to 2 000 – from 810 650 to 1 825 580. The rapid expansion of education programmes at the same time enhances the quality of this expanding labour force.

The economy is to a large extent integrated with that of South Africa and other states in Southern Africa. This means that raw materials and intermediate goods, financial and other services as well as an export market are readily available. In addition, the generous incentives provided by the South African government for industrialists who establish factories in Transkei will remain operative after independence.

Gross national income increased from $106 million in 1960/61 to $468 million in 1973/74, while in the same period income per capita increased by 8,9 per cent a year – from $67 to $201. The average annual increase in prices – 3,5 per cent – in this period was considerably lower than the growth in income per capita. This indicates a substantial increase in the economic welfare of the population.

In five years the cash income of Transkeians doubled to $170 million (in 1974/75). This points to an expanding domestic market for goods and services which will continue to have a stimulating effect on the commerce and services sector of the economy.

As far as physical infrastructure is concerned, Transkei, with its network of roads, railway lines and telecommunications and its abundant water supply, is better endowed than most other developing countries in Africa.

After 1963, when Transkei was granted self-government, the foundations for an efficient government administration were laid. This sound administrative base, together with Transkei's stable political climate, will enhance the process of economic development. The Transkei government has been giving increasing attention to the identification of goals and objectives and to the programmes required for their achievement.

Even now, Transkei may be described as an "achiever", as opposed to a "loser" among the developing countries. Achievement outlined in this chapter already puts Transkei in the "upper bracket" of Third World countries.

Economic co-operation between Transkei and the rest of Southern Africa is assured and Transkei has the makings of a worthy partner in the community of Southern African states.

Chapter Twelve

Political Evolution

"*Something started around 1450. The conquest of the world by Europe, followed by colonialisation.*
It is we who have discovered the world. Nobody discovered us. This era lasted for five hundred years. The year 1950 marked the end of the period. India became free in 1947, Mao came to power in 1950. In my book there is the perspective of the end of a civilization, just as we were at the end of the Roman Empire. We are actually between civilizations – the colonial one and the decolonised one – which we do not really know yet but only sense" – *André Malraux.*

The great change to which Malraux refers affected South Africa possibly more than any other country because, all other considerations aside, as a casual glance at the demographic facts of South Africa shows, Africa, Asia and Europe come together here. And although South Africa was directly affected by the decolonisation process and the coming to independence of the peoples of Asia and Africa (possibly the single most important event of the 20th century), the answer which elsewhere applied, namely the simple withdrawal of the European powers, did not and does not apply in South Africa's case. A different answer had to be found, and Transkei is part of that answer.

The background

Independence for Transkei is a milestone in the

Transkei designed its own flag – ochre, white and green – in 1963 when the territory was granted self-government by the South African Parliament in Cape Town. The flag was retained unchanged when the country became a sovereign state in October 1976.

realisation of South Africa's policy of multinational development which is designed to provide for full self-realisation for several disparate peoples which history has brought together within the confines of one state.

Even the most casual glance at the composition of South Africa's population will reveal that it does not comprise an amorphous mass of 23 million individuals, some of whom merely happen to be White and others who happen to be Black.

There are four major demographic divisions: Whites, Coloureds, Asians and Bantu (Black) South Africans.

Predominantly of Indian origin, the Asians were first brought to South Africa as indentured labourers by the British colonial authorities in 1860. Today there are 700 000 of them, concentrated mainly in the provinces of Natal and Transvaal.

The Coloureds are of mixed origin, the descendants mainly of the early indigenous Hottentots and Bushmen, Whites, Blacks and Indonesian slaves. Today they number 2 200 000.

The Black peoples of South Africa are not a single, homogeneous group, but comprise nine disparate peoples or ethnic units. Each has its own culture, language, and social system and territory. Each is an established ethno-political unit. In order of numerical importance these peoples are the following: Zulu (four million), Xhosa (four million), Tswana (1 700 000), North Sotho (1 600 000), South Sotho (1 500 000), Shangaan (740 000), Swazi (500 000), Ndebele (420 000), and Venda (360 000).

The four million Whites are hardly a group of settler-exploiters or temporary intruders on the African continent. The first Whites (Hollanders) arrived at the Cape of Good Hope in 1652. This was only 32 years after the Pilgrim Fathers set foot on American soil and about 130 years *before* Australia and New Zealand were colonised. There were stable White communities in the South African interior long before most Latin American republics were founded.

Today, by all accepted historical and demographic criteria, the Whites are a permanently established nation in its own right. Afrikaans, the mother tongue of the major segment of this nation, was developed on the continent of Africa and is spoken nowhere in Europe. Indeed, Afrikaner nationalism was the *first* of all African nationalisms and Afrikaners fought the first wars of national independence in Africa. The customs and traditions of the White nation are rooted in those of Europe, particularly the Netherlands, Britain, Germany and France, but in the course of three centuries these have been adapted to the needs and conditions of Africa. The parliamentary system of government, however, is distinctly British in origin and content.

In 1657 the first free burghers were permitted to become private farmers. Soon afterwards the expanding community of farmers began to extend their settlement which about a century later encompassed an area of some 170 000 km² – more than twice the size of Austria. The only indigenous peoples they met during this period were nomadic Bushmen and Hottentot tribes. Their first substantial contact with Black people occurred in the 1770s – about a thousand km north-east of Cape Town, roughly the distance between London and Rome. These were Xhosa-speaking tribes, the vanguard of a southerly Black migratory movement from the vicinity of the Great Lakes in Central Africa, which by the end of the 15th century had reached as far as present-day Zambia, Rhodesia and Mozambique and some time later crossed what are today the northern borders of the Republic of South Africa. The Black migration was not a single, coherent movement, but rather a succession of waves of small tribes representing four Black ethnic groups – Nguni, Sotho, Venda and Tsonga – responding to the push and pull of economic conditions and tribal conflicts.

A member of the family has been married and there is a new hut to be thatched. This is usually the job of the women of the tribe. Against a sultry summer sky this Thembu matron is returning home after a successful day with the sickle.

In 1806 the Cape was finally ceded to Britain and during the 19th century the Boer-Afrikaner farmers, descendants of the Dutch settlers, became increasingly dissatisfied with British colonial rule. From 1835 onwards nearly a quarter of the Cape's White population left the colony in a series of organised movements collectively known as the Great Trek. The general direction was northwards over the Orange River, as far north as the Limpopo River, and then eastwards into Natal. The movement coursed over vast tracts of empty land, depopulated of migratory Bantu or Black tribes by the *Mfecane* – a series of Black reigns of terror over a period of about 25 years of internecine warfare and devastation of the most appalling proportions. (See Chapter 2: The People).

By the end of the 19th century there were two Boer-Afrikaner republics – the South African Republic (Transvaal) and the Orange Free State. British South Africa comprised two colonies – the Cape and Natal – and three areas of Black hegemony – the protectorates of Bechuanaland, Swaziland and Basutoland, homelands of respectively the Tswana, Swazi and Sotho peoples. In 1902, after the two Boer republics had been defeated in the Anglo-Boer War, this entire area became British South Africa.

In 1910 the four colonies – Transvaal, Orange Free State, the Cape of Good Hope and Natal – were amalgamated into the Union of South Africa, a British dominion like Canada and Australia. The three protectorates of Bechuanaland, Swaziland and Basutoland were specifically excluded from the new Union.

Given the situation at the time – world-wide European and White ascendancy – it seemed expedient and logical to create a Union of four territories in which White interests were paramount. But in retrospect, in view of subsequent events, this was a curious arrangement, to say the least. *Excluded* from the new Union, quite logically, were three homelands of Black peoples, Basutoland, Swaziland and Bechuanaland. *Included* in the Union, however, were certain areas in Transvaal, the Cape and the Free State into which the peoples of Basutoland, Swaziland and Bechuanaland had overspilled in the course of time. These areas have since been designated Black homelands and are Lebowa (North Sotho), Qwaqwa (South Sotho), Swazi, and Bophuthatswana (Tswana). *Included* also were the homelands of several other Black peoples. The current names for these territories are Ciskei and Transkei (Xhosa-speaking peoples); Venda (Vhavenda); Gazankulu (Machangana/Tsonga); and KwaZulu (the Zulu nation).

Initially the door was left open for the eventual

incorporation into the Union of the three protectorates, but these plans were finally abandoned in the late 'fifties and in the 'sixties these protectorates became independent Black states.

Meanwhile, in 1913, the Union Parliament passed the *Bantu Land Act* which defined and scheduled some 8,9 million hectares of land in the four provinces as permanent and inalienable Black territories. In 1936 the *Bantu Trust and Land Act* set aside another 6,3 million hectares of land to be added to the Black homelands.

The total of some 15,4 million hectares (or 154 000 km²) is larger than England and Wales combined, and four times the size of Switzerland. The largest homeland, Transkei, was larger than Wales, Belgium or Switzerland.

It is true that the total of some 154 000 km² is only 13 per cent of the total land area of the Republic of South Africa, but this fact has to be seen in perspective.

In their south-eastward migration the various Bantu peoples, who were stock-farmers and hunters, sought out the best-watered regions of Southern Africa. Thus, today the Black homelands include some of the best farming regions of South Africa. About half of the total of 100 000 km² with a wet, temperate climate is situated in the Black homelands. More than 75 per cent of the Black territories receives more than 500 mm of rain a year, while the mean annual rainfall for South Africa as a whole is only 430 mm. It has been calculated that on average 100 hectares in the homelands have the same potential as 147 hectares in the rest of the country.

It is also pertinent to point out that the combined area of all territories involved in the dispensation of 1910 was just over 1 800 000 km². Of this more than 770 000 km² will eventually be Black territory. This is the total area of Lesotho (formerly Basutoland), Botswana (formerly Bechuanaland), Swaziland and the various Black homelands within the borders of the Republic of South Africa.

This then was the position in the Union (later the Republic) of South Africa when in the late 'fifties the process of decolonisation in Africa gathered pace. South Africa's leaders were very much aware that the Black peoples of the Republic could not be isolated from the stirrings elsewhere on the continent. Dr H. F. Verwoerd, who became Prime Minister in 1958, spelled out the message in no uncertain terms to the White nation who at that time was in full control, politically and economically, of the entire country. The Whites could not merely withdraw and leave the entire country to the Blacks. After all, the Whites knew no other homeland than that part of South Africa which they had settled in the course of two centuries. But suppression was not possible either: provision had to be made for the legitimate aspirations of the various Black peoples within the borders of the country.

The constitutional and political system with which South Africa as a country was launched in 1910 was a direct product of European (notably British and Dutch) colonialism. The European-descended settlers inherited a political culture which assumed the primacy of Western values and European interests; and the political system which was created in 1910 gave White South Africans a monopoly of formal or institutionalised power. What participation persons of colour enjoyed in the governmental system was nominal, largely indirect, and for the main part ineffectual. Two observations need to be made here. Firstly, this arrangement was undertaken with British approval; and secondly, South Africa was accepted without reservation in the international community. Indeed, South Africa played an important role in the development of the British Commonwealth of Nations; the League of Nations considered South Africa respectable enough to give it a mandate over the former colony of South-West Africa; Pretoria was the conference centre of Africa; South Africa established international trade, commercial, cultural, sporting and other relations without hindrance; South Africa's participation on the side of the Allies in both world wars was welcomed; South Africa made a significant contribution to the establishment of the United Nations; and the counsel of South African leaders (notably General J. C. Smuts) was everywhere sought. The change in the international climate as far as South Africa was concerned came immediately after the Second World War. And it was a change which came suddenly.

The first clear indication was the criticism levelled at South Africa at the United Nations at the very first session of the General Assembly in 1946. The charge related to South Africa's internal race relations policies and in particular its treatment of the Asian section of the population. The suddenness and the vehemence of the attack caught South Africa by surprise, and a disillusioned General Smuts, the main author of the preamble to the Charter, on his return to South Africa after attending the United Nations described that body as a mixture of "emotion, passion and ignorance".

This antagonism to South Africa had its origins partly in the universal post-Nazi reaction to racism, which included the USA, and partly in the pressure on European powers to withdraw from Asia and Africa.

Multinational development

There were really only two courses the country could adopt. First, there was integration, which meant that the institutions of government should be opened to persons of colour and political power shared on a basis of eventual, if not immediate, adult suffrage with full representation in parliamentary institutions of a common society. The alternative was a system of multinational development which implied that parallel institutions of government would be created for the various Black peoples, based in those parts of the country which, historically, were their homelands and the only parts of the country to which they could justly lay claim. The implication was clear that these territories could eventually opt for full sovereign political independence.

In 1948 – and at every election since that year – the White electorate of South Africa chose the latter course. They and their leaders have done so for many sound reasons which may be summarised as follows:

Neither the White nor any of the Black nations has a prior claim to all of South Africa, but only to that part of the country which history allotted as a homeland to each.

Integration would mean a new kind of colonial subjugation for the White nation, for in a so-called common society it would no longer be the master of its own political and economic destiny. If it is wrong for a Black people to be subjugated to a colonial power, it must be equally wrong for a White people to be so subjugated.

Similarly, if a Black nation has a right to self-determination, so has a White nation.

Various *nations,* not conglomerates of individuals, find themselves within South Africa's borders – not by choice, but as a legacy of British imperialism which turned this part of Africa into one multinational state. More or less the same happened in India (now India, Pakistan, and Bangladesh), Malaya (now Malaysia and Singapore) and the Central African Federation (now Malawi, Zambia and Rhodesia). In fact, in modern history there is no example of two or more disparate nationalisms being successfully accommodated within the confines of one geopolitical entity or state.

A typical Transkeian homestead or cluster of huts. Every family unit has its own patch of garden which is usually planted to maize, the staple food. When a log has to be transported it is simply hitched behind a team of oxen and dragged across the veld.

The political system of the White nation is inalienably Western. Every five years the electorate has a choice of candidates representing at least two political parties. This system has been rejected by virtually every independent Black African state in favour of a one-party system. This is neither a good nor a bad thing. It seems to suit Black Africans better in their present stage of development. But such a system would inevitably be anathema to the White nation whose tradition of Western democracy has a history of three centuries.

The concept of integration is unacceptable not only to the White nation, but also to the smaller Black ethnic groups, the Coloured and the Asian community. As peoples they would be extremely reluctant to be at the mercy of the numerically superior Black majorities. Incidentally, one of the worst racial riots in the history of South Africa – that of 1949 – was not between Black and White, but between Blacks and Asians. Integration would surely lead to the rapid disappearance of many of the minority groups in South Africa who have so far not only multiplied their numbers but also substantially improved their socio-economic position under the present dispensation.

These, in summary, are the basic considerations underlying the policy of multinational development. It seeks to ensure the full development of all the peoples or nations which history has gathered within the borders of the Republic of South Africa. As far as the Black peoples are concerned, the policy envisages a number of sovereign nation-states, based on the historical and inalienable homelands of these Black peoples. Thus, the policy does not envisage the westernisation of individuals with a view to absorbing them in the mainstream of White political development. In view of the realities of the situation – various distinctive peoples within the borders of the same state – the policy has as target the upliftment in all spheres of peoples or nations in their entirety. As far as the Black nations are concerned, this programme is therefore no different from the process of national evolution by which virtually all states of the world have been established. Indeed, the objective of the policy is self-determination for each people and elimination of domination of one group by another, which would be inevitable in a so-called common society.

The government's commitment after 1948 to a policy of independent political advancement for the Black peoples of South Africa was consciously and decisively taken. However, at different times prior to 1948 various prominent South Africans had also urged this course. Thus General Smuts in 1917 and again at the Paris Peace Conference in 1919 extolled the advantages of developing dis-

tinctive institutions for the various peoples of Southern Africa. In line with the "self-determination of peoples" precept which dominated thinking on political matters at that time, it was generally accepted that every nation was entitled to rule itself in accordance with its own customs, traditions and ideals.

Recognition of territorial integrity was the first step. The next was the distinctive development of the various peoples. In his Savoy Hotel speech in London on 22 May 1917, General Smuts described the consequences of this process as far as South Africa was concerned in these terms:

"Thus in South Africa you will have in the long run large areas cultivated by Blacks and governed by Blacks where they will look after themselves in all their forms of living and development, while in the rest of the country you will have your White communities, which will govern themselves separately according to accepted European principles."

And in 1925 General J. B. M. Hertzog, then Prime Minister, declared in the terminology of that time in a political speech at Smithfield:

"The Native question cannot be allowed left hanging like a threatening sword over the heads of White and Black for lack of a solution . . . The aim must be to develop and train the Native to enable him to take charge of his own affairs in his own territories."

Under Hertzog's premiership substance was given to this approach with, specifically, the *Representation of Natives Act* and the *Bantu Trust and Land Act,* both of 1936. The former laid the basis for the distinctive political development of the Black peoples. Those Blacks in the Cape Province who had always voted on the common voters' roll, were placed on a separate roll, with the right to elect three White members of the House of Assembly and three members of the Cape Provincial Council. In addition, Black electoral colleges were constituted in all four provinces to elect four White members of the Senate to look after the interests of Blacks throughout the country. Provision was also made for the establishment of the Natives' Representative Council, an advisory body comprising Blacks from all over the country.

The *Bantu Trust and Land Act,* as pointed out earlier, enlarged by about 70 per cent the area of

The kraal or cattle pen is usually circular. Note the square pen where the small stock, sheep and goats, are kept. Rainfall in Transkei is abundant and in a good year stretches of water or natural dams are commonplace.

the established homelands of the various Black peoples inside South Africa.

Another person who about this time added weight to this approach to political development in South Africa was the philosopher Alfred Hoernlé. Professor Hoernlé, regarded as one of the fathers of South African Liberalism, distinguished three possible courses of action which a liberal might support. In his words, these were parallelism, assimilation and separation:

"Speaking solely for myself, I suggest that . . . total separation should be the liberal's choice. Separate areas of liberty for separate racial groups seems the only alternative to domination in a racial caste society. At any rate, if the liberal choice among the three schemes were for total separation, there would be, at once, created a more favourable psychological atmosphere for co-operation with all those who are keen on the development and enlargement of the Native reserves; and who do not in principle oppose Native progress along the lines of European culture; and who contemplate, and would welcome, the growth of a vigorous and self-reliant spirit among the Native peoples (*South African Native Policy and the Liberal,* 1939).

Also of relevance in this regard is the fact that the United Transkeian Territories General Council (or Bunga as it was more generally called), which was originated in 1931 as a form of local government for Transkei, repeatedly petitioned the South African government for wider powers, and in 1944 it actually asked that Transkei be declared a "Union Native province or state with sovereign rights in the administration and government of its affairs and peoples".

This request was turned down, as well as one in 1946 that Transkei become a fifth province of the Union.

What these several statements and enactments show is that official policy after 1948 had antecedents. And, as has been pointed out, Britain acknowledged the diversity of the population of Southern Africa when in 1910 the former protectorates of Bechuanaland (now Botswana), Basutoland (now Lesotho), and Swaziland were excluded from the Union of South Africa.

Prior policy statements and government steps notwithstanding, Transkei and the other homelands were shaped by a series of decisions and legislative enactments determinedly pursued in the years after 1948. An important motive behind official policy was clearly stated by Dr W. W. M. Eiselen, Secretary of the Department of Bantu Administration and Development at the time, in

an article in *Optima* (March 1959):

"It stands to reason that if all were thrown together into one social melting pot, an entirely new society, definitely not European in character or culture, would emerge. White South Africa is numerically not strong enough to absorb and can therefore only choose between being absorbed or surviving by the maintenance of separate communities. It has chosen the latter alternative".

As far as implementation is concerned, the exclusion of Black Africans from the existing political institutions was accomplished mainly through the following legislative enactments. In terms of the *Bantu Authorities Act* of 1951 the Natives' Representative Council ceased to exist. It had last met in January 1949 when its meeting ended in deadlock as a result of Dr Verwoerd's insistence that matters of a political nature lay outside its scope. The *Promotion of Bantu Self-Government Act* of 1959 among other things provided for the removal of the three Whites in the Assembly and the two representatives in the Cape Provincial Council elected by Blacks in the Cape, and the removal of the four White Senators elected by Blacks in all four provinces. This provision therefore finally terminated all Black representation in the legislative branch of the central government. The *Prohibition of Political Interference Act* of 1968 excluded Blacks from membership of political parties and political activities of the dominant system. The Act was designed to encourage the formation of political movements by Blacks in their homelands where they themselves would play the dominant role.

The following legislative enactments have been instrumental in creating the alternative political systems which were the main goal of official policy after 1948. Although these systems were initially subordinate to the South African government, the intention was that they would develop to independence. The *Bantu Authorities Act* of 1951 substituted for the Natives' Representative Council a system of local government which in the words of Dr Eiselen "starts from the principle of tribal authorities, corresponding in great measure to the old Bantu tribal councils, whose opinion had always to be taken into account by the chiefs, and which will govern in accordance with Bantu customs as far as these can be reconciled with civilised standards". The *Promotion of Bantu Self-Government Act* of 1959 was probably the most important legislative plank in the implementation of official policy. According to the

The Transkeian army was trained by White officers and instructors of the South African Defence Force. At independence, the army consisted of one battalion of 280, comprising inter alia a headquarters company, a rifle company and a mounted platoon.

long title of the Act, it ". . . provides for the gradual development of self-governing Bantu national units and for direct consultation between the government of the Union and these national units in matters affecting the interests of such national units". This was the Act which set up the hierarchy of Bantu authorities, culminating in self-government.

By 1970 the political and economic development of the homelands had reached such an advanced stage that the government decided to take the overall blueprint a step further. The *Homelands Citizenship Act* was enacted by Parliament which bestowed on the government of each homeland the right to issue a certificate of citizenship to all its citizens, wherever they may be living and working in the country. This served both to enhance the status and prestige of the various homeland governments and to strengthen the ties of Black citizens with their respective homelands which, in terms of government policy, are independent states in the making.

All these measures clearly applied to Transkei. But in addition there were certain enactments which specifically applied to this territory, which was the first to be granted self-government.

Transkei

The first is the *Transkei Constitution Act* of 1963, the provisions of which encompassed the composition and powers of the Legislative Assembly, the composition of the Executive or Cabinet, citizenship, and matters such as a national anthem and flag. The Transkei Legislative Assembly consisted of four paramount chiefs (or their representatives), a maximum of 60 additional chiefs and 45 elected members.

The Assembly was therefore indirectly controlled by the central government, since under the *Transkei Constitution Act* the government had a crucial say in the appointment of the chiefs and could remove them from office and consequently from the Assembly. Certain matters were expressly excluded by the constitution from the Assembly's legislative power. These included control of the South African Police, defence, foreign affairs, communications, railways and national roads, currency, public loans and banking, customs and excise. The Assembly was also disallowed the power to amend the constitution. Legislative authority on all these matters continued to reside with the South African Parliament. In addition, all enactments passed by the Assembly required the assent of the State President of South Africa who, following parliamentary practice generally, acts on the advice of the Cabinet.

While the constitution expressly excluded certain powers from the Legislative Assembly, it was equally explicit in what powers the Assembly enjoyed: direct taxation on citizens of Transkei (whether resident within or outside Transkei) and on property situated within Transkei, education, agriculture (including soil and veld conservation, stock improvement and water supplies), establishment and administration of inferior courts, organisation and control of a local police force transferred to Transkei, land settlement and registration of deeds, public works, labour matters, welfare services, collection of and control over all revenue payable to the government of Transkei. The schedule of powers also included a provision whereby the powers of the Legislative Assembly could be extended to any matter which the State President deemed to be in the interests of Transkei.

With the *Bantu Laws Amendment Act* of 1972, control of prisons, motor carrier transportation, road traffic and the licensing of drivers and vehicles was transferred to the Transkei government. Later in the same year the Transkei government assumed control of housing schemes for citizens, legal aid, tourism, auction dues, and the establishment and control of all forms of entertainment, cultural services and public resorts. Health and hospital services followed in 1973, as did the power to raise public loans, subject to prior approval by the Minister of Finance of South Africa.

In terms of the *Transkei Constitution Act* of 1963 the executive function of Transkei was performed by a Cabinet elected by the Assembly. The Assembly elected a Chief Minister by secret ballot from among its own members. One day later five other ministers were elected in the same way. The Chief Minister assumed the portfolio of Finance, and then allocated the other portfolios: Justice, Education, Agriculture and Forestry, and Roads and Works. Until the constitution was amended in 1971, the principle of collective responsibility (an important feature of which is that the Prime Minister appoints his Cabinet) did not apply in Transkei.

Professors Carter, Karis and Stultz in their book *South Africa's Transkei* (London, 1967) said that the *Transkei Constitution Act*

". . . placed Transkei in the same constitutional position that had been occupied by most British and French colonial territories in the early 1950s. The fact that government-appointed chiefs held a majority of the seats in the Assembly was comparable to the official majorities that were commonplace in these colonies then. Indeed, the British Crown still retained as great reserve powers in 1963 in Basutoland as the South African government held in respect of Transkei . . . In this context, South Africa's domestic colonialism for Transkei might be looked upon as the first step towards full self-government. How the development in the Transkei is, in fact, to compare with that in former British and French colonies and in neighbouring Basutoland – which by 1966 was to be independent Lesotho and a member of the United Nations – remains to be seen".

An indication of how South Africa would proceed was shortly forthcoming.

During its 1968 session the Transkei Legislative Assembly approved a motion that the Republican government be approached to do all within its power to speed up independence.

In response to this request the Republic's Minister of Bantu Administration and Development said in Parliament a few months later that the government was certainly not averse to early independence for Transkei but pointed out that the government held that certain requirements had to be met before independence could be granted. These were considerable administrative experience in the management and control of government departments and functions of state, particularly budgeting and finance; sustained economic development which would permit the Transkei government to provide jobs for its own people; and a democratic way of life and a firm desire for peaceful co-existence with neighbouring countries.

Nevertheless the South African position was clear: the government was committed to granting independence, and in April 1972 the Prime Minister said in Parliament:

"If there is a Bantu people that believes the time has arrived for it to become independent, it can come and discuss the matter with me . . . When I speak of independence, I mean independence in the normal sense of the word, the independence which Botswana or any other country has".

During its 1974 session the Transkei Legislative Assembly appointed a 27-member recess committee to consider various implications of independence for Transkei, and to draft a constitution for consideration by the Assembly. At the same time, the South African government was requested to grant independence within five years. The recess committee's report was finalised at the end of 1974, when negotiations with the South African government commenced.

Black opposition
So much for the goals and assumptions of official

policy after 1948 and the steps which were taken to implement these, so laying the legal and administrative basis for the independence of Transkei and other Black homelands. But Black Africans, and Transkeians in particular, have not been passive onlookers.

South Africans of colour did not participate in the deliberations which led up to Union, nor were they really consulted. The vast majority of Blacks were concentrated in rural areas and isolated from the mainstream of South African life. Most were fully integrated in traditional and mainly non-Western subsystems of authority. No significant modern Black African point of view was articulated at the time. The British decision on the protectorates underlines this point: by keeping the protectorates out of the Union of South Africa, Britain acknowledged the existence of differences between these territories and the rest of Southern Africa and, by implication, also admitted that they constituted distinct political entities.

After Union, as the evangelisation and education of Blacks expanded and urbanisation and their participation in the economy increased, the nature of Black political aspirations altered: an increasing proportion of them demanded participation in the dominant political system. A new Black élite emerged, composed chiefly of teachers and ministers of religion, to be joined later by traders and persons from the "prestige" professions (doctors and lawyers).

At the mass level there were grievances which this élite could articulate, and political organisations were not slow to materialise. In fact, while there was virtually no Black political activity at the time of Union, during the 'twenties and the 'thirties it assumed alarming proportions as far as the government of the day was concerned. In the main, three organisations were responsible for this – the African National Congress (ANC), the Industrial and Commercial Union (ICU), and the independent African churches.

From its inception in 1912 until approximately 1937, the ANC pinned its hopes for a reduction of racial discrimination and greater participation in the dominant political system on the influence of liberally inclined Whites. For the most part, its activities during this period took the form of representations and petitions to the government.

The cathedral of St John the Evangelist in Umtata. Sunday is widely observed by Christians and traditionalists alike. As far as cultural and educational development is concerned, Transkeians owe much to the endeavours of the early missionaries.

There was no sudden renunciation of traditional institutions and forms of political association, however. Thus, the leadership of the ANC during the 'twenties and the 'thirties was drawn from both élites – from the newly emergent professional class as well as from hereditary rulers. Moreover, paramount chiefs were honorary vice-presidents, and no decision could be taken which was in conflict with the expressed desires of the majority of the chiefs.

During the 'twenties the ANC was overshadowed by the Industrial and Commercial Union. Described by the historian Professor Eric Walker as "the first attempt at a Bantu mass-movement", the ICU was founded in 1917 by Clements Kadalie, who came from Nyasaland (now Malawi). Originally it sought to organise dock-workers, but was soon imbued by the idea of a federal organisation of trade unions and by 1925 it housed nine types of workers and had a reputed total membership of 200 000. It also had its own newspaper the *Workers' Herald*. Before Kadalie retired into obscurity in 1931 and his organisation disintegrated into a few isolated and short-lived unions, the ICU had made a considerable impact on South African politics.

The establishment of independent Bantu churches had its origin, as one writer put it, "in over-much study of the more sanguinary portions of the Old Testament". The Bantu people, and every sect in particular, were seen to be the Chosen People and the Whites the Philistines who had to be overcome. This line of reasoning had produced some 160 Bantu sects by the early 1920s. While most of them tended to be latently seditious, probably the most notable instance of overt political action on the part of independent churches was the so-called Israelite uprising with its tragic denouement when in May 1921 police moved in on a Black African religious sect illegally squatting on the farm Bulhoek in the Queenstown district, killing 163 of them.

Following the Bulhoek affair, the government of the time appointed a commission to inquire into the Israelite movement and the wider question of independent churches. The Commission subsequently reported that "there is a growth of race consciousness with its natural outcome of social and political aspirations of the natives of the Union". The commission did not believe that this was something which could be checked, but it suggested that these expressions should be guided into safe channels.

After the 'thirties, all the determinants of political socialisation continued to work on Black society. Urbanisation increased, as did involvement at

more sophisticated levels in a now fully industrialised economy. To factors such as education, commercialism and Christianity were added two new ones: the independence movement in the rest of Africa, and international hostility to South Africa and its policies.

The presence of seven Whites representing Black interests in the Parliament of South Africa, and possibly more important, the existence of the Natives' Representative Council with its considerable possibilities, kept Black alienation from the dominant system at a level at which co-operation with White liberals was possible until well into the 'forties. But as the failure of this body became clear, the nature of Black political activity, with the ANC setting the pace, began to change.

Gradually the techniques and demands of the ANC became more militant. In the 'forties it concentrated on building an urban movement. In the early 'fifties it attempted to bring all Blacks into a mass movement, and later still it sought to establish an alliance of Blacks, Asians, Coloureds and Whites, based on what was called the "Freedom Charter". In the late 'fifties younger Black leaders urged greater militancy, racial assertiveness and identification with developments elsewhere in Africa.

Communist influence on the ANC increased during this period. In 1947 Moses Kotane, general secretary of the central committee of the South African Communist Party, was elected to the executive of the ANC. In 1950 J. B. Marks, a member of the Communist Party, was elected Transvaal leader of the ANC. Subsequently Dr Moroka, national leader of the ANC, declared Marks's election null and void, and the organisation was rent with dissension for some time.

The ANC and its offshoot the Pan African Congress (PAC) were behind the defiance campaign which in 1960 led to a confrontation with the authorities, culminating in the tragedy of Sharpeville in which 69 Blacks were killed by the police. Both the ANC and PAC were banned after Sharpeville and have engaged in illegal political activities ever since that time.

The increasing communist influence in both the ANC and PAC apart, these and other organisations were demanding what was entirely unacceptable to the White nation. For reasons stated, the

Before a girl becomes eligible for marriage in traditional society, she has to undergo an initiation ceremony called intonjane *during which she is secluded behind a screen in a hut for a period of a few weeks to a month when no man, not even her father, may see her.*

Whites believed and still believe that a common society would mean the end of their birthright: control over their political destiny as a nation.

While the Whites were not prepared to countenance political integration, they accepted that alternative arrangements had to be made to provide for the expression of the legitimate political aspirations of Blacks. Thus, throughout the 'sixties, the establishment of political institutions in the Black homelands was actively encouraged and promoted. Transkei was first in the field with a Legislative Assembly and maintained its lead in development, until now, finally, it has become a fully independent state.

Self-government

The point has been made elsewhere that the territory today known as Transkei came into existence as a consequence of successive British colonial annexations, beginning in 1878 and culminating in 1894. Prior to the extension to Transkei of British jurisdiction and corresponding administration, the peoples of Transkei were integrated into their own system of rule, as described by Prof W. D. Hammond-Tooke in his book *Command or Consensus* (Cape Town, 1975). This pre-colonial system of government rested heavily on the traditional institution of chieftainship; and even though the powers of the chiefs were somewhat reduced, they continued to figure prominently in the forms of government evolved for Transkei after British occupation and also after Union.

But they lost much of the autonomy which they enjoyed as, in the first instance, the process of annexation united and incorporated these chiefdoms into the wider bureaucratic structures first of the Cape Colony and later, after 1910, of the Union. The magisterial system which was introduced had arbitrarily defined jurisdictions which did not correspond to tribal boundaries or to long established chiefdoms. Also tending to weaken the traditional system of rule was the introduction in 1894 with the *Glen Grey Act* of a third element – the District Council system, which stood entirely outside of the traditional and bureaucratic-magisterial systems. Members of the councils were required to be neither traditional leaders nor civil servants, although chiefs and headmen predominated among those elected. The district councils had no decision-making authority; their function was to advise the administration on reforms and on matters of local concern.

An important line of constitutional development was for various district councils to merge to form larger and more extensive bodies, as more and more district councils were created. The culmina-

tion of this development was the establishment in 1931 of the United Transkeian Territories General Council (or Bunga), which consisted of 108 members: the 26 magistrates, three paramount chiefs (those of Tembuland, and Eastern and Western Mpondoland), and three representatives from each district council, elected from among themselves. This interaction of traditional, bureaucratic, and elective advisory bodies was the pattern of local government in Transkei until 1956, when the UTTGC voted at a special session to accept the provisions of the *Bantu Authorities Act* of 1951, which gave statutory recognition to the traditional Black power structure, at the base of which is the tribal authority. The Act also provided for the establishment of regional and territorial authorities whose administrative and legislative powers would be gradually increased. It was left to the Blacks themselves to decide whether they would accept the provisions of the Act. By the end of 1968 – five years after Transkei had acquired Legislative Assembly status – there were eight territorial authorities, 632 tribal and 75 regional authorities.

While Transkei decided to fall in with the *Bantu Authorities Act,* the composition of tribal authorities in that territory differs materially from those in other Black homelands. In the latter, tribal authorities are usually not elected but comprise the traditional leaders of the community. In Transkei, however, the ordinary tax-payers have the right to elect some of the members of the tribal authority. In addition, unlike those of other homelands, Transkeian tribal authorities not only have the power to impose taxes but are also charged with specific functions.

Commentators have remarked that although Transkeian Blacks were always alert to the importance of national representation as a means to secure political rights, the General Council or Bunga was generally conservative regarding political activities in Transkei itself. There was nothing like a political party in Transkei and until the early 1940s little notice was taken of the African National Congress. Two important reasons for this were the district councils' lack of effective power and the key role traditional leaders played in them. The way was cleared for the emergence of political parties only after the *Transkei Constitution Act* of 1963.

Transkei's first general election was set down for

A new session of the Legislative Assembly of Transkei being opened in the Bunga building in Umtata. According to the constitution, the Parliament of Transkei, which superseded the Legislative Assembly at independence, will have 150 members.

20 November 1963. In terms of Transkei's constitution, the franchise was opened to all citizens of Transkei over 21 years of age, and to all tax-payers over eighteen. Registration of voters commenced on 17 June and was completed on 17 August. No effort was spared in publicising the election and the importance of registering. As a consequence, about 630 000 voters (or about 97 per cent of those deemed eligible) registered in Transkei itself, and about 250 000 Transkeian citizens (or 50 per cent thought eligible) registered outside the territory. This gave a total registration of over 880 000, which was an impressive 77 per cent of the estimated eligible voting population.

The next phase of Transkei's first general election was the nomination of candidates for the 45 elected seats in the Legislative Assembly. The principle of single-member constituency representation had been adopted, and nomination courts were specified within each of the nine regions of Transkei. The nomination procedure was very similar to that of the Republic of South Africa itself, even as regards the deposit (at $23,00 very much lower than in the Republic) candidates were required to make. About 180 members were nominated – on average four candidates per seat. Of these a notable 25 per cent were teachers or retired teachers, 20 per cent headmen and 20 per cent farmers. There were also two clergymen, an attorney, a medical doctor, and two women.

Although some candidates in the same region formed electoral pacts, and others assumed party political designations, an important feature of Transkei's first general election was that it took place prior to the formation of political parties. This unquestionably influenced the character of the subsequent campaign which was conducted at two levels.

On one level, the two candidates who had declared themselves in the running for the position of Chief Minister, Kaiser Matanzima and Paramount Chief Victor Poto, vied for the support of the 62 other chiefs, who, in terms of the constitution, would be *ex officio* members of the Assembly. Carter, Karis and Stultz liken this aspect of the campaign to ". . . the struggle between two presidential aspirants for delegate support at an American party's national nominating convention". On the other level, the nominated candidates competed for electoral support in their respective constituencies.

However, some degree of interaction occurred between the two levels of activity as particular candidates for electoral office attached themselves to the political coat-tails of the two aspirants for the Chief Ministership. This aspect of the campaign also had the effect of ensuring that electioneering turned more on policy differences than on personalities, because both Matanzima and Poto had clear and strongly held views on the major issues facing an increasingly self-governing Transkei.

Matanzima was at the time described by independent observers as undoubtedly one of the ablest and best-trained personalities on the Transkei political scene. He was 48 years of age and a graduate (1939) in law and politics of the University College of Fort Hare. He had completed his articles and was a practising attorney in Umtata. In 1958 he was recognised as Senior Chief of Emigrant Tembuland and, therefore, traditional leader of some 88 000 tribesmen. He was generally said to be sympathetic, until the early 'fifties, to the organisations which had figured so prominently in Black politics, notably the African National Congress. Although, from his student days, he is reputed to have known most of the ANC leaders, many of whom were Xhosa, he was apparently never a member of the ANC.

Paramount Chief Victor Poto (62) lacked university training. On the other hand, his experience in government was considerable. In varying capacities, his involvement in the administration of Transkei stretched back to 1918 when he became Paramount Chief of the Western Pondo. He had also been a member of the Natives' Representative Council from its inception until its abolition in 1951.

Chief Matanzima favoured increased powers of self-government for Transkei and spoke in his manifesto of "independence". He revealed a strong sense of Black self-reliance: he wished to see the training of Blacks accelerated so that they could increasingly take over the administration of Transkei. He called for the establishment of a Black army, supported the claims of the traditional leaders for an integrated role in the governmental process of Transkei, and insisted upon the extension of the territory of Transkei. As far as the future status in Transkei of Whites and Coloureds, who jointly numbered 24 000, was concerned, he advocated the primacy of Black Xhosa citizenship.

There is little doubt that in South Africa itself Chief Matanzima was perceived to be favouring official policy. Indeed, in a press statement in March 1963 he said that "whereas the United Party and Progressive Party both wish to maintain White leadership, the National Party is making an honest offer of race separation which provides Blacks with the opportunity of governing themselves". The policy of separate development, he went on to say, "was the only practical solution to possible race friction in South Africa". This is a statement well worth the attention of overseas commentators.

On the other hand, Paramount Chief Poto did not mention the concept of independence in his manifesto. He accepted the constitutional developments of 1963 as only a temporary arrangement. Although he, too, stressed the importance of traditional rulers, he advocated their inclusion in the governmental process through an upper chamber or House of Review, and held that all members of the Legislative Assembly should be democratically elected. All "non-Africans" who were prepared to give their allegiance to a Black government would be welcome in Transkei. He advocated a "government which is truly representative of the population comprising the inhabitants of the territory over which it has authority".

Broadly speaking, in terms of formalised White political attitudes in the Republic, Paramount Chief Poto was seen to be identifying with the declared objectives of the United Party and, perhaps more directly, the Progressive Party.

Polling day was set down for 20 November. In the end, 601 204 votes were cast. In Transkei itself the highest percentage poll (75,4 per cent) was recorded in Nyanda (Chief Poto's region). The highest turn-out in urban areas outside Transkei was in Port Elizabeth (72,4 per cent) and the lowest in Cape Town (29 per cent). In view of the fact that voting had not been on party lines, there was really no way of ascertaining how the main issue, the race for Chief Ministership, had been decided. Paramount Chief Poto claimed that he was supported by 38 of the 45 elected members and indeed it seemed that a good majority of the electorate had supported his policies.

When the Chief Minister was elected in the Assembly, however, Chief Matanzima emerged the victor by 54 votes to 49. Three days later the Assembly met to elect the five Cabinet Ministers, in accordance with the constitution. The Matanzima faction submitted five names and the Poto faction one. Over the week-end the latter had decided not to participate in the new government but to constitute an opposition. Consequently, the Matanzima nominees were all elected, and Transkei's first Cabinet was constituted as follows: Chief Kaiser Matanzima (Chief Minister and Minister of Finance), George Matanzima (Minister of Justice), B. B. Mdledle (Minister of Education), Columbus Madekezela (Minister of Agriculture and Forestry), M. Selby Mvuse (Minister of Roads and Public Works) and Chief Jeremiah Moshesh (Minister of the Interior).

Two points should be made. Four of the five Cabinet Ministers were popularly elected members of the Assembly; and Paramount Chief Poto's decision not to serve in the new government but to

lead an opposition laid the basis for the emergence of political parties. In fact, within weeks of the crucial executive elections in the Assembly, the first moves were made towards the establishment of parties. Paramount Chief Poto and his followers formally founded the Democratic Party on 7 February 1964 and, with Poto as leader, the DP held its first conference in Umtata on 6 April. After lengthy initial discussions, Chief Minister Matanzima announced on 11 March the founding of the Transkei National Independence Party and issued a programme of principles. The TNIP held its first congress in Umtata on 23 April.

Both political parties developed relatively sophisticated organisational structures, policy-making procedures, and recruiting systems.

Several other parties were established in Transkei in the years following the 1963 elections. None was of lasting significance, however, and interest in Transkei politics continued to centre on the struggle between the TNIP and the DP.

Transkei's decision under the leadership of Chief Minister Matanzima to seek self-government on a distinctive territorial basis was something of a watershed in South African politics generally. Apart from Black commitment to official policy which this entailed, it was a decision which put to the test the sincerity of the South African government's promises of unlimited development opportunities in the Black areas.

Chief Matanzima and other homeland leaders who have opted "to work within the system", have increasingly been able to justify their stand in terms of certain tangible advantages or benefits. At one level, self-government has enhanced Black political self-respect; provided national political platforms; and created a basis for Black-White dialogue and for future Black-White political interaction. At another level, self-government has provided educational, administrative, professional, economic and technical opportunities which would otherwise not have been available to Blacks, and generally contributed to the social and economic advancement of Blacks in the homelands. Moreover, homeland leaders have not hesitated to use their bargaining power to press for similar improvements for Blacks domiciled outside the homelands.

Recent years have seen several "summit" meetings

Umtata's manual telephone exchange is due to be replaced by a fully automatic exchange which will link the country with South Africa's national automatic network. Most jobs in the communications services of Transkei have already been taken over by Transkeians.

between the chief ministers of the various homelands and the Prime Minister of the Republic of South Africa. Discussions at these meetings are wide-ranging, frank and comprehensive. Invariably, issues of major significance, which are raised by the homeland leaders but cannot be satisfactorily resolved during the meetings, are referred to departments of state or other bodies for study and action.

These advantages aside, the fact is that Matanzima and other homeland leaders have disarmed all but their most implacable critics with their particular formulations of government policy. Thus Matanzima in October 1963 said that to him separate development meant the expansion of educational opportunities for Blacks, the opening up of economic opportunities for Blacks, and the Africanisation of the public service.

In fact, the pace at which Transkeians have taken over from Whites in the civil service has been remarkable. In 1963, when Transkei was granted self-government, 455 posts in a total complement of 2 446 were filled by Whites seconded by the government of the Republic of South Africa. At independence, only 350 of a total of 10 620 officials (or three per cent) were Whites.

While the TNIP has consistently adhered to this basic position on official policy, the DP has been equally consistent in opposing it. Both Paramount Chief Poto and Mr Knowledge Guzana, his successor, have favoured the "non-racial" or "multiracial" approach. In a nutshell, the DP favours an undifferentiated and uniform citizenship for all persons within South Africa as a whole and has firmly rejected the view that Transkei has a distinctive destiny separate from that of the rest of South Africa. In fact, both Poto and Guzana have at various times pressed for the inclusion of Transkei and the other homelands as provinces within the Republic of South Africa.

This difference in outlook on official policy has also influenced positions on other issues. Thus the TNIP has taken a strong line in favour of more land for the homelands and the consolidation of existing land allocations, while the DP's attitude has tended to be lukewarm, because it views claims for more land as implying acceptance of the premises of official policy. Similarly, whereas the TNIP wishes to see White traders replaced by Blacks, and favours only controlled investment by Whites in Transkei, the DP adopts an almost *laissez-faire* approach.

In all this, the TNIP has not had reservations about the ethnic basis of government policy, and has all along promoted a sense of Xhosa national con-

sciousness and identification.

By contrast, the DP is committed to "non-racialism" or "African unity" and thereby implicitly rejects ethnicity. It would seem that in this respect most homeland leaders in power agree with the Transkeian Chief Minister to a greater or lesser degree. Even Gatsha Buthelezi of KwaZulu, who is most frequently cast in the role of "non-racial" leader, has often used terms such as "the Zulu people", "Zulu pride" and "Zulu state". Recently he revived a national cultural movement of which the objective is promotion of national consciousness among the Zulu people.

The point which is made here is important because it bears on the validity of one of the fundamental assumptions of government policy, namely, that the population of South Africa, while unquestionably multiracial, is also multinational.

The TNIP came to power in Transkei's first general election with a very small majority – largely because it gained only nine of the 45 elected members of the Legislative Assembly. Subsequently its position improved somewhat as a result mainly of "floor-crossing", and at the dissolution of the first Legislative Assembly immediately prior to the 1968 election the line-up was:

	Chiefs	Elected members	Total
Transkei National Independence Party	56	15	71
Democratic Party	8	27	35
Transkei Freedom Party		2	2
(One vacancy)	64	44	108

The issues in the 1963, 1968 and 1973 elections were essentially the same, but by the time of the 1968 election, the issues were clearer, party programmes more detailed, and party organisation better than ever before.

Three parties contested the 1968 elections – the TNIP, the DP, and the Transkei Peoples' Freedom Party (TPFP).

There was a considerable degree of consensus among them on educational policy, improved health services, removal of race discrimination, the abolition of restrictions on Transkei labourers in South Africa, the promotion of agriculture and

The streets of Umtata represent a fascinating blend between the old and the new, between traditional tribal dress and Western clothes. Note the elaborate headdress of the woman in the picture, which is a throw-back to the traditional styles followed by most tribes.

economic opportunities for Blacks in Transkei, and the importance of the institution of chieftainship.

The main point of difference lay in their attitudes to the future of Transkei.

The TNIP sought territorial autonomy and the development of Transkei as a geopolitical entity distinctive from the rest of the Republic of South Africa. This meant the achievement ultimately of independent statehood, the gradual withdrawal of Whites from Transkei, and increased political and administrative autonomy in the running of the affairs of Transkei. These goals were anathema to the DP, which continued to advocate a single, undivided South Africa of which Transkei would be an integral part. It did not support claims for more land; it opposed insignia of independent statehood such as a distinctive anthem and flag; and it opposed the idea of Transkei becoming constitutionally, administratively, and politically increasingly independent of the rest of South Africa. In its attitude on the chieftainship the DP differed slightly from the TNIP, in that it stressed the desirability of traditional rulers adjusting themselves to Western-oriented or modernist approaches. The Transkei Peoples' Freedom Party shared the DP's commitment to the more rapid modernisation of Transkeian society, but supported the goal of Transkeian independence. As a matter of fact, it appeared to be impatient with the pace which the TNIP had set on this issue.

Polling took place on 23 October 1968. Interest in the election was not as high as in that of 1963: the percentage poll was a little over 50, compared with 68 in 1963. Whatever the reason for the drop may have been, by African standards this was not a poor performance. The results revealed a pronounced swing towards the TNIP and away from the DP. The composition of the Legislative Assembly after the 1968 election was:-

	Chiefs	Elected members	Total
Transkei National Independence Party	56	28	84
Democratic Party	8	14	22
Independents		3	3
	64	45	109

The percentage breakdown in round figures of the votes cast was TNIP, 44 per cent; DP, 36 per cent; Independents, 18 per cent; and TPFP, two per cent. The really significant feature of this election was the increase in the TNIP's number of popularly elected seats – from nine in 1963 to 28.

Independence

In the 1973 election the TNIP not only gained a majority of popularly elected members, but also an absolute majority of the total votes cast – 55 per cent compared with 27 per cent for the DP, and 18 per cent for the Independents. The significance of this election, and in particular the result, lies in the fact that it took place after a motion calling for full independence had been debated during the Legislative Assembly's 1972 session. In fact, the 1973 general election may be described as Transkei's "independence election". This goal was boldly stated in both the collective manifesto issued by all TNIP candidates and the manifesto issued by Chief Matanzima. Mr Guzana and other DP candidates made their position equally clear: they rejected official policy and reaffirmed their view of Transkei as an integral part of South Africa. The results of the 1973 election were:

	Chiefs	Elected members	Total
Transkei National Independence Party	63	23	86
Democratic Party	9	11	20
(There were three vacancies)	72	34	106

Early in March 1974, at the instigation of delegates from the Western Cape Province, the annual congress of the TNIP adopted a motion in support of independence for Transkei within five years. This indicates that by this time the ideal of independence was shared by Transkeians residing and working in urban areas in South Africa. On 27 March the Transkei Legislative Assembly decided "that in the opinion of this Legislature the government should consider the advisability of approaching the Republican government to grant full independence to Transkei within a period of five years . . ."

The motion continued by stipulating that independence should be preceded by the transfer to Transkei of the outstanding land set aside in terms of the *Bantu Trust and Land Act* of 1936 and, moreover, that independence would not prejudice Transkei's claims to certain other districts. The Assembly also agreed to the appointment of a recess committee to explore all the implications of independence and to draft a constitution.

The recess committee completed its work in early 1976 and provisionally set 26 October 1976 as the date for independence.

A prematurely born baby is placed in an incubator in a hospital in Transkei. The country has built up a sound and comprehensive infrastructure of health services which even now make available the minimum services to people in all the outlying districts.

The constitution of the Republic of Transkei is discussed in another chapter. A point that needs emphasis here is that the draft constitution was drawn up by the representatives of the people of Transkei. The South African government or its agencies had no part in it. The constitution is therefore completely autochthonous or indigenous, as is evidenced by the preamble which states: "We, the people of Transkei, rightfully represented in this Assembly, do hereby adopt, enact and give to ourselves this Constitution . . ."

The draft constitution was thoroughly debated in the Transkei Legislative Assembly and amended in certain respects.

Meanwhile the South African Parliament adopted the *Status of Transkei Act* which provided, inter alia, for the transfer of sovereignty over Transkei from the Republic of South Africa to the government of Transkei as a fully sovereign and independent state.

During the year preceding independence, a committee of experts from both the Republic of South Africa and Transkei concluded various agreements designed to facilitate the process of the transfer of power and to ensure the least possible dislocation in administrative and other services.

It was agreed that Transkei would remain in the Rand monetary system and that it would be a member of the South African Customs Union, which hitherto comprised the Republic, Botswana, Lesotho and Swaziland. The South African Railways would continue to run the rail and road transportation services in Transkei and would train and employ as many Transkeian citizens as possible in these services.

Appeals against decisions of the Transkei High Court will be heard by the Appellate Division of the South African Supreme Court in Bloemfontein. Meanwhile all functions of the Bantu Appeal Court in Transkei have been transferred to the Transkei High Court.

It was also agreed that all existing laws of the Republic, except for those Acts specifically repealed in the Transkei constitution, would continue to apply in Transkei until such time as they are revoked or amended by the Transkei Parliament.

The Transkei civil service was reorganised to make provision for the execution of the additional functions which would devolve at independence. The South African government agreed to put at the disposal of the Transkei government such officials as the latter would need for as long as they were

required. Meanwhile training programmes for Transkeians have been speeded up for it remains the ideal that all functions in the government service should be performed by Transkeians as soon as possible.

Whites and Coloureds in Transkei did not automatically become Transkeian citizens when the territory became independent. They could choose either to become citizens of Transkei or to remain citizens of the Republic of South Africa. Properties of those Whites and Coloureds who wish to return to South Africa after independence will be bought by the South African Bantu Trust and all land registered in the name of the Trust will be transferred to the Transkeian government.

All towns in Transkei which at the time of independence were under White management, are now under the control of the Transkei government. Municipal officials who do not wish to remain in service after independence will be absorbed into similar jobs in the Republic.

Black Transkeians living or working in the Republic of South Africa will lose their South African citizenship and become citizens of Transkei. They will, however, forfeit no other existing privileges or advantages. In fact, when he introduced the second reading of the *Status of Transkei Bill* in the South African Parliament, the Minister of Bantu Administration and Development said that a new dispensation would have to be introduced in the Republic to ensure that citizens of Transkei were not treated like foreign Blacks from other independent states beyond the borders of the Republic and, therefore, less favourably than Blacks from homelands within the borders of the country.

Other agreements arrived at between the Republic and Transkei are those governing the continuation of the supply of electricity by the national Electricity Supply Commission (ESCOM), the rationalisation of postal and telecommunications services between the two countries, the continuation of certain survey services and research and development projects in Transkei by the renowned Council for Scientific and Industrial Research (CSIR) of Pretoria.

At a lower level, there are agreements designed to ensure the least possible inconvenience to citizens of both South Africa and Transkei as a result of the new dispensation. For instance, it has been agreed

Construction of the new government buildings in Umtata was a race against the clock. Most Transkeian government departments and ministerial offices will be accommodated in this new high-rise building which has become the major landmark in the city.

that third-party insurance on South African motor vehicles will continue to be valid in Transkei. This means that South Africans motoring in Transkei will not have to enter into the same complicated insurance procedures normally necessary to take their cars into other foreign countries.

The Transkeian Army was trained by White officers and instructors of the South African Defence Force. Training started in August 1975 near Cape Town where about 70 Transkeians completed a basic course which included military law, musketry, fire-fighting and regimental procedure. Advanced instruction was given at Lenz near Johannesburg in 1976. This included training as signal officers, medical orderlies, drivers, mounted infantrymen, and military police. Since that date several other groups have completed similar training programmes to bring the combined strength of the new army to one battalion of 280 comprising a headquarters company, a rifle company, a mounted platoon, infantrymen and a ceremonial company complete with band. Future training will take place at Umtata, capital of Transkei, and the South African Defence Force has agreed to assist for as long as necessary.

As far as land is concerned, during the 1975 session of the South African Parliament the *Transkei Constitution Act* of 1963 was amended to provide for the incorporation in Transkei in December 1975 of the districts of Herschel and Glen Grey, and for the enlargement of the Legislative Assembly of Transkei to include members representing these districts. The White-controlled town of Port St Johns was handed over to Transkei in November 1975.

In addition, it has been agreed that what land is still to be added to Transkei in terms of the *Bantu Trust and Land Act* of 1936, will be gradually incorporated as funds for expropriation become available, even after independence. These are comparatively small areas and have been incorporated in all maps of Transkei used in this publication. The South African government has consistently refused all *additional* land claims on the grounds that the Black homelands can lay claim only to what is historically theirs. Moreover, in terms of both agriculture and industry, the Black nations have only just embarked on a proper exploitation of their existing lands.

Conclusion

This chapter set out to describe the political developments and events in Transkei which culminated in independence. The history of the Xhosa people reaches far beyond their first contact with the White pioneers in the 18th century,

although the boundaries of Transkei itself were determined in the second half of the 18th century. The concept of Transkei as a distinctive geopolitical entity from the rest of South Africa was entertained from early after Union in 1910, but it was only after 1948 that independent statehood became a conscious goal of official policy. Like the origins, the motives for the policy, too, were a compound of idealism and realism, of genuine concern for the maintenance of established group identities in general, and also of pure self-interest. However, the question should be asked: Is there an objective justification for the course South Africa has taken? Can the developments which have led to Transkei independence be justified in a more general context?

The assumption in this chapter is that although South Africa, like any other country, has its distinguishing characteristics and its particular difficulties, its basic problems are not very different from those of any other developing society. Thus South Africa shares with other African countries the problems of national integration or nation-building, of economic development, and of the generation of the personnel needed to keep the machinery of a modern nation-state going. There is the additional factor that, with its highly heterogeneous population, its numerous cultures and languages, and its various levels of technological development, the South African situation poses the question: What manner of distributing power will best promote the interests of the entire population, safeguard the interests of each ethnic group, including minorities, and guarantee individual interests?

The main thrust of political change in South Africa, of which Transkei is possibly the most dramatic product, has centred on an increasing evolution of institutionalised power on territorial and communal lines. And in terms of the experience of other similarly diverse societies, a strong case can be made for this policy as a response to the very considerable pluralism of the society. As a matter of fact, this aspect of policy has seldom been assailed. Most criticism is directed at practical aspects of implementation and the seeming limitation of the political system. Thus, Professor Carter in a widely publicised Hoernlé Memorial Lecture of 1966 stipulated certain conditions for the success of government policy. In the main these were the territorial expansion of the homeland areas, a more realistic sharing of the country's material

While new buildings rise to mark the new era in the history of Umtata and Transkei, the old townhall clock tower remains as a symbol of stability and a gentle reminder that there is much to be proud of in the endeavours of the pioneers.

resources, the elimination of discrimination on grounds of colour, and greater consultation in the formulation and implementation of policy.

Since 1966 there has been considerable progress in these and other aspects. In fact, the South African political system has demonstrated an impressive capacity to adapt to the fundamental demands which have and are being made upon it. An interesting development of importance is the series of meetings which have of late been held between the Prime Minister and other Cabinet Ministers of South Africa and the political élites of the Black and Coloured population groups. In fact, from about the middle of 1972 a subtle, almost imperceptible, yet crucially important change has taken place in inter-group dynamics at the policy formulation level. The days of White dictation are over; South Africa has entered an era in which the key concepts are consultation, dialogue and negotiation.

Progress in relation to discriminatory practices and segregation has been slower and more difficult. As in the United States of America, the first visible breakthroughs have been in sport – in the form of visits by internationally famous Black sportsmen and sportswomen, the convening of "international" sporting events, the acceptance of merit selection regardless of colour for national teams for all Olympic sports.

More generally, the last few years have seen the South African government move boldly forward, both in world councils and domestically, in reaffirming the broad premises of its policy and its objective of eliminating discrimination on grounds of colour. At the same time it has sought to put its unrivalled experience of African conditions and circumstances at the disposal of all those seeking a genuine and just solution to the problems of Southern Africa. Thus, in 1975 the South African Prime Minister played a not insignificant role in initiating constitutional talks in Rhodesia between the government of Mr Ian Smith and Black Nationalist leaders.

In July and September 1976, the Prime Minister, Mr B. J. Vorster, had a series of meetings with the American Secretary of State, Dr Kissinger, which, if nothing else, once again underlined the fact that without the co-operation of South Africa there was little point in devising schemes for peaceful development in Southern Africa.

There can be no doubt that an independent Transkei will play a significant role in the unfolding of South Africa's policy of constructive co-operation in Africa in general, and Southern Africa in particular.

Chapter Thirteen

System of Government

The constitutional framework for Transkeian growth towards independence is implicit in the goals and propensities of the Promotion of Bantu Self-Government Act of 1959 (No. 46 of 1959). In terms of this Act the South African government committed itself ". . . to create self-governing Bantu national units" (par. 10). The Transkei Constitution Act of 1963 and the Republic of Transkei Constitution Act are the logical sequences to this Act of 1959.

The decision to accept independence was made by the Transkeian people themselves, however, and independence was in no way forced upon them. In fact, the Transkei Constitution Bill was not tabled in the South African Parliament but in the Transkei Legislative Assembly. This procedure is a unique deviation from the normal constitutional pattern followed in the case of colonial territories being granted independence.

In terms of the new constitution, Transkei is a sovereign unitary republic, modelled on the lines of the Westminster type of democracy. This entails the separation of powers, legislative supremacy and a parliamentary executive, the members of which are appointed from the ranks of members of Parliament. The legislature is only partially elected by way of general elections contested among the existing political parties.

Paramount Chief Kaiser Matanzima, Chief Minister of Transkei since the territory was granted self-government in 1963. His Transkei National Independence Party won the elections of 1968 and 1973 and seemed set to win that of 1976 as well.

The President is the head of state. He is a titulary functionary and is the symbolic head of both the legislature and the executive. While separation of powers between the latter two branches of government is maintained, close collaboration is ensured by the system of parliamentary responsibility of the Executive. This implies that the Executive must be members of Parliament and accountable to it. Because the President is elected by Parliament, he is also held accountable to Parliament.

The Transkeian constitution is entirely flexible, with no entrenched clauses, and amendments may be made in the same manner as to ordinary laws of Parliament.

The constitution comprises a preamble, 76 sections and 11 schedules. There are provisions to define the territorial limits of Transkei and determine the capital (Umtata), to prescribe a public seal, national flag and anthem and the official language, and to establish executive, legislative and judicial branches of government and define the relationship between them. Xhosa is the official language, but Sesotho, English and Afrikaans may also be used for official purposes.

The President

Executive power in Transkei is said to vest 'in the President acting on the advice of the Executive Council'. The relevant section (17,1) also states: '. . . and any reference in this Act or any other law to the President shall, unless it is expressly otherwise provided or must necessarily be otherwise implied, be construed as a reference to the President acting on the advice of the Executive Council'.

Acting on the advice of the Executive Council, the President performs a variety of functions of a legislative as well as an executive nature. These include inter alia the power to confer honours; to appoint, accredit, receive and recognise diplomatic representatives; to pardon or reprieve offenders, and to remit fines and penalties. He also has the power, subject to the relevant provisions of the constitution, to determine the times for the sessions of Parliament and to prorogue Parliament, and to declare war and make peace. In his capacity as Commander-in-Chief, the President, subject to the relevant laws, may mobilise or call out the Defence Force 'for operational purposes or otherwise for the maintenance of law and order, the preservation of peace, the protection of life, health, or property or the provision or continuance of essential services'.

The transfer of sovereignty from the Republic of South Africa to the Republic of Transkei is reflected in a provision which gives the President as Head of State 'such powers, such authorities, and functions as were immediately prior to the commencement of this Act possessed by the State President of the Republic of South Africa in his capacity as Head of State of that Republic by way of prerogative'.

The President is elected for a term of office of seven years by the National Assembly sitting as an electoral college under the chairmanship of the Chief Justice or another judge. No incumbent is eligible for re-election, unless the National Assembly expressly decides otherwise by resolution. The constitution stipulates only three qualifications for the office: candidates should be thirty years of age or older; they should have resided for a period of five years in the Republic of Transkei; and they should qualify to be a member of the National Assembly, which implies mainly that they should be registered voters and citizens of Transkei.

The constitution describes the method of election of the President in detail. The Speaker of the National Assembly calls for the nomination of candidates. Such nominations must be in writing and must be signed by two members of the National Assembly as well as the nominated candidate, unless he has otherwise signified his willingness to be a candidate. If only one person is nominated and qualifies in terms of the constitution, he is declared elected. If more than one candidate is nominated, the electoral college votes on all the candidates, with the candidate receiving the lowest poll falling away until somebody emerges with the majority of the votes cast. Voting is by secret ballot and no debating is allowed.

The President is elected for seven years. He may resign at any time by submitting his resignation in writing to the Speaker. An elaborate impeachment procedure is provided for by the constitution. The incumbent President may be removed from office on the grounds of misconduct or inability to perform the duties of office. His removal on purely political grounds seems to be excluded in terms of the constitution.

The Executive

The President exercises his powers subject to constitutional conventions and the real authority is wielded by the Executive Council or Cabinet on whose advice the President acts. The constitution makes no mention of the office of Prime Minister, but it does refer to certain South African parliamentary conventions which will be followed. The assumption may therefore be made that the Prime Minister will lead the strongest party in the National Assembly and that he will appoint a Cabinet in his own discretion, subject to the formal approval of the President. Unwritten conventions of this nature are a typical manifestation of the Westminster system.

The constitution provides that for the discharge of the business of the Republic, the President may establish such departments of state as he may consider necessary, and may appoint persons (not exceeding fifteen in number) to administer such departments. These are Ministers of State, and while holding office they constitute the Executive Council. No person shall assume the office of Minister of State unless he is a member of the National Assembly, and has taken the prescribed oath. The constitution provides also for the appointment of no more than five Deputy Ministers. Although the qualifications for Deputy Ministers are the same as those for Ministers, the former are expressly excluded from membership of the Executive Council.

In accordance with parliamentary conventions of almost universal application, in the event of a no-confidence vote, either the Executive Council would resign or be dismissed by the President, or the President would exercise his power to dissolve the National Assembly and call for fresh elections.

Transkei's Cabinet prior to independence: From left to right, top and bottom, the Ministers are in alphabetical order: Mr A. N. Jonas (Education), Mr Z. M. Mabandla (Agriculture and Forestry), Chief G. M. Matanzima (Justice), Mr J. D. Moshesh (Health), Chief G. S. Ndabankulu (Roads and Works) and Miss S. N. Sigcau (Interior). The portfolio of Finance was administered by the Chief Minister, Paramount Chief Kaiser Matanzima.

Legislature

The legislature in the Westminster system consists of the monarch and Parliament (or 'the King/Queen in Parliament'), and this concept has been retained almost everywhere the Westminster model has been introduced. Thus the constitution of the Republic of South Africa states that '. . . the legislative power shall be vested in the Parliament of the Republic which shall consist of the State President, a Senate, and a House of Assembly'. The constitution of Transkei has a similar provision: 'The legislative power shall vest in a Parliament consisting of a President and a National Assembly'. Parliament is furthermore said to be '. . . the sovereign legislative authority in and over the Republic, and shall have full power to make laws for the people, order and good government of the Republic'.

In the case of written constitutions in particular, constitutional lawyers distinguish between 'legislative supremacy' and 'constitutional supremacy'. The former refers to the primacy of Parliament in relation to, say, the judiciary in the making of laws. Constitutional supremacy refers to the primacy of the constitution in relation to all other laws: in the case of a conflict between a constitutional provision and another law, it is the former which prevails. In the case of Transkei, the constitution puts the matter beyond all doubt by declaring 'no court of law shall be competent to inquire into or pronounce upon any Act'. This provision, coupled with the fact that the constitution may be amended by ordinary legislative enactment, places Parliament above the constitution.

The doctrine of constitutional supremacy therefore does not apply in Transkei, and in this regard the constitution echoes the long-established rule in British constitutional theory and practice of the supremacy of Parliament. The constitution of the Republic of South Africa contains an almost identical provision.

As regards the composition of the National Assembly, the constitution perpetuates the basis of representation adopted in 1963 when Transkei was first granted self-government. The main components are the five paramount chiefs, 70 chiefs representing the districts of Transkei in which they hold office; and 75 elected members.

The authority and role of paramount chiefs and chiefs are discussed in detail in Chapter 3. Suffice

The head of the parliamentary mace of Transkei. The nine ivory rings on top are bound by a gold band to symbolise the traditional tribal government by the aristocracy of the people. The basket is peculiar to Transkei and is used to store grain.

it to say here that the chiefdom in the traditional political structure of Transkei has a territorial authority, and each chief was and is free from interference in his internal affairs from the paramount chief, whose authority, according to Professor Hammond-Tooke in *Command or Consensus* (Cape Town, 1975), is social and ritualistic rather than political. '(The paramount chief) is head of the royal lineage, to which they all (that is, the chiefs) belong, and is consulted by them, or consults them, in all matters concerning the royal family, e.g. marriage. Ritually he is responsible for sacrifices on their behalf to the shades, as is any other lineage head . . . But the crucial difference between the spheres of authority of the paramount and cluster chiefs is in the concept of sovereignty. There is no idea of a territory 'owned' by the paramount, other than his own particular chiefdom, and no obligation on the part of the cluster chiefs to provide military aid to him . . .'

According to Professor Hammond-Tooke the following description of the kingdom of France in the early 12th century is a fairly accurate characterisation of the historically evolved relationship between paramount chiefs and chiefs: 'It was a group of small feudal states under hereditary rulers who were the final judicial, fiscal, and military authorities within them, each in nominal dependence on a king (himself the ruler of such a state) whose paramount authority was undefined and largely moral'.

The determination of the framers of the constitution to acknowledge the claims to participation in the legislature of traditional rulers alongside the popularly elected members is significant – particularly in view of the fact that the Parliament of Transkei is unicameral as was the Legislative Assembly before independence. As this could prove controversial in certain circles, it should perhaps be looked at more closely.

In most African countries the problem of political integration has taken two forms. Firstly, with their largely arbitrarily drawn boundaries, their multiplicity of cultural and ethnic groups, and the general lack of social cohesion, most African countries have experienced difficulty in translating the slogans of nationalism on which independence was won into a genuine sense of nationhood. It is to this aspect that Dr K. A. Busia, formerly Prime Minister of Ghana and author of *The Challenge of Africa* (New York, 1962), refers when he writes: 'Often one of the first tasks to be accomplished when independence is gained, is to complete the structure begun by colonial powers – to build a nation out of the different groups colonialism has brought together. For an administrative framework provides neither an inner unity nor the

The national flag of Transkei.

sentiment of nationhood. It points the way, and helps toward it, just as do the greater physical contacts that new and improved communications make possible'.

Secondly, most African countries have also experienced difficulty in harmonising the two kinds of leadership which have emerged in the post-colonial era – traditional and modernist (sometimes called Westernised). In most countries independence was called for by leaders of the second sort who then set the goal for reform and the pace of change, while the traditional rulers were thrust aside and their authority consciously undermined. In other countries traditional rulers have been accommodated in upper houses; in a minority of

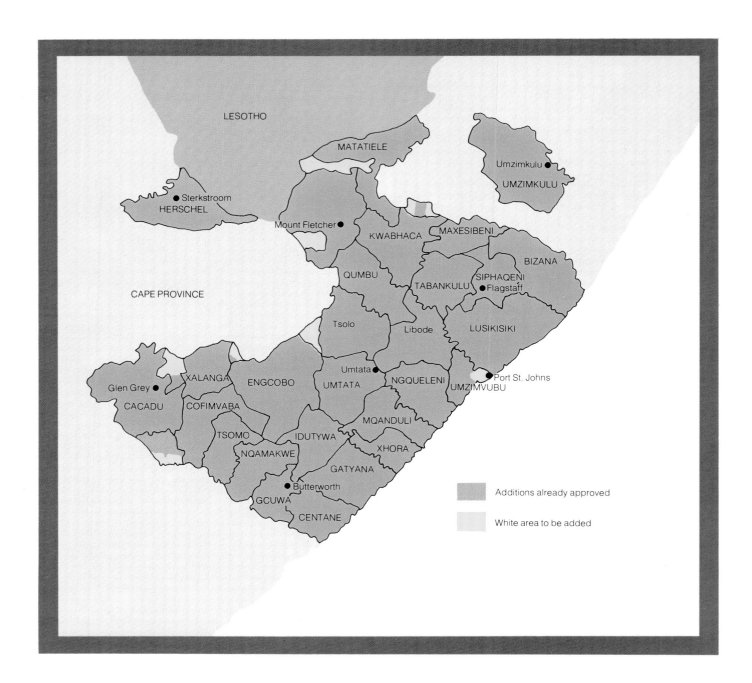

countries the traditional rulers themselves have set the seal on government; and in a few situations a traditional head of government has himself happened to be a modernist.

The decision of the framers of the Transkei constitution to give traditional rulers representation does not appear to have occasioned any controversy among the Xhosa people themselves. Indeed, this feature of the new state's system of government was justified in rather matter of fact terms when the draft constitution was discussed by the Transkeian Legislative Assembly. What is more, it is a decision which is entirely in line with experience elsewhere in Southern Africa, where traditional élites have not been excluded from government. Thus in Swaziland the Ngwenyama or King and the Swazi National Council (an exclusively traditional body) are pivotal in that country's constitutional system. Traditional rulers are also officially recognised in Botswana and Lesotho. Apart from the fact that the heads of state in these countries are leaders by tradition, both countries have bicameral legislatures of which one chamber is constituted by chiefs. In Botswana it is known as the House of Chiefs and in Lesotho as the Senate.

As a matter of interest, Professor Hammond-Tooke asks whether, in view of the possible incompatibility between the time-honoured view of the proper role of the traditional ruler and the hurly-burly of political involvement, a bicameral parliament is not a more desirable way of involving the traditional élite also in Transkei. 'If it is indeed deemed good to emphasize the traditional leadership, it might be wiser to withdraw the chiefs from participation in the political give and take on the floor of the Assembly by constituting a House of Chiefs which could exercise, if so desired, some control over laws emanating from the Legislative Assembly itself, and yet not be subject to criticism by commoner members. Only in this way would it seem possible to maintain the dignity and influence (as is desired) of the traditional rulers.' Time and experience alone will tell.

A matter which did occasion lengthy debate when the Legislative Assembly considered the draft constitution, was the question of whether, in addition to the special provision for their representation, chiefs could also seek election to the National Assembly in competition with those seeking popular election. The charge was made that this had indeed happened in terms of the 1963 constitution. The independence constitution is very clear on this point. It declares: 'The total number of Paramount Chiefs and chiefs in the Assembly shall at no time exceed seventy-five . . .' although it should be pointed out that the constitution does not expressly mention that chieftainship is a disqualification for election to the National Assembly.

Elections

For the purpose of elections, the constitution provides that Transkei will be delimited into 28 electoral divisions, and the 75 seats for popularly elected members of the National Assembly distributed among them in proportion to the total number of registered voters in each division – with the proviso that at least one member shall be elected from each division. The electoral divisions are described in a schedule to the constitution and correspond exactly with the 28 magisterial districts. (See map).

A system of universal adult suffrage applies. Entitled to vote are all those who are Transkeian citizens, over the age of 21 or, if they are taxpayers, over the age of 18 years. There are also detailed grounds on which registration as a voter will be refused.

All persons who are over the age of 21, who are citizens of Transkei and registered voters, may stand as candidates for election to the National Assembly. The last qualification means, in effect, that candidates for election and voters may be disqualified on the same grounds.

The constitution provides that the life of a Parliament shall be five years calculated from its first meeting, and contains a miscellany of provisions relating to quorums, voting in the Assembly, and to rules of procedure. This and the usual privileges are applicable to members of Parliament and parliamentary procedure.

Legislative process

The procedure for the passage of legislation is that which normally applies in the parliamentary system, namely, three readings of the Bill and a committee stage. A Bill becomes law following presidential assent to it, and the recording of the Bill in Xhosa (together with copies in English and Sesotho) with the office of the Registrar of the Supreme Court of Transkei. As an Act of law it becomes operative on publication in the *Government Gazette*.

The Judiciary

The judicial function of the Republic of Transkei is vested in a Supreme Court, which the constitution provides shall consist of a Chief Justice and as many other judges as the President may from time to time feel are needed. The Supreme Court has jurisdiction over all persons residing in Transkei. It not only determines civil and criminal matters,

but is also a council of appeal from all inferior courts in Transkei and has the power to review their proceedings. (The legal system is discussed in detail in the chapter: System of Justice).

The administration of justice is placed under the control of the Minister of Justice who has all powers and authorities relating to the prosecution of offences. Apart from this general statement, the constitution is even more specific on the responsibilities of the Minister of Justice. The attorney-general and other functionaries in the administration of justice exercise their powers '. . . under the direction and control of the Minister of Justice who may set aside or vary any decision of the Attorney-General and himself, either generally or with reference to a particular matter, exercise or perform any power, authority, or function of the Attorney-General'.

Citizenship

Probably the most vexing problem faced by the framers of the constitution was the question of citizenship, because of the need to reconcile the point of view of the framers of the constitution of Transkei on the one hand, and that of the government of South Africa on the other.

The point has been made that the Republic of Transkei is a nation-state of the Xhosa people. This was common ground between the two governments, and there was therefore no disagreement about the citizenship of Xhosa resident in Transkei, or whose place of domicile is in Transkei but who have sought employment in the Republic of South Africa. However, some difficulty arose in relation to those Xhosa who regard the Republic of South Africa as their permanent domicile: the issue was whether they should have a right of choice as far as citizenship is concerned.

In the debate on the draft constitution in the Transkeian Legislative Assembly, Chief Kaiser Matanzima expressed the view that the franchise was the essential feature of citizenship. Transkeians, he said, had never been citizens of South Africa because they had never had the franchise. 'Up to 1963 (when Transkei attained self-government) the people of these territories were not citizens of the Republic of South Africa, and anybody who says we were citizens of that country should turn to his dictionary or to constitutional law to understand exactly what is meant by a citizen

The Bunga buildings in Umtata, the capital. The building has for many decades served as the seat of the Transkeian 'parliament' in one form or another – from the United Transkeian Territories General Council to the pre-independence Legislative Assembly.

of a country. A citizen of a country should participate in the framing of the laws of that country . . . We never participated in the House of Assembly in Cape Town, and therefore we could never claim we were citizens of South Africa'.

The Transkei constitution provides for a number of categories of persons who will be citizens of Transkei at independence. These categories comprise persons born there or descendants of such persons, and any person who was a citizen of pre-independence Transkei in terms of section 7 (2) of the constitution of 1963.

In regard to the acquisition of future citizenship, the *jus soli* and the *jus sanguinis* are applied alternatively, with the usual exceptions of children of diplomatic personnel, prohibited immigrants, persons who had no right of permanent residence, persons born in enemy-occupied territory, interned enemy nationals; but with the inclusion of children adopted in accordance with the law, including customary law.

Finally, the constitution provides for two categories of persons eligible for citizenship by registration, namely adults who are South African citizens and who were domiciled in Transkei for a period of five years; and persons who have language and cultural ties with a Transkeian tribe.

However, the Transkei Parliament may either amend the present provisions or by legislation provide for further categories, and for the renunciation, deprivation or loss of citizenship.

Finances

There are two provisions dealing with the finances of the new state. The first stipulates that all revenues from whatever source shall vest in the President (that is in the Executive). The second provides for the continuance of the Transkei Revenue Fund established by the Transkei Constitution Act of 1963, and the payment into this of all revenues raised or received by the President; and for the withdrawal of moneys from the Revenue Fund only under appropriation by Act of Parliament. The principles embodied in these provisions are consistent with general constitutional practice.

Fundamental rights

Neither in the British constitution itself, nor in any of the older Commonwealth countries, is there any comprehensive statement of human rights. Recently, however, one new country after another has included in its constitution statements of fundamental rights.

In general, the practical value of such statements is questioned by constitutional lawyers and political theorists – certainly in the case of many new countries which have had difficulty in maintaining even a semblance of political stability, and in most instances have only managed this with one-party political systems.

The Transkei constitution does not contain anything like a bill of rights. The closest it comes to guaranteeing fundamental rights is in the preamble, which is reproduced here in its entirety:

'In the Name of God. Amen. In the faith that the One Eternal God is the source of all authority, wisdom, justice and morality, and in humble acknowledgement that we and all mankind are subject to His Laws; We, the people of Transkei rightfully represented in this Assembly, do hereby adopt, enact and give to ourselves this Constitution. We solemnly resolve to constitute Transkei into a sovereign and independent Republic wherein its citizens and all others who dwell lawfully within its borders are assured of social, political and economic justice, freedom of speech, assembly and worship, and unimpeded access to and equality before the Law. And we do further determine to use the powers which we do hereby take to ourselves for the promotion of the spiritual and material well-being of all in our midst, the maintenance of law and order, defence of our country against its enemies and the furtherance of peace among the nations of the world'.

The commitment in the passage above is, of course, little more than a statement of intention, as preambles are not legally enforceable. At most, therefore, this is a morally persuasive commitment.

The future

In the rise to independence of the peoples of Asia and Africa, many new states have retained the broad form of government inherited at independence, but the liberal-democratic assumptions underlying Western systems of government have not weathered well, particularly in the more rugged conditions of Africa. Democracy as conceived at the time of independence has all too often come unstuck as a result of the ethnic and cultural diversity of African countries and the absence of unifying factors. The process of converting the slogans of nationalism on which independence was won

Prior to independence a great many preparatory discussions took place between South Africa and Transkeian ministers and officials, either in Pretoria or in Umtata. The picture shows a group of Transkeians on the airstrip of Umtata prior to departure for Pretoria.

into genuine nationhood has proved much more difficult than was originally thought. Competitive party political systems have virtually disappeared, and in most countries constitutional authority has been concentrated in the hands of a single political leader. In fact, experience in the new states of Africa and elsewhere has compelled constitutional lawyers and political scientists to re-examine their assumptions on the workability of Western concepts of democracy in developing countries.

Against this background, what are Transkei's prospects? And in anwering this question, what criteria is one to apply? Sir Ivor Jennings, in his *Problems of the New Commonwealth* (Cambridge, 1958) cites four conditions which should be satisfied before power is transferred and a country becomes independent, if the transfer is to produce a workable, democratic government. There should be a sufficiently large group of educated politicians to whom power can be transferred; the balance of power should be settled before independence; there should be a transitional constitution, so enabling the local politicians to gain experience; and time must be allowed for the permeation of the public service with local men.

How does the transfer of power to Transkei stand up to this test? Transkei has enjoyed a considerable measure of self-government for nearly two decades. In its broad outlines, the independence constitution and the system of government which it creates follow closely the system of government practised in Transkei for the past nearly 20 years. In fact, the first general election was held in the territory in 1963, and in the intervening years political parties have developed, a new political élite has emerged, and a class of politicians has emerged which is experienced in most aspects of politics and government (see chapter on Political Evolution). So Transkei would certainly seem to fulfil the first and third of these conditions.

The same may immediately be said of the fourth condition, namely, permeation of the public service by local men. Under the aegis of experienced, senior civil servants from South Africa, Transkeians have steadily occupied the more important positions in the administration. Some South Africans remain, but experienced and able Transkeians now constitute the hard core of the country's civil service.

Transkei also fulfils the second condition. There was no balance of power to be settled before independence. Unlike many new states in Africa, Transkei has no politically significant ethnic or cultural differences. Its population is homogeneous; it is a nation-state in the very best sense of that term.

Chapter Fourteen

Transkei and the World

The South African government has committed itself unequivocally to granting independence to the Black people of South Africa in their traditional homelands.

The first concrete manifestation of this commitment was the granting of sovereign independence to the Transkeian people on 26 October 1976. On this date the South African government relinquished all control over Transkei and the new state assumed complete sovereign status on equal footing with all other members of the community of nations.

The implications of Transkeian independence are both far-reaching and profound. First of all, it signals the final stages of a bold experiment in state-building and the politics of multinational development, with the ultimate aim of achieving a *status nuovo*. Inevitably, because of the magnitude of this task, it is the most difficult and daring venture political leadership can opt for. Here one is reminded of Machiavelli's classical statement that "there is nothing more difficult to carry out nor more doubtful of success, nor more dangerous to handle, than to initiate a new order of things". When Transkei finally assumed its independence, it signified the success of an evolutionary process set in motion by White and Black leadership in South Africa to achieve such a new order of things

The wig factory at Butterworth. Most industrial development on the agency basis has taken place at this town and at Umtata, the capital. The Transkei Development Corporation has been instrumental in launching and maintaining most of this development.

in human relations and multinational development in this part of the world.

Secondly, success of the Transkeian venture into independent nationhood is extremely important to the future unfolding of the South African government's policy of peaceful change and the accommodation of the legitimate political aspirations of the other national entities still within the borders of the Republic. In fact, this step has been described as a hinge upon which much of the South African government's future stance will turn – both with regard to race relations in South Africa and the Republic's place and role in the rest of Africa.

In the third place, Transkeian independence has far-reaching implications as far as future international attitudes vis-à-vis South Africa's domestic affairs are concerned. The policy of multinational development and homelands independence is seen by many observers as the only practical way whereby racial discrimination can be phased out or dismantled in South African society. Racial discrimination has always been the major reason given for international antagonism and enmity towards South Africa. Attitudes following upon Transkeian independence will supply the litmus test – will the world accept South Africa's good intentions to bring about a new order of things whereby the moral discrepancies in the South African society will be eradicated, or will the intransigence of past decades endure despite the proof supplied by granting political self-determination to the people of Transkei?

Fourthly, from the Republic of Transkei's point of

view, it obviously is of supreme importance to the leaders and people of that country that Transkei should prosper. In the words of Chief Minister Matanzima: "The example of our success will, we trust, inspire other homelands to follow in our footsteps and thereby contribute to the peaceful break-up of the Republic of South Africa in its present unsatisfactory form, and, eventually, to a coming together of the parts in a new association of free men and women of all races in a mighty industrial state straddling the subcontinent" (Politikon, Vol 3 No 2). Echoing these sentiments, Professor Mlahleni Njisane writes in the same volume ". . . we are girding ourselves with independence in Transkei for the task of making our contribution to the reshaping of South Africa, participating with dignity according to our own definition of the situation. We wish to inject our own definition and conception of man by re-emphasising our value of humaneness. Transkeian leadership realises quite clearly therefore that the success of their country could greatly influence the status and position also of (other) Blacks in South Africa in future".

Finally, of cardinal importance to the success of Transkei are the attitudes of the international community towards the new state. By their stance, international organisations and individual governments can hinder or help Transkei in its efforts to take its rightful place in the community of nations.

The question most often raised is that of recognition of Transkei sovereign status by other states. It is a pity that this should be an issue at all, because at stake here are the rights of three million Blacks in a country with a sound historical base. In the history of the world during the past 25 years the emergence of new states was a normal thing. In this respect, Transkei will not be unique. Brierly, eminent specialist in international law, clearly states ". . . generally in modern times a new state has been formed by the division of an existing state into more states than one" (*The Law of Nations*, OUP 1963, p. 137). When proposing the second reading of the Status of the Transkei Bill in the South African Parliament, the Minister of Bantu Administration and Development remarked that the independence of Transkei "revolves around the consummation of the natural course of development of a Black nation on the pattern followed by nations over the whole world throughout the ages in attaining self-realisation and fulfilment by developing separately. This occurred in Europe

The bus terminus at Idutywa, south-central Transkei. Most passenger bus services are owned and run by Transkeians, thanks to the efforts of the Transkei Development Corporation which has helped many fleet operators with capital and expert advice.

and other continents with large states and smaller ones, and this was right and natural; it was accepted by all! Until very recently this still occurred on our own continent of Africa, in fact on our borders and also encircled by our South African territory and also in the form of comparatively small states. This was also right, also natural and they were also quite rightly recognised and accepted! Why and in what respect is the same process then wrong when it is now to take place in so far as Transkei is concerned?"

Objectively, there can be no doubt that the emergence of Transkei to statehood accords completely with the classic emergence of a state in international law, defined by Brierly as follows: "A new state comes into existence when a community acquires with a reasonable probability of permanence, the essential characteristics of a state, namely, an organised government, a defined territory, and such a degree of independence of control by any other state as to be capable of conducting its own international relations" (p. 137).

It is abundantly clear that Transkei satisfies these requirements and there can be no doubt that it will exist as a state.

But international law is not rigorously followed by individual states and international bodies in all spheres of international conduct. The question of recognition is one area where not only international law is ambiguous, but international organisations and states prefer to follow the dictates of their self-interest. Instead of merely using it as a declaratory act, e.g. confirming the existence of a factual situation, some states regard recognition as a "constitutive" act whereby a legal personality is conferred on the entity seeking entry into the community of nations. It therefore stands to reason that, given the background and circumstances of Transkei's emergence to statehood, for the first few years of its existence it could well experience difficulties in this regard in the international community. While this is unfortunate and undeserved, there is one major redeeming feature. The widespread use of recognition as a political weapon in an international system based on ideology and organised into blocs, and the resulting emergence of numerous states which are recognised by some countries but not by others, has greatly strengthened the view among international lawyers that recognition is essentially unimportant to the existence or continued existence of a state. It would seem countries function quite satisfactorily in the international community, even if they are recognised by only some countries.

In any event, much of the opposition to Transkei taking its rightful place in the international com-

munity is highly specious. There are those who claim that Transkeian independence is wrong because it violates the territorial integrity of South Africa. In the first place it should be pointed out that sovereignty has been transferred from the legally constituted government of one country to the legally constituted government of the other. But there is also an element of double-standards in this charge. So far, territorial integrity has not generally been considered an obstacle to any country gaining independence where circumstances allowed this. In 1920 the people of Southern Ireland attained their independence from the United Kingdom. In more recent times Bangladesh emerged as an independent state out of the territory of another country. There are several other examples.

It is also said, again by persons who presume to have the interests of the majority of the population in South Africa at heart, that by taking independence Transkeians have left their fellow-Blacks in the lurch. Quite apart from the role which Transkei as an independent country can and, no doubt, will play in the promotion of change in race relations in Southern Africa as a whole, Lesotho (an independent enclave in the Republic of South Africa) did not hesitate to take independence for its population – despite the fact that as many Sotho-speaking people were living and working in South Africa. In direct reply to this criticism, Mr D. S. Koyana, a senior official in the Transkeian diplomatic corps, has written of the other independent countries of Southern Africa:

"The Transkeians applaud the independence of Lesotho, and of the 500 000 people of Swaziland, and the 650 000 of Botswana, for the obvious reasons that the number of Blacks under White rule was thereby reduced – and the areas of freedom in Southern Africa increased. It is difficult to see how the independence of the four million people of Transkei in an area more than the size of Denmark cannot have the same effect".

Apart from the parallel provided by the development of the former British High Commission territories in Southern Africa to independent nation-states, there are also very convincing historical arguments backing up Transkei's quest for independence.

In 1976, during the final pre-independence session of the Transkeian Legislative Assembly, the

Tanks being manufactured at the sheetmetal works in Umtata. This is the kind of primary product for which there is a substantial demand in Transkei where the economy is still largely agrarian. The metal is imported from South Africa.

Chief Minister preceded his introduction of the draft constitution by an exposition of the history of Transkei, "in order that the world should understand the unique position of Transkei". After describing the various territories which Transkei historically included, he argued that Transkei was not a 'Black homeland' in the sense in which the South African government used the term in the exposition of its policy. It had come into existence as a result of British colonial annexation in the 19th century. He maintained that Transkei was a territorial entity which pre-existed the 'homeland' policy. It had fallen under British colonial rule as part of the "scramble for Africa" and Transkei, like other countries on the African continent, was now regaining its independence.

This statement is of more than passing interest, because it introduces a perspective on Transkeian independence which should give food for thought to interested foreign parties, whether international organisations, governments or individuals.

The Chief Minister also referred to the nature of Transkei nationhood. Outsiders, he said, consistently referred to Transkei as a tribal area. "We feel this is an insult to our nationhood. There are twelve tribes in Transkei; Transkei consists not of a tribe but of a nation". This, too, is a perspective of more than incidental interest.

However, the new Transkeian state's existence can be justified on more than historical and moral grounds. The quality and size of the country's physical and human resources leave little doubt that it has the capacity for stability and progress in the years ahead, but also that it will play a constructive role in regional and international politics. In any case, the size of a country, the size of its population or the way in which a state became independent has never been the criterion for international acceptance. The USA became independent by rebellion, Bangladesh by partition after civil war and Rwanda after separation from Burundi on UN instructions.

There are those who decry Transkei's independence, because it is not economically viable. According to contemporary world and particularly African standards, this is a fiction. From a developmental or viability point of view, Transkei is indeed one of the leaders among Black states in Africa. The argument that Transkei is not a viable state, in so far as it does not possess the economic resources and skilled personnel to maintain a truly independent posture, particularly in relation to its powerful neighbour, is, to say the least, highly specious. In terms of all important indices of development, Transkei outranks the majority of African member states of the United Nations.

Table 1 Transkei compared with other African countries

	Surface area	De facto population, 1970	Scholars and students as percentage of de facto population, 1970	Persons per hospital bed		Percentage economically active population in agricultural sector, 1970	GNI per capita, 1972	Average annual growth in GNI per capita, 1960-72
	'000 ha	'000	%	Number	Year	%	$	%
Transkei	4 400	1 930	24,2	391	1973	78,5	161	6,8
Southern Africa:								
Malawi	9 538	4 440	8,3	800	1965	87,5	90	3,6
Zambia	75 223	4 136	18,9	340	1967	69,4	343	2,0
Botswana	56 958	611	14,7	410	1968	87,4	216	5,5
Swaziland	1 736	423	19,9	280	1968	82,1	235	6,3
Lesotho	3 033	923	20,5	410	1968	88,7	89	—
East Africa:								
Somalia	64 766	2 828	2,1	560	1964	82,3	72	—0,6
Uganda	23 604	9 814	8,5	550	1968	85,9	136	2,2
Burundi	2 783	3 544	5,4	910	1968	85,6	63	1,1
Tanzania	93 797	13 270	6,8	1 120	1967	85,9	108	2,9
Central Africa:								
Zaïre	234 541	18 800	17,9	270	1968	78,3	90	3,3
Congo	34 200	899	29,5	170	1967	45,3	270	0,9
Cameroon	47 544	5 836	17,7	650	1968	81,8	181	4,0
West Africa:								
Niger	126 700	4 020	2,6	1 850	1968	91,4	82	—0,4
Nigeria	92 377	55 070	7,1	2 230	1968	67,0	117	2,0
Dahomey	11 262	2 708	7,3	770	1965	52,3	99	0,9
Ghana	23 854	8 640	17,7	920	1968	54,8	270	0,0
Mali	124 000	5 018	4,7	1 570	1968	91,1	72	2,1
Ivory Coast	32 246	4 941	11,4	510	1968	81,1	307	4,2
Guinea	24 586	3 980	6,5	820	1968	83,5	82	0,0
North Africa:								
Tunisia	16 415	5 075	21,6	420	1968	46,4	343	3,1
Sudan	250 581	15 695	6,2	—	—	79,9	108	—

The exchange rate of the Rand as at 1976/08/31 was R1,00 = $1,15.

The accompanying table shows that in gross national income per capita in 1972 Transkei ranked ninth among the countries listed. At the same time, it should be pointed out that in the period 1960-72 Transkei's average annual growth rate in gross national income per capita exceeded that of all countries listed, including Nigeria, Tanzania, Ghana and Tunisia. In addition, the number of students as a percentage of the total population in 1970 outranked that of all countries except one (Congo).

By these criteria, there can be little doubt that the independent Transkei will be off to a good start. No doubt there will be difficulties in the initial stages. But whatever these initial difficulties may be, the Transkeian leadership has a very clear idea of what independence means to the country and its people in the world of nation-states, and of what their foreign policy objectives are. Chief Minister Kaiser Matanzima has interpreted independence as follows:

"Independence will bring definite advantages to the people of Transkei. Independence means freedom for Transkei to enter on its own initiative agreements with friendly states in relation to defence, communications, and financial matters, and to recruit agricultural and other technical experts from anywhere in the world. Independence means the freedom to abolish discrimination in Transkei and it means freedom of movement – subject only to our own statutory provisions and to international law – in Southern Africa. Independence means the freedom to plan the future of Transkei ourselves. It means the freedom for ourselves to determine our role in promoting the common destiny of Southern Africa, and in defending its interests. And it means the freedom to introduce legislation combating communism and other foreign ideologies in our state".

From the above it is clear that Transkeian leadership has clear-cut ideas on the country's future foreign policy. As far as style and purpose of foreign policy are concerned, Transkei will no doubt adopt a typically African posture, moderated however by the experience of its politicians and administrative corps as well as the uniqueness of its Southern African environment.

On the multilateral level of international politics, Transkei will seek membership of the United Nations and the Organisation of African Unity, and there is nothing in the constitution of either organisation in terms of which Transkei can be barred. But political considerations also figure in the admission of new states to international organisations, and it seems that for the first few years of its independence, ulterior motives will militate against Transkei's admission.

Chief Minister Matanzima has also indicated that his country will apply for membership of the British Commonwealth of Nations. He maintains that when the Union of South Africa came into being in 1910, Transkei had the same status as Lesotho, Botswana and Swaziland, and it is purely an act of history that Transkei was incorporated into South Africa while these three countries were declared British protectorates.

But whatever bilateral relations the Republic of Transkei may establish with other countries, its relationship to South Africa will be of particular significance. Quite apart from the fact that Transkei has emerged as an independent state out of former territory of the Republic of South Africa, and is seen by the government of South Africa as the product of its policies, the interests of the two countries are interrelated to an extraordinarily complicated degree. There are Transkeians living in South Africa, and South Africans living in Transkei; the economies of the two countries are inextricably intertwined; and they share the same communications and transportation network and a host of other services. All these involve constant political interplay. In fact, relations between Transkei and South Africa are closer even than may be realised on either side. This interdependence is reflected in a host of agreements on many matters entered into between the governments of the two countries immediately prior to independence (see chapter on Political Evolution). But this interdependence also poses a number of questions the answers to which are vital to the future peaceful co-existence of the two countries. These questions relate to arrangements in the fields of trade, transport, labour, electricity supply, development assistance, monetary matters, tourism, etc.

In any event, the leaders of both the Republic of Transkei and South Africa realise the advantage of co-operation in a wider association. This has a significant bearing both on the relations between the two countries and on inter-state relations generally within Southern Africa. A decade ago, the then Prime Minister, Dr H. F. Verwoerd, spoke of the possibility of a commonwealth of nations emerging in Southern Africa. Other government spokesmen since then have returned to the theme. Mr M. C. Botha in his speech introducing the *Status of Transkei Bill* in the South African Parliament in 1976 spoke as follows:

"The diversity of national groups here in South Africa, independent or semi-independent, Black and White, and also the Brown groups and those of Eastern origin, will therefore all, in their diversity, have to continue to live here alongside one

243

another, but in a friendly and tolerant manner, and together, and interdependent on one another.

"For this reason, in this extensive multinational dispensation, we will have to design an organisatory framework, already named a commonwealth, a constellation, a common market, a power bloc, an association, etc. Within this framework the national groups will have to consult with each other in a comprehensible and orderly procedure whereby the course of action of the people of the national groups concerned, as individuals in their own countries, but, in particular, also in the other man's country, can be determined".

On various occasions Chief Minister Kaiser Matanzima and other Transkei leaders have expressed similar sentiments. Thus Chief Kaiser has written:

"Independence does not mean alienation from the Republic. Dr H. F. Verwoerd as Prime Minister often spoke of the possibility of the Republic and the homelands developing into a South African Commonwealth of Nations. I believe that this is a very real likelihood – given the fact that in so many ways our fundamental interests overlap . . ."

Transkei defence policy will be quite independent of South Africa's. But aggression by any power against the states of Central and Southern Africa will certainly be seen as a threat to Transkeian independence to be met in collaboration with sub-continental states with mutual interests. The Republic of South Africa is clearly such a state, and co-operation in defence matters is therefore likely. In fact, Transkei's defence force, which stood at only battalion strength immediately prior to independence, was initially trained and equipped by South Africa. The two countries have also concluded a non-aggression pact.

From the official South African point of view, the grant of independence to Transkei and the policy decisions which preceded this, are seen as an essential step in the process of achieving an equitable redistribution of political power among South Africa's peoples. What the South African government no doubt realises is that independence confers equality. As a consequence of historical links, because of racial implications, because of numerous African and international considerations, Transkeian independence is inextricably linked with the whole question of Black-White equality.

A scene in the bus maintenance workshops at Idutywa. There are several private operators of large passenger bus fleets throughout Transkei and Transkeians are trained to undertake all maintenance work. The demand for transport is likely to increase substantially.

Naturally, an independent Transkei will move into a position of equality with South Africa in accordance with international conventions and law. This is, of course, a formal equality – the equality which Botswana or Lesotho enjoys with South Africa. But because Transkei has evolved out of South African territory; because the South African government views it as of South Africa's making, South Africa is bound consciously not only to ensure that Transkei receives equal treatment but also that it receives as much assistance as possible in achieving equality in fact.

The race relations issue clearly also has implications for an independent Transkei. Even if it wished to, Transkei would not be able to stay aloof from the debates on race relations in Southern Africa. Transkeian leaders have often expressed themselves in terms critical of official policies in South Africa, and they have described their own policies as being directed to building up a non-racial democracy in Transkei. But the objectives of their policy aside, Transkeian leaders, for both international and domestic reasons, are bound to maintain a lively interest in race relations in South Africa. For example, they will be watching to see that discrimination on grounds of colour is not practised against their citizens.

A well-disposed Transkei can help provide White South Africans with what they need most – a sense of security. This security is necessary if they are to continue to make their very considerable contribution to sustained economic growth for everyone in the region. Conversely, a well-disposed South Africa will greatly contribute to what Transkei needs most – economic growth. South Africa's support – in capital investment and technical aid – could be decisive, for it is clear that in the rest of Africa assistance of this kind from elsewhere, whether from the East or the West, is limited and inadequate.

The above are some of the more important aspects of the Republic of Transkei's relations with the Republic of South Africa. It is a complex and dynamic relationship and could present some serious difficulties. An independent Transkei will also be speaking out on matters such as South-West Africa and Rhodesia, and the pros and cons of closer relations between the Republic of South Africa and the rest of Africa. It would be surprising if there were not differences of opinion between the two countries. However, the course to independence itself was not without differences of opinion. These were overcome, and there seems to be no reason why, with statesmanship and diplomacy which is conscious of the interests which the two countries share, post-independence difficulties should not be surmounted as well.

Chapter Fifteen

Nature Conservation and Tourism

Until Transkei was granted self-government in 1963 and assumed the function itself, the responsibility for nature (fauna and flora) conservation in the Territory was that of the Provincial Administration of the Cape Province of South Africa. In that year the Division of Fauna and Flora and Tourism was created in the Transkei Department of Agriculture and Forestry. The main functions of the division are control of hunting, shooting and fishing, protection of game, establishment of game sanctuaries, protection of indigenous flora, stocking inland waters and streams with fish, and control and eradication of vermin.

The enabling legislation is titled the Nature Conservation Act (No. 6 of 1971) which permits the Minister of Agriculture and Forestry to establish nature reserves on forest reserves or any other state land for the propagation, protection and preservation of fauna and flora.

The first nature reserve in Transkei was established in 1974 in the Dwessa and Cwebe forest reserves and opened to the public in 1976. These are coastal forests on either side of the Bashee River. A development plan has been prepared by a firm of landscape architects for the Dwessa forest, and game previously indigenous to Transkei, such as buffalo, eland, blesbuck and other species, are

The first nature reserve in Transkei was established in 1974 in die Dwessa and Cwebe forests reserves into which species previously indigenous to Transkei, such as buffalo, eland, blesbuck (picture) and other species, are now being introduced.

now being introduced with the help of the various parks boards of South Africa.

All forest reserves are actually treated as game sanctuaries and are closed to all hunters. Nevertheless, foresters and forest guards have to be continually on the look-out for poachers.

Many of Transkei's perennial springs dried up after severe droughts during successive summers up to that of 1973/74. The result was that antelope such as bush-buck and blue buck deserted some of their traditional grazing areas. Heavy rains fell during the past two seasons and it is expected that some of these antelope will return to their usual haunts as soon as the water resources have been replenished.

Inland fisheries

The potential for fish-farming in the inland waters of Transkei is substantial. Several comparatively large dams have been built which are ideally suited to fish-breeding. Several more dams are being planned or constructed for irrigation and all these might eventually be used for the economic production of freshwater fish. On the whole, the people of Transkei are not fond of fish, but even if they were not to overcome their prejudice against this food, fish-farming could be of considerable economic significance to the country, as a lucrative export trade to the Republic of South Africa and other neighbouring territories could be built up.

Progress so far has been only moderate, due partly to the successive droughts of a few seasons ago when dams dried up and much of the pioneering work was lost. Aischgrund carp has been success-

fully spawned at Xume Dam on the Tsomo River and in 1972 fingerlings were placed in stock-watering dams to test their suitability for growing carp. All the fish were subsequently lost when the dams dried up, but breeding operations were continued in order to maintain a stock which is now being transferred to the experimental production ponds constructed in 1975 at the Tsolo College of Agriculture.

The breeding scheme for large-mouth bass at Tsolo has been highly successful. Most of the larger dams throughout Transkei have been stocked and fish of up to 2,5 kg have already been taken out by anglers. Waters too small for bass have been stocked with *Tilapia sparmannii*, also produced at Tsolo.

The first rainbow trout fingerlings and yearlings in Transkei were distributed before 1910 and all suitable streams and rivers have been stocked at some time or another. Until recently all these fingerlings and yearlings were obtained from the trout hatcheries at Stellenbosch, Western Cape and Pirie, near King William's Town, but a small hatchery is now being developed at Mhlahlane near Umtata, capital of Transkei. It is envisaged that the country will soon be in a position to supply its own fingerlings for stocking its waters.

The mountain streams of Transkei have for many years been renowned for their trout, but the recent droughts devastated the trout waters and it will be some time before recovery will be complete. Another complicating factor is the severe soil erosion in the catchments of some river systems. The burden of silt carried along by floodwaters year by year reduces the number of rivers which can be fished. Good fishing is nevertheless still to be had in streams rising in and flowing through forests and plantations.

Several fishery research projects are being undertaken by South African universities on behalf of Transkei. They concern the distribution of freshwater fish and the occurrence of eels and the feasibility of establishing an eel industry.

Tourism

There is no doubt that the tourist potential of Transkei is considerable. The climate of the country is ideally suited to the development of a substantial tourist industry. Most rain falls in summer

The arum lily, indigenous to Southern Africa. The Division of Fauna and Flora and Tourism was created in the Department of Agriculture and Forestry in 1963 to protect the indigenous flora and fauna of Transkei against the ravages of man.

and the autumns and winters are dry and comparatively mild. Snow is rare on the central plateau and usually falls only on the high mountains in the west. Summers can be very hot but the climate on the whole is equable.

Transkei offers much of absorbing interest to the tourist, particularly those from abroad. Transkeians are a courteous and friendly people, with a dignified and leisurely life-style. The youngsters will start singing and dancing almost at the drop of a hat. Eighty per cent of the population of Transkei still follow the traditional way of life of their forefathers. Most of the customs and rituals of yore have survived intact and are practised as assiduously as ever. There is a bewildering kaleidoscope of dress and headdress styles, each with its own significance and charm.

The clusters of huts on the slopes of the hills, each group home to a closely knit family, are the first things to fascinate the visitor from beyond the shores of Africa. Each cluster has its own kraal (cattle pen), patches of maize and vegetables and is surrounded by communal meadows where the family's cattle graze by day. These groups of huts are remarkably evenly dotted throughout the country, except perhaps for the more mountainous areas in the west and north-west.

If the country offers a great deal for the observant student of humanity and a populace in transition, the potential for the holiday-maker is as yet largely undeveloped. And herein lies one of the greatest potential sources of revenue for the Transkei of the future. Mother nature was particularly lavish in her endowments to Transkei. From the majestic peaks of the Drakensberg in the north-west, through the rolling green hills and fertile valleys of the midlands to the enthralling desolation of the coastline, Transkei is blessed with a natural beauty which at all times is pleasing to the eye.

Where else in the world does one find a 250-km coastline undeveloped and unspoilt? The rugged splendour of the 'wild coast' has a fascination and charm all its own. In time this could become the playground of thousands of holiday-makers from all over South Africa and even further afield. The warm Mozambique current flows only a few kilometres off-shore on its way to the south.

The Transkei Department of Agriculture and Forestry, which promotes and controls the development of the tourist industry in Transkei, is firm in its resolution that the unique 'wild coast' of the country will not be spoiled by injudicious development. Care will be taken that the unrivalled splendour of the beaches and the natural vegetation is perpetuated for generations to come.

Captions to following colour plates.

Pondo women chatting by the roadside.

Catching the early bus to town.

Tea will be served shortly!

Carrying some fresh produce home for dinner.

Thembu woman preparing for the next brew.

A Gcaleka boy dressed up for a festival.

A Thembu boy and girl ready for the dance.

Horsemen cantering in street of Flagstaff.

Making bricks with hand moulds.

Pondo women with home-made grass mats.

Mouth of the Umgazi River.

Village in the mountains.

Young girls stamping maize.

A band of nubile women dressed in their best finery.

A young initiate at a waterfall near Umtata.

Who needs a glass when there is so much water?

In the backyard of a remote trading store.

This couple decided on a Christian wedding.

Priests about to enter a church.

Huts being thatched.

Shopping at the local store.

The wayside watch vendor.

Pondo couple building their mud hut.

The crane is revered by Transkeians.

Eland in a game reserve.

Collecting firewood is an important task for the young.

Enjoying a cheerful pipe.

A Gcaleka girl with elaborate beadwork.

Gcaleka boys engaging in a stick fight.

Seascape on the Wild Coast.

Sunrise at Port St. Johns.

Waiting for transport to church.